Mien Relations

Mien Relations

Mountain People and State Control in Thailand

HJORLEIFUR JONSSON

Cornell University Press   *Ithaca and London*

First published 2005 by Cornell University Press
First printing, Cornell Paperbacks, 2005

Printed in the United States of America

Library of Congress Cataloging-in-Publication Data

Hjorleifur Jonsson.
    Mien relations : mountain people and state control in Thailand / Hjorleifur Jonsson.
        p. cm.
    Includes bibliographical references and index.
    ISBN–13: 978-0-8014-4338-1 (cloth : alk. paper)
    ISBN–10: 0-8014-4338-5 (cloth : alk. paper)
    ISBN–13: 978-0-8014-7284-8 (pbk. : alk. paper)
    ISBN–10: 0-8014-7284-9 (pbk. : alk. paper)
    1. Yao (Southeast Asian people)—Thailand, Northern—Government relations. 2. Yao (Southeast Asian people)—Thailand, Northern—Ethnic identity. 3. Mountain people—Thailand, Northern—Government relations. 4. Minorities—Government policy—Thailand, Northern. 5. Thailand, Northern—Ethnic relations.   I. Title.
    DS570.Y35H52 2005
    323.1195'970593—dc22
    2005017715

Cornell University Press strives to use environmentally responsible suppliers and materials to the fullest extend possible in the publishing of its books. Such materials include vegetable-based, low-VOC inks and acid-free papers that are recycled, totally chlorine-free, or partly composed of nonwood fibers. For further information, visit our website at www.cornellpress.cornell.edu.

Cloth printing   10 9 8 7 6 5 4 3 2 1
Paperback printing   10 9 8 7 6 5 4 3 2 1

Til stelpnanna minna, Mánu og Sóleyjar,
fyrir jarðsamband, hugarflug og tungumál.

CONTENTS

ACKNOWLEDGMENTS

Many kind people have shared ideas and experiences that helped me toward my perspective in this book. I may never be able to thank them fully, but I can acknowledge their generosity and hope that the book shows that I have learned something. The book is primarily about Thailand's Mien and their past, but my own research has been more varied. I did field-work among lowland Shan farmers in Thailand in 1988, visited Mien set-tlements in northern Thailand for the summer of 1990, did fieldwork among Tampuan and other ethnic minorities in Ratanakiri Province of Cambodia in the first half of 1992 and among Thailand's Mien from Octo-ber 1992 to August 1994. Later I did consultancy work that brought me among Stieng and other minorities of the central highlands of Vietnam for a month in 1996. I was back among Mien in Thailand in 1998, in 2000 while exploring ethnographic museums in Vietnam and Thailand, and again briefly in early 2001 for an ethnic festival. All of this work has influ-enced my perspective, as have various encounters less easily specified. My deepest gratitude is to Nora A. Taylor and our two daughters, Mána Hao and Sóley Nai. They were forgiving and fun while the book was taking shape, and they did their best to keep me in the real world.

Tom Kirsch, Davydd Greenwood, and David Wyatt advised me on the first version of this project. Each not only provided solid advice but also left me with questions that I am still trying to address. Cornell's Southeast Asia Program was an important part of my training. Oliver Wolters challenged me in a gentle manner to think more seriously about regional history. I also studied with Paul Durrenberger and Nicola Tannenbaum, and my research with Shan was as Nikki's assistant. For their teachings, encouragement, and support, they have my lasting gratitude.

For support of my research, I thank the National Science Foundation, the Wenner-Gren Foundation for Anthropological Research, the Nordic Institute for Asian Studies, and the Walter F. Vella Scholarship Fund. For subsequent support, I thank the College of Liberal Arts and Sciences (Faculty Grant-In-Aid), the Center for Asian Studies, the Program for Southeast Asian Studies, and the Department of Anthropology, all at Arizona State University. For my research I had a permit from the National Research Council of Thailand. I was affiliated with Phayap University, the Tribal Research Institute, and the Social Research Institute of Chiangmai University. While my research permit was long approved, the visa authorization from Bangkok never reached Chiangmai's Immigration Office. In some ways my ability to conduct research was dependent on the kindness of the immigration officials in Chiangmai who gave me a temporary stamp every two weeks on trust. Farmers from Mae Jedi Mai helped me out after a traffic accident that could have ended my research before it even started. *Yin di jad nak.*

During my fieldwork in Thailand, I relied on the kindness and generosity of many people. Tang Tsoi Fong (Phaisal Srisombat) and Pung-Si Fam Kwe were my hosts in the village of Pangkha. Their household was the setting for much of my education about the past and present and about dealing with spirits and government officials. Le Tsan Kwe was an occasional host in Phale; he told great stories, gave helpful advice, and was a link to various histories. Tang Tsan Seng, a spirit medium in Pangkha, was a source of wisdom and history and helped me toward a comprehension of ritual chants. Tsan Kwe and Tsan Seng are now both in the spirit world. Of the many other Mien who were instrumental in allowing me to comprehend some of their lives, histories, and larger contexts past and present, Kidakarn Athornprachachit and Kittisakr Ruttanakrajangsri deserve special thanks. To them and numerous other Mien people, *leng tsing tsam o.* In Chiangmai, Graham Fordham, Heather Montgomery, Nikki Tannenbaum, Kate Gillogly, Pat Symonds, Geoffrey Walton, Peter Vail, Ronald Renard, and Ratanaporn Sethakul provided good company, comparative and historical perspective, and welcome distraction.

Some of the material in the book has appeared previously in a different form. In chapter 1, I draw from "Yao Minority Identity and the Location of Difference in the South China Borderlands," *Ethnos: Journal of Anthropology* 65, no. 1 (2000): 56–82, copyright Taylor and Francis on behalf of the National Museum for Ethnography, Stockholm. In chapter 3, I make use of "Moving House: Migration and the Place of the Household on the Thai Periphery." *Journal of the Siam Society* 87, nos. 1/2 (1999): 99–118, copyright Siam Society and "Does the House Hold? History and the Shape of Mien (Yao) Society," *Ethnohistory* 48, no. 4 (2001): 613–54, copyright American Society for Ethnohistory. Chapter 4 is partly based on "Serious Fun: Minority Cultural Dynamics and National Integration in Thailand," *American Ethnologist* 28, no. 1 (2001): 151–78, copyright American Anthropological Association and "Mien Through Sports and Culture: Mobilizing Minority Identity in Thailand," *Ethnos: Journal of Anthropology* 68, 3 (2003): 317–40, copyright Taylor and Francis on behalf of the National Museum for Ethnography, Stockholm. I thank these organizations and am indebted to the editors, Wilhelm Östberg and Don Kulick at *Ethnos*, Ron Renard at the *Journal of the Siam Society*, Neil Whitehead at *Ethnohistory*, and Carol Greenhouse at the *American Ethnologist*, and their anonymous readers for their insightful engagement with my work. Unless otherwise specified, all translations in the book are my own. I took all of the photographs as well.

Davydd Greenwood, Rich O'Connor, Sumit Mandal, Anne Brydon, Ken George, Carolyn Epple, Doug White, Nikki Tannenbaum, Yoko Hayami, Jim Eder, Jim Ockey, Pat Symonds, Jane Hanks, and many other kind people have helped me think through some of the ideas about ethnography. From a distance, John McKinnon and Peter Hinton generously answered my queries via e-mail. The pseudonymous Karl Coogan, who did a video documentary with me on a Mien festival, taught me things about words and images that have slowly influenced my understanding of ethnography and its possibilities. I regret that Tom Kirsch, Oliver Wolters, and Peter Hinton are no longer around, as their work remains an inspiration.

A Visiting Research Fellowship at Kyoto University's Center for Southeast Asian Studies was the context for the final revisions of the manuscript. I am indebted to Koji Tanaka, the center's director, Yoko Hayami, my institutional counterpart, Yukio Hayashi, Noburo Ishikawa, Jojo Abinales, Donna Amoroso, Junko Koizumi, Akio Tanabe, and many others for intellectual stimulation, new perspectives, and various pleasantries in and around Kyoto.

In much different form, the manuscript was read by Lorri Hagman of the University of Washington Press. She encouraged me to rewrite it from scratch, which I did, with many delays and occasional despair, several times. Years later the manuscript landed at Cornell University Press, first with Catherine Rice, then with Sheri Englund, later with Roger Haydon, and last with manuscript editor Karen Laun. To them and their anonymous readers I owe much of the current shape of the book.

NOTES ON LANGUAGE, TIME, AND PERSPECTIVE

Both Mien and Thai are tonal languages. In the book, I do not represent tones, nor do I generally distinguish open and closed "o" (as in *bog* versus *boat*) or short and long vowels. I ask linguistic purists forgiveness for this choice. Thai authors are noted by first name, following Thai convention, both in the text and in the bibliography. Japanese authors are listed by family name. Mien names, as in Vietnam and China, start with a lineage name and are followed by a "first" name usually consisting of two parts. Regarding time, I use the terms BCE and CE to indicate years "Before the Common Era" and "Common Era" in synchrony with the Western calendar now in use around the world. In the bibliography I give Buddhist Era dates for works published in Thailand, but in citations they are indicated by Western year only. The citation to "Theraphan 1991" is listed as "Theraphan 2534/1991" in the bibliography. The Thai dates matter, but the text sidesteps the dual chronology.

I use the ethnolinguistic references *Thai* and *Tai* to distinguish Siamese (Central Thai) from northern Thai, Shan, Lü, Khün, and others. These are relevant but problematic distinctions, as the book makes clear. I refer to Mien and other highland ethnic minority peoples rather interchangeably as uplanders, highlanders, and hinterland peoples. These are relational terms that imply the group's position relative to lowlanders and those in the cities. My tendency to use the term "upland–lowland relations" is deliberate. Unlike the contrasts *high* versus *low* or *up* versus *down*, upland–lowland is meant to suggest a disjuncture that has been a significant feature of this social landscape. Binaries do not always work straight.

Conversations with many non-academic Mien and Thai people have informed my views and interpretations, as have those with academics in the
"West" and "East." Mien stories written and unwritten, indigenous chronicles from within Southeast Asia, and past and present writings on China's
highland peoples have been essential to this project. Regional and local histories and identities have become part of my perspective on reality. I take
full responsibility for the interpretations contained in the book, but I have
also been influenced in many ways by the people, places, and issues that the
book is about.

I do not repeatedly call attention to the contingency of my understanding or use quotation marks to emphasize the assumed but problematic reality of certain terms (e.g., "hill tribes"). Most or all things and terms are
contingent, and their reality lies in relations and histories. In northern
Thailand, basic matters of land rights and citizenship are everyday concerns; at the same time it is possible to imagine a harmless, promising, and
interesting future. As an ethnographer and otherwise, I find the latter senti-
ment a precious object, and I hope that this account of often political matters is marked more by optimism and surprise than by their many opposites.

Mien Relations

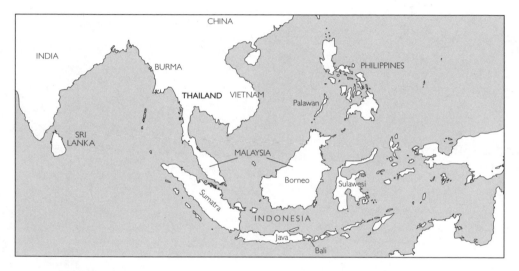

Southeast Asia

Introduction: Ethnic Landscapes

> The observations of colonial administrators, missionaries, ad-
> venturers and anthropologists were filtered through a grid of
> western preconceptions, assumptions and expectations about
> "tribes," "social structures," "societies" and the like. . . . The
> locus of the problem lies with the flaws of western theoretical
> and methodological preferences rather than in any intrinsic
> peculiarity of the upland peoples.
> —A. Thomas Kirsch, *Feasting and Social Oscillation*

About five hundred people of Thailand's Mien (Yao) ethnic minority came together for a festival in 2001.[1] The four-day event was held in
the northern part of Chiangmai Province at the end of March, and Mien
people from sixteen other villages came to compete in sports, to socialize,
to participate in the cultural program, and to enjoy the event as spectators.
The daytime program was similar to many other village festivals around the
country. Sports competitions at school grounds have to some extent replaced Buddhist temple festivals as the most prominent way of mobilizing
rural villages for common activities and to link them to one another in
ways that simultaneously imply societal integration and state control.

Such village festivals in the Thai countryside do not commonly, if ever,
feature displays of traditional culture, but in this case the cultural program
was very deliberate. The event was organized by the Mien Association, an
identity and advocacy group formed about a decade earlier to articulate
Mien interests in relation to national integration and development and to
work toward the preservation of Mien culture. Cultural programs featuring
dress, dance, and music are common as evening entertainment in contem-

porary Thailand, even at academic seminars. As edifying entertainment, such displays may be taken as an indication of nationalist ideas as much as expressions of globalization. Both national and global contexts assume that nations or ethnic groups share a cultural essence that is manifest in traditions that can be displayed on stage for a general audience (cf. Handler 1985).

While a relatively small and local event, this recent gathering is suggestive of how the lives of people in supposedly remote villages are entangled with national and global worlds (cf. Piot 1999). The daytime sports events consisted of volleyball, soccer, handball, basketball, *betong* (*pétanque, bocce*), *takraw,* and table tennis (ping-pong), all derived from Thai schools and Thailand's involvements in international sports. There was live commentary over loudspeakers for some of the action, most of it in the Mien language but some also in Thai, the national language. The competitive sports, the cups awarded for the top three finishers in each sport, and the broadcast commentary lent this local and ethnic festival the air of an event for a national or international audience.

In the evenings the action was different. There was singing in the archaic song language (*nzung wa*); the enactment of a wedding reception accompanied by musicians playing a double-reed oboe, drum, gongs, and cymbal; and the display of a color photocopy of an old illustrated scroll in ancient Chinese dealing with Yao origins. These presentations have some connection with traditional Mien culture, but other features suggest entertainment more in line with national television, such as a quiz show, dancing by teenage Mien women to a popular Thai tune, and a duet in the Thai language. For each of these elements of the evening program, there was commentary in the Mien language (*mien wa*).[2] The evening performers all received small wrapped gifts for their contributions.

The combination of Thai and Mien elements in this event is significant in a number of ways. The Mien are a highland ethnic minority group who have stood in a sometimes uneasy relationship with national society and state authorities, which have viewed the social, cultural, and agricultural practices of highland people as something to be overcome in the name of national integration and development. The event manifested a significant disconnection from the way Mien appear in ethnographic work from the 1960s when there was no concern with staging the elements of their culture for a general audience. At that time, their social life revolved around farming, rituals, and the incorporation of new household members through marriages and purchase adoptions (Kandre 1967; Miles 1974; Lemoine 1983). The apparent change from patterns described forty years earlier may suggest that Mien culture and social organization were traditional up until the 1960s and that they have become increasingly modern since.

Writing on the Karo of Sumatra, Indonesia, and on the Akha of northern Thailand, respectively, Kipp (1993) and Tooker (2004) suggest a fundamental shift regarding culture and identity in Southeast Asia's hinterland communities, from the integration of culture with all aspects of daily life and livelihood in the past to its dissociation from everyday life in the era they associate with modernity—the integration of communities into orbits of national administration, capitalism, and the like. Their analyses evoke a familiar expectation among Western theorists about the destructive potential of modernity that typically is based on a contrast with the coherence associated with tradition (Berman 1982; Englund and Leach 2000).

Appadurai has suggested that "the landscapes of group identity . . . around the world are no longer familiar anthropological objects, insofar as groups are no longer tightly territorialized, spatially bounded, historically unselfconscious, or culturally homogenous" (1996, 48). This sense of ethnic groups and the past may be fundamentally misguided, at least regarding cultural and social dynamics in the hinterland areas of Southeast Asia and adjacent regions. The Yao/Mien case suggests that identities have always been contingent and contested, never descriptively adequate, and always anchored to tenuous conflations of nature, culture, society, identity, and history. Ethnic identities have entered history to the extent that they were the basis for local and translocal claims to rights, recognition, and power. As far back as historical records go, identities have been entangled with the negotiation of rights and relationships within and among groups of people. In that sense, there has always been a regional and political dimension to "local" identities.

Mien forms of society and culture may have never matched the "familiar anthropological object." Yao peoples were historically confined to the forested mountains, and this spatial demarcation was from its inception entangled with dynamics of state control of identity, settlement, and political rights. The other components of Appadurai's characterization of premodernity, that people were historically unselfconscious and culturally homogenous, is an implausible depiction of Yao, Lawa, and other hinterland peoples of Southeast Asia and adjacent regions past or present. Perhaps most seriously, this terminology systemically precludes recognition of culture as inherently political, as a component of internal debates and inequalities, and as a feature of state control as much as a feature of the social life of so-called ethnic groups. Ethnic identity and culture have long been central to contestations regarding political position and the landscape of history. Allegations that certain peoples, who in this case suggest the image

Fig. 1: Soccer players at the Mien festival in 2001. Unlike at sports contests a decade earlier, villages now have team outfits.

of traditional tribal peoples, were historically unselfconscious are questionable and may simply reproduce certain Western expectations concerning history and culture that have served to discredit particular claims to identity and history since the colonial era (Sahlins 1985; Thomas 1989, 1994; Trouillot 1995).

The sports and culture fair in 2001 suggests some of the involvement of Mien peoples with national realities in contemporary Thailand. Their ethnic minority status has everything to do with the national classification of identity, and Mien are known as one of Thailand's "mountain peoples" (*chao khao*), who are assumed to be lacking in development, manners, and loyalty to the nation. At the fair, Mien showed themselves to be not only competent in modern Thai ways but also loyal to the principles of nationhood—the event started with a parade and the singing of the national anthem. The components of the festival suggest different aspects of who the Mien are. It was a festival of their identity; a competitive event; a social event on an unprecedented scale; an act of allegiance to the modern nation of Thailand; a reassertion of minority identity that had not received any positive public recognition; and a forum for organizing that accommodated several different perspectives on identity, culture, and the position of

Mien peoples within the contemporary state of Thailand. Some of these features appear to be contradictory, in particular the celebration of minority identity and the various declarations of allegiance to the Thai nation.

Much anthropology on Southeast Asia has shown that ethnic groups are not bounded or self-contained entities. Ethnicity implies a position within a network of identities, which are not always mutually exclusive (cf. Leach 1954; Moerman 1965; Lehman 1967a, b). Thailand's Mien are a highland ethnic minority group, and this book is in part concerned with what that entails and how this came about. The distinction between lowland peoples—peasants, fishermen, craftspeople, and urbanites in stratified societies—and upland peoples—farmers in the forested highlands whose social organization has in general not been stratified—is one of the basic features of the social landscape of Southeast Asia and the adjacent regions of South and East Asia. The spatial divide has simultaneously implied various differences in livelihood, ethnicity, ritual and other cultural practice, and relations with state authorities. Aspects of this upland-lowland distinction were the focus of much ethnographic work in the twentieth century.

With national integration measures during the latter half of the twentieth century, these differences between upland and lowland peoples have become less pronounced or taken a different form. The festival in 2001 had everything to do with the contemporary reality of the Mien peoples involved; their marginal status and their quest for acceptance in Thai society; their competency in the ways of the modern nation; notions of culture as a presentable heritage belonging to an ethnic group; and inequalities of wealth, location, and gender in the representatives of the Mien as a people and a culture.

The recent dynamics of sports competitions and the politics of identity may appear to stand in fundamental contrast to Mien social life in the past. Such contrasts might reinforce the contrast of tradition and modernity, but the book's aim is to suggest that in terms of society, culture, politics, and identity, the worlds of Mien and other hinterland minority peoples have always been found in region and history. Their apparent isolation in an "out-of-the-way place" (Tsing 1993) has not only rendered them adequate to ethnographic research about traditional peoples but simultaneously defined them as the focus of government interventions. The issues that the book deals with—ethnic and other identity, social organization, ritual, state-minority relations, nation-building, and the politics of culture—are all central to anthropological concerns and debates, both regarding Southeast Asia and more generally. Mien identity, society, and culture must be understood in terms of their relations within a larger social landscape where the distinction between upland and lowland peoples has been of fundamental importance. Focusing on different aspects of this regional setting, the book revolves around various cosmographic narratives—deriving from states, Yao or Mien peoples, ethnographers, or interactions among these different players—and their relations to identity and the practices of social life.

Approaches to the Uplands

Any discussion of the region's upland peoples and their identity in relation to lowlanders is indebted to Edmund Leach's *Political Systems of Highland Burma* (1954). His case concerned various peoples known collectively as Kachin but who oftentimes varied greatly in language, dress, ritual, political organization, and ethnic identification. He showed that there had been numerous shifts between egalitarian and hierarchic arrangements to these social formations and that Kachin stood in various relations to stratified lowland societies that were ethnically Shan. Kachin peoples sometimes became Shan, and ethnic shifts in the opposite direction were less common. In general, Kachin were upland shifting cultivators whose political units ranged from a few households to large collections of ranked settlements, whereas Shan were lowland wet-rice cultivators whose villages were under the command of princes who ruled states of varying scope.[3] Social life was often suffused with debate concerning its principles and the kinds of relations that people had with one another. Many of the ideas that informed hierarchic social organization among Kachin were actually borrowings from the stratified Shan society. The diversity and instability that Leach described for social life in the Kachin Hills makes highly problematic any notion that things had been stable and somehow traditional in upland communities up until recent national integration measures.

A focus on "a people," even if the notion of an ethnic group as socially or culturally uniform may be of dubious value (cf. Hinton 1979, 1983), allows for an exploration of differences in how people within a social category act. The recent Mien festival was not only a response to a historical situation, it was also an active engagement with a particular setting that influenced both the place of Mien within Thailand and the relative position of individual people and settlements. In addition, it lent a particular shape to the relations of men and women in the public sphere. Leach insisted that ritual was not unreflective practice but rather a language of argument constitutive of social positions and relations. He made a similar case concerning myth, as stories that were central to how people continually fashioned their social realities. "Myth and ritual are modes of making statements about structural relationships" (1954, 264).

Kirsch (1973) followed up on this focus on ritual with his study of how patterns of feasting contributed to the shifts between hierarchical and egalitarian social organization in upland societies. Drawing on the ethnographic literature concerning the upland regions of Burma and Laos in particular, he argued that ritual and feasting provided a much closer match to local, indigenous concerns than did Leach's emphasis on political maneuvers. Kirsch centered his study on patterns in who could make offerings to what spirits and invite what people to a subsequent feast and their meaning in terms of social organization. Hierarchical settings were marked by ranked and differentiated feasting and the differential status of kin-groups, which impacted patterns in marriages, for instance. More egalitarian settings were highly competitive and sometimes quite litigious. The ethnographic cases showed significant variation but no explicit directionality toward either egalitarian or hierarchic organization.

At first glance there may seem little connection between the cases made by Leach, Kirsch, and various other scholars of the region and the contemporary reality of Thailand's Mien. National integration has turned highland peoples into ethnic minorities and placed various restrictions on their farming practices. The previous autonomy regarding ethnic affiliation and political organization has disappeared, as have the competitiveness of feasting, ritual, and household formation and the freedom to move households or settlements. This shift indicates a radical change in the position of upland groups within a larger landscape and thus a change in the composition of the region. The structures of identity and social life have changed. States, highland minorities, the upland-lowland divide, hinterland livelihood, and the relations of livelihood to identity and political organization are all different from what they were forty years ago, a hundred years ago, and earlier.

The analytical emphasis of scholars such as Leach and Kirsch was conditioned in part by trends in upland social life at the time. Kinship, ritual, feasting, and engagements with lowland societies have changed in significance and/or taken new forms. The comparative and historical emphasis of these earlier studies is valuable, as is their focus on local patterns in the ongoing production of communities and social relations through ritual, exchange, and the telling of stories. This study of the Mien in regional context is a product of another time and place, it does not aspire to replicate or refute earlier anthropology but rather to complement it and to offer a perspective on the historical contingency of the worlds it described.

In Thailand between the 1960s and 1980s, the highland ethnic minority peoples were generally viewed as a national problem that could be solved to the extent that highlanders "became Thai"; lived in permanent, lowland settlements; grew wet-rice; and abandoned their ethnically different ways. In this context, one that involved military attacks on highland settlements in many areas, Western ethnographers affiliated with the Thai government's Tribal Research Center conveyed each ethnic group as traditional, adapted to the highland environment, and (more or less implicitly) endangered by the forces of modernity and national integration. The situation of Thailand's hinterland peoples was different at the time of my research, in the period between 1990 and 2001. The area was peaceful, and there was in general much greater acceptance of ethnic diversity than there had been a few decades earlier.

Most contemporary ethnography on Southeast Asia's upland regions, island and mainland, is situated in relation to state control, nation-building, and other aspects of recent historical context.[4] There is a growing body of work on similar issues in southern China emphasizing the relations of marginality and minority status to the rhetoric of nationalism and state control (e.g., Litzinger 2000; Schein 2000). As across Southeast Asia, the civilizational discourses of state control in China were significant to the reproduction of an upland-lowland divide (Harrell 1995; Turton 2000). In both places there has been growing acceptance of ethnic difference, one that draws on changes in nationalist imagery, modernist notions of traditional peoples, and the importance of cultural tourism by domestic as well as international clients.[5]

Tsing's (1993) study of the Meratus Dayak of Kalimantan, Indonesia, was consciously aimed against the conventions of the "tribal" ethnography of that region, in particular the emphasis on stable and shared cultures. Instead, her focus was on how state control and modernization had marginalized Meratus and other upland peoples and how these dynamics of inequality and marginalization informed local realities. While increasingly unavoidable dealings with Indonesia's state structures and development rhetoric had accentuated gender inequalities among Meratus Dayak people, Tsing shows quite clearly that inequality was already manifest in their notions of gender in relation to power and mobility. Men dealt with spirits and the outside world, assembling communities around them as the men's prowess became known. Dealings with states and a dangerous and often violent outside world were central to how men established their reputation and created settlements (Tsing 1996). In the same historical setting, the global political economy of logging and other resource exploitation has exposed Meratus Dayak areas to further marginalization (Tsing 2003), while transnational rhetoric of environmental preservation and indigenous eco-wisdom has availed other connections to the outside world that may offer some protection of local claims to livelihood (Tsing 1999).

This book is situated within the same currents as this recent work. I pay similar attention to the relations of marginal identities and state control, but I seek to go one step further in questioning the historical character of ethnicity in my suggestion that prior to the colonial era ethnic identity was analogous to rank in the pervasive tributary systems of the time. The engagement with early states is partly about cultural notions and the classification of peoples as inseparable from political economy. The cultural aspect of state control classified the natural and social landscapes in such a way that the position of hinterland peoples in the forest seemed somehow natural to ecologically minded anthropologists, an adaptation to nature. Classifications of types of people and environments, as much as the notions of historicity that have entered the historical record, have always been entangled with the politics of culture and situated in relation to political economy and state control.

This book's engagement with origins is in part simply a consequence of the research setting, as Yao/Mien identity has roots in relations with Chinese states that may stretch back over a thousand years. The case cannot be proven in any simple sense, but scholars all too often confine their historical contextualization to the colonial era and that of modern nation-states. This strategy of not confronting earlier history may leave the impression of a traditional or ahistorical period prior to the advent of capitalist expansion and colonial rule. Because the telling of history inherently implies a definition of identity, rights, and agency, it seems imperative to go beyond Western historical dynamics to show that the modernist expectation of a fundamental break between past and present, from tradition to modernity, does not hold. The alternative, it seems, is to convey the Mien as having been a traditional people and culture cut off from the dynamics of history and region until the recent past—but this strategy misconstrues both the so-called mountain peoples and the dynamics of history and reinforces the notion of "the West" as the sole agent of history and modernity.

Situating the Mien

To some analysts, engaging with ethnic minority formations of culture and society "runs the risk of imputing an authentic subject position to the Other" (Litzinger 2002, 428). But limiting the analytical focus to the present context of ethnic minorities and state control, for instance by taking it for granted that the Mien are fundamentally an ethnic minority and the nation's Other, which can be comprehended in terms of their marginalization, ends up only reproducing some of the inequalities that Mien people have had to contend with. Not confronting the histories and contingencies of the categories that animate social landscapes "has reduced the value of the categories for research and has obscured the epistemologies of other cultures" (Epple 1998, 280).

Mien identity and social formations are in and of history, and they inform particular historical understandings among Mien people. The current marginalization of ethnic minorities in Thailand is an important component of contemporary Mien understandings of who they are, but their responses to this condition are varied. The Mien ethnic festival offers a glimpse of some of the current self-definitions, such as that of progressive villagers whose sports competition shows them as very compatible with the rest of the country; the ethnic group as a carrier of heritage that would be of interest to a general audience; and the ethnic group as a carrier of eco-wisdom. Each of these self-fashionings suggests different relations with a larger context of identity and state control, and each carries a particular definition of the Mien as an acting subject.[6]

Different versions of Mien social organization have expressed the social visions of particular sets of actors, such as individual householders, multi-village chiefs, and lately village headmen, schoolteachers, and various others. Mien agency, the ability to impose specific designs on social life around them, has always related to regional contexts of culture and political economy. Any manifestation of Mien society, the mobilization of labor, resources, and attentions through particular channels, has always downplayed a range of alternatives. Sports contests have become integral to social life in rural Thailand. Sports, village fairs, fund-raising, and competitions for awards such as "model development village" make villages an unquestioned reality. Villages are equally real for their inhabitants, for fun-seeking visitors, and for political and royal personages who distribute attention and favors on them unequally.

In a recent conflict with a wildlife sanctuary, Mien farmers insisted on establishing their legitimacy as players on the national landscape of modernization and development, whereas the authorities in many ways tried to discredit them and to define them as simple recipients of the state's leadership—they were not to act on their own initiative. The current denial of rights to various ethnic minority peoples in Thailand is based on national history in relation to a specific landmass. Mien people are increasingly positioning themselves on this landscape of national sovereignty, and their emphasis on ethnic identity and local cultural practice has been far from uniform.

Scholars of Southeast Asia commonly argue that premodern state formations were characterized by centrist ideologies that manifested an emphasis on control over people rather than land (Reid 1988, 129; Carsten 1997, 257–58). Earlier states were "nonbounded kingdoms" that did not concern themselves with border demarcation. In this earlier political context, "the tribal people wandering in the mountain forests were subjects of no power" (Thongchai 1994, 74, 73). But the recorded origins of the Yao peoples in southern China and those of the Lawa people in the Lanna and Shan areas of what are now northern Thailand and Burma suggest a different historical scenario. It was not just that premodern states had various links to hinterland regions, the upland-lowland divide that reinforced the position of "tribal peoples wandering in the forested mountains" was also an outcome of the state's project of mapping rank and identity on the landscape. The origins of the Yao and the Lawa do not so much concern the long history of some peoples. More importantly, they reveal the roots of an Asian "savage slot" (cf. Trouillot 1991)—a category of uncivilized people through which members of the civilized state fashion their identity, superiority, and agency—in the historical dynamics of state formation. Establishing an accurate history is in this case very nearly impossible and may simply reproduce the biases of the historical record. Instead, the writing of history and the formation of mountain peoples were expressions of the same process of defining state society, where sovereign command was the principle of history as much as of the various identities that were consolidated in relation to the state. These dynamics are the focus of chapter 1.

Identity and history referred to the rankings of tributary rulers, and history was repeatedly rewritten in ways that fused past and present. Peoples such as the Yao and the Lawa were defined as hinterland savages standing outside tributary systems because they did not share the rhetoric or practices that defined state society. Contracts exempting Yao and Lawa from the trappings of the state were repeatedly reissued, for reasons that concerned the state as much as they did the highland peoples. Defining "savages" was not simply about marginalization; it was a general process of aligning cosmography, society, and politics in the consolidation of a state. Rank and tributary duties were central to state-defined society, which was charted between the opposing poles of savages in the forested hills and slaves within but "below" society. The identities that have entered ethnography as ethnic were entangled with rank, tribute duties, and sumptuary categories in ways that conflated categories of nature, culture, society, and politics. Changes in state control and political economy during the nineteenth century undid the previously common tributary states and, with them, the entanglements of identity and rank, all of which had various repercussions for the social relevance of ethnic identity.

The case of Thailand during the twentieth century provides an example of how ethnic identities were reconfigured in relation to nation-states in the region, a process described in chapter 2. Thai and Western ethnographic writing alike show a trend toward racialization as the link between nation and terrain became the principle for classifying peoples—defining their identity and rights by their relations to land and history. The process was all about establishing the sovereignty of Bangkok-based authorities over the terrain. Ideas of race and evolution recast the ethnic landscape toward the categorizations that the Western ethnographers affiliated with the Tribal Research Center later inherited and extended in their studies of the nation's minorities as hill tribes.

The category of "hill tribes" draws on this international contact zone and was consolidated in relation to border controls and projects of national integration and development. After military campaigns against highlanders and communist insurgents came to an end, a proliferation of museums in northern Thailand contributed to the refashioning of the national public sphere. Museums project particular understandings of the world, and in Thailand they center on royalty and Buddhism as the principles of identity and history. This is not simply celebratory hegemonic rhetoric: ethnic minority highlanders as much as other people in Thailand are repeatedly reminded that they come into being and agency through their subservient devotion to the pillars of nationhood.

State structures have long influenced the realities of the region's varied mountain peoples. The assumed disconnection or autonomy of mountain peoples from state power that forms the basis for various contrasts between tradition and modernity may be, like the idea of tradition itself, a product of modernity's worldview (cf. Knauft 2002). In the late nineteenth century, various upland leaders had titles from lowland states, and they delivered tribute or rendered services to these authorities. Two such Mien strongman leaders are known from the ethnographic record, and they serve as good examples of the centrality of chiefly rule in highland areas prior to national integration. In Thailand, some Mien settlements were connected to a monopolized trade in opium. The village of Phulangka was central to this opium production and trade among the Mien. The titled leader of this Mien area ran a household of 120 people, which is quite extraordinary for trends in upland household formation but also revealing of various changes that took place in the twentieth century. As links to tributary rulers faded into oblivion, uplanders' articulations of prominence shifted focus from military prowess to success in farming. This shift helps to contextualize the exceptionally large household in Phulangka and also the opposite and then prevalent trend of small households and highly mobile settlements. Chapter 3 is concerned with these histories.

Not only were Mien people on unequal footing in relation to the state, there were also various internal inequalities regarding manifestations of Mien ways. Normative Mien practices, the cultural and ritual dynamics that constitute the ethnic group, have been the privilege of the more affluent. Poor people have had no voice when it comes to articulations of ethnicity, and this emphasis on ethnic ways also tends to silence women's voices and agendas. "Even in classless societies, cultural ideologies empower some, subordinate others, extract the labor of some for the benefit of those whose interests the ideologies serve and legitimate. Cultures are webs of mystification as well as signification. We need to ask who *creates* and *defines* cultural meanings; and to what ends" (Keesing 1987, 161–62).

During the 1960s, foreign ethnographers did pioneer research in northern Thailand among peoples who were largely unknown to the world of anthropology—or so it seemed. There appeared to be a good fit between the category of tribal peoples and the minority ethnic groups then living in the highlands of northern Thailand. The biases of the ethnographic record need to be situated in relation to political economy and anthropological expectations (Pels and Salemink 1999). Such a critique of previous ethnographic conventions is still necessary, but it yields little insight beyond the worlds of universities and governments and risks making ordinary people and their histories or politics unimaginable. Going beyond such critique requires the refocusing of ethnography, including a historical contextualization detailing which local voices have been dominant in upland settlements (in this case) at different points in time.

Patterns in Mien social formation and agency draw on their uneven position at various interfaces with state control and the regional political economy. Recent social and cultural dynamics in the ethnic minority hinterlands of Thailand show an increasing emphasis on the village as the fundamental unit of ritual and social relations. This process is clearly related to national integration, as described in chapter 4. Villages are the smallest administrative unit of the Thai nation-state.[7] Political and economic changes have undermined the articulations of being and agency that centered on households. Like previous household centrality, the village focus is not simply a reaction to regional political economy but a creative project of self-fashioning that aligns people as individuals and collectivities in particular ways with the larger world. Many contemporary activations of the village center on sports, which are derived from national schools. Education and national administration inform new ways of being Mien and institute new inequalities. But Mien people are also drawing on international frameworks for indigenous people in refashioning themselves. There is some tension between this "indigenous-people" emphasis, one that focuses on eco-wisdom as a key to gaining land rights, and a concern with culture and identity as matters of staged displays in the countryside.

These efforts, manifest in the activities of the Mien Association, are forward-looking projects that reach into the past in order to align the Mien as an ethnic group to nation and state in Thailand. They contribute to the public silencing of older people who assume farming households as the central element of identity and social life, thus refashioning Mien identity on the ruins of previous articulations. The Mien society, like the state, is a framework for establishing the coordinates of identity, history, and social practice. The alignment of identity, history, rights, and agency is what creates and sometimes reifies projects such as the state or the Mien. Neither the Mien nor the state exist in a thing-like fashion, they are projects that mobilize people in their terms and thus create the effect of an ethnic group or of the state. But states tend to appear dominant because they employ various means to inscribe themselves into the social landscape and as the principle of history and identity, often using violence to erase alternatives.

When the warfare against highlanders and communists ended in 1982, the state declared many forested areas out of bounds for settlement, both to preclude continued resistance and to inscribe itself into the landscape in new ways through protected forests. Among the repercussions of these efforts was an impressive protest by Mien farmers against a wildlife sanctuary and its director, both of which had caused them many grievances. Chapter 5 concerns the politics of rights and recognition. After some destruction of property and many meetings and petitions, the protest came to nothing. The Mien protest emphasized their position as citizens, iterated their history as an official settlement, and pleaded for their right to improvement in their lives through education, health care, and trade. That is, while the event was in some ways violent and flirted with the possibility of further violence, it rested on the notion of Mien farmers as proper, modern Thai subjects.

The conclusions section addresses some of the matters of classification that pertain to the Mien and mountain peoples more generally, including the implicit state biases of scientific and common definitions of history. The Mien people have been constituted at various interfaces of state control and ethnography. They have also constituted themselves through relations with their ancestor spirits. Their chants to ancestors reveal some of the entanglements of worldview and economy. Spirits are cordially invited and treated deferentially, a deal is made with them, and they are paid. When it is clear that they have received the payment, then the spirits are sent off, after which people may sit down to a feast where interactions among hosts and guests inform a different set of identities. When Mien householders invite and later send off the ancestor spirits at their rituals, the distinction between the spirit world and the human world is very important for their sense of who they are. These two worlds are never quite separate, though people sometimes talk and act as if they were; spirits have long been integral to the various aspects of Mien lives, and without people to sustain them through offerings the spirits would cease to exist. The separation between humans and spirits constituted the identity of the two and the parameters of their subsequent relations. The book concludes with the words to one such encounter.

Upland and lowland worlds have been entangled from the very beginning, somewhat like the worlds of people and spirits. The bifurcation between peoples of the plains and those of the forested mountains contributed to the structure of the region's social landscape. The upland-lowland divide set the terms for the diverse constructions of identity and history that informed social relations as much as ritual practice. The Mien and other upland peoples have lent shape to this part of Asia just as the region has informed the parameters of their identity. The book rests on such relations between parts and wholes. The notion of the Mien, like the notion of a household with its ancestors, suggests considerable continuity and even permanence, whereas the relations through which they have been constituted have always been tenuous and negotiable and have had varied outcomes in different times and places. The book traces frameworks of interaction and identity in different settings; the interpenetration of local, regional, and global dimensions in the social and cultural dynamics that have been constitutive of the Mien and mountain peoples more generally.

Once I sat with Le Tsan Kwe and other Mien people in Phale and they were telling me stories—"rare stories, not like the ones you would hear in Pangkha." As always, Mien ancestry in the tale about the dog Pien Hung came up. One of the men asked me about the ancestry of Westerners. I drew a blank. Then another old man said he had heard it was a monkey. Over time, this encounter brought the idea of human evolution into a whole new light for me. The following chapters may reflect some of that Mien-related light on matters of history, identity, ethnography, and the state.

CHAPTER ONE

Yao Origins and the
State of Nature

Wild men from the hills can be bought to serve as slaves. Families of wealth may own more than one hundred; those of lesser means content themselves with ten or twenty; only the very poor have none. These savages are captured in the wild mountainous regions, and are of a wholly separate race called *Chuang* [brigands].

—Chou Ta-Kuan, *The Customs of Cambodia*[1]

Mountain peoples were captured for slavery during the reign of Angkor rulers in the thirteenth century. This suggests some of the relations of inequality that accompanied the spatial distinction between the people in the region, the upland-lowland divide. The account mentions that those of the mountain peoples "who understand the language of the country are sold in the towns as slaves," contrasting them with others who "refuse to submit to civilization and are not familiar with its language. They have no houses but wander about in the mountains" (Chou 1992, 25). The description is very similar to those of the mountain peoples in southern China at the same time. Bellwood, working from the archaeological record, suggests that "the 'hill tribe phenomenon' of mainland Southeast Asia—the expansion into high altitudes from the north of shifting agriculturists—is a relatively recent development" (1992, 120). It is likely that prior to the consolidation of states in relation to areas of intensive wet-rice cultivation, land-use and the categorization of people were more diverse and place-specific. O'Connor argues from archaeology and history that the predominance of irrigated rice cultivation in Southeast Asia largely emerged in the early second millennium CE, replacing an earlier emphasis on house gardens and flood management (1995, 970). The category of forest or mountain peoples became possible once the cleared lowlands had become a principle for society and identity, and this holds both for lowland notions of "savages" in remote locations and for mountain people's notions of themselves as a particular kind of people. Highland shifting cultivation as the basis for livelihood and identity was thus a product of and a response to state formation. This assertion cannot be proven in any simple way. The issue is similar to that of gender differences; it may be a fact to some that men and women differ in a given set of ways, but this does not get us very far in explaining the range and historicity of differences that are projected on these apparently natural categories.

The differentiation between mountain peoples and lowlanders was not an event but rather an ongoing process of reproducing social categories in terms of livelihood, residence, political organization and relations, group identity, and cultural practice. There was considerable family resemblance in this differentiation within the large region that stretches from southern China, across Southeast Asia, and to certain parts of South Asia.[2] The similarities may be compared to the colonial era when particular patterns of political economy and statecraft aligned with traffic in imagery to anchor notions of race, progress, and civilization that informed an increasingly global worldview regarding the types of people. The family resemblance among colonial-era ideas about kinds of people does not suggest homogenization but rather the organization of diversity along a select set of features that were shared among different and only partially connected societies.

For the premodern regionalization of Asia in all its cultural, political, and other diversity, notions of civility and hierarchy were central to the consolidation of lowland society and the mapping of its opposite on the forested mountains. Only one aspect of these complex dynamics is the focus here: the consolidation of Lawa and Yao highlander identities in the Lanna and Shan areas and in southern China, respectively, as examples of a more general process of the creation of an Asian region through related categories of society and its outsiders. The discussion of these "local" cases provides a sense of the bigger picture of how states engendered the conflation of politics, identity, residence, livelihood, and cultural practice that informed the category of mountain peoples. The key element of this case about previous history is that ethnicity was primarily about rank within schemes of tributary

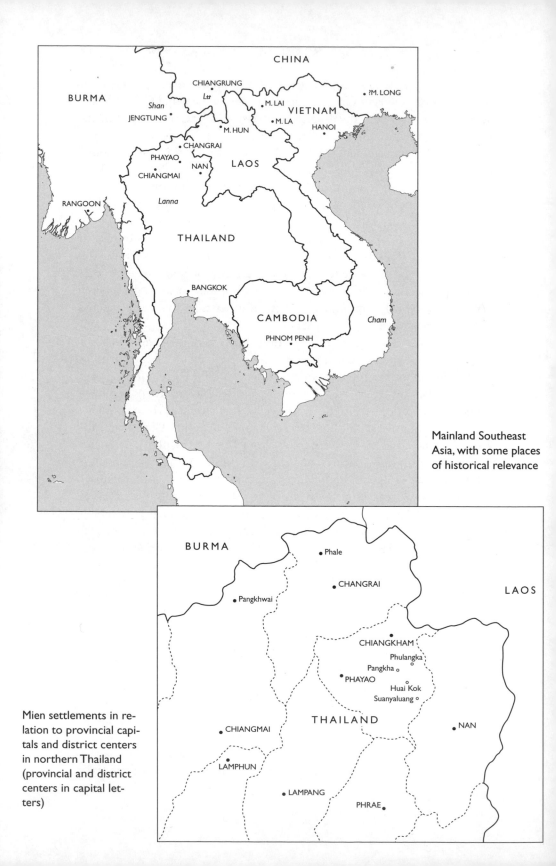

CHINA

CHIANGRUNG
Ltt
BURMA   ?M. LONG
                    Shan   M. LAI
JENGTUNG   VIETNAM
                    M. HUN   M. LA
                                         HANOI
            CHANGRAI
    PHAYAO
        NAN   LAOS
CHIANGMAI

            Lanna

RANGOON

        THAILAND

            BANGKOK

                CAMBODIA   *Cham*

                PHNOM PENH

Mainland Southeast
Asia, with some places
of historical relevance

BURMA   Phale

                        CHANGRAI
                                        LAOS
        Pangkhwai

                    CHIANGKHAM
                        Phulangka
                    Pangkha
                    PHAYAO
                        Huai Kok
                    Suanyaluang

        CHIANGMAI   THAILAND   NAN

Mien settlements in re-
lation to provincial capi-
tals and district centers
in northern Thailand   LAMPHUN
(provincial and district
centers in capital let-
ters)   LAMPANG
                            PHRAE

relations and rested on various aspects of state control. The making and re-production of mountain peoples as a category reflects one aspect of region-alization. It suggests the consolidation of a limited set of identities in rela-tion to livelihood, political status, and state control that were simultaneously local and regional. The entanglements of identity and political economy during the historical era (roughly 900–1900 CE) should lay to rest any no-tion of uplanders' isolation from the dynamics of history and politics prior to the colonial period.

Making Lawa around Chiangmai and Jengtung

The Lawa (Lua') are commonly viewed as an ancient people in northern Thailand, an autochthonous population (cf. Condominas 1990; Penth 2000). They are mentioned in early northern Thai chronicles and state-founding stories (Aroonrut 2000, 2002). In these accounts, the Lawa were already living in these regions when the Thai states were established, and a part of the founding of the kingdom (queendom, rather) of Hariphunchai (later Lamphun) involved driving the Lawa into the hills, where they have remained ever since. Some dimensions of the Lawa origins parallel the case of the Yao vis-à-vis the Chinese state discussed below. More than showing how the state has marginalized certain peoples, the Lawa and Yao cases il-lustrate the interconnectedness of the region's varied peoples and the sig-nificance of ethnic identity in these entanglements.

The *Jengtung State Chronicle* (Sao Saimong 1981) provides one version of the account of Queen Jamathewi (Camadevi, Cammadevi) that involves the marginalization of the Lawa by the conquering Thai or Mon (Condom-inas 1990; Swearer and Premchit 1998). Taken at face value, this narrative provides ample support for a political reading of the social landscape, as one ethnic group marginalizes another one. But it is not a given that "Thai" and "Lawa" were separate ethnic entities before this encounter or that being in the hills was the equivalent of marginalization. It is only so if the ultimate reference to social position lies within the state. The engagement between Lawa and Thai brought a restructuring that involved ethnic labels and, further, provided multiple terms of engagement that are glossed over with the narrow focus on peoples as either having or not having power.

The queen constructed villages and towns with appropriate grades and classifications, together with places of worship, and named the capital Haribhunja. . . . At the time there was a Lva [Lawa] named Lango, who was the overlord of all Lvas, residing in Usupabbatta [arrow mountain,

Doi Suthep], and he was very strong and powerful. When that Lva learned that the queen had come to reside in the kingdom he had a desire to have Nang Cammadevi as his wife. . . . When she learned that the Lva man had a desire to have her, she thought to herself thus, "The Dammilva is base and low; no matter how powerful he may be, he is not suitable for me. Were I to reply in brief words it would not be proper; I must think of means to demolish the power of the braya of the Lvas" [which she then did, and after an attack by her army the Lawas] were utterly destroyed and fled. (Sao Saimong 1981, 221–24)

This description concerns the establishment and expansion of Buddhist domains, a civilizing project that has two sides to it—driving away the Lawa and establishing the hierarchy of lowland settlements. Queen Jamathewi established a hierarchy of settlements and linked them to Buddhist temples, and she named the court-town where she presided. Hers was a spatial project of linking the identity and rank of both people and settlements, stringing together a social order centered on her court. Her project was not simply the state, but also the state's social and ecological exterior, where the Lawa and the forest became mutual references. The expulsion of the Lawa served as a means to establish a Buddhist state that joined civilization and hierarchy. Projecting barbarism on the Lawa conveyed what the state was not, and this aligned forests with any manifestation of disorder. The fixing of an ethnic label on highland peoples in northern Thai regions emerged from a cultural project that naturalized political control over the social landscape through the allocation of identities (ethnic, rank, and so on) as within or outside the state.

Stately order was made by a ruler's distribution of rank within a universal domain. Each new ruler had to constitute the domain through the ranking of people and places and through the defining of their relations (O'Connor 1983, 11). The making and remaking of uplanders' identities was a part of this process, not as an inherent quality but in general where a domain had important relations with the peoples of the forests. Consider coronation ceremonies in Jengtung in what is now the Shan State of Burma. Right before the coronation of King Namthun, Lawa people from two villages "were brought down [from the hills] to sit and eat their food on the gem-studded throne in the palace. While they were eating, the Lva were driven out and the [King] took their place" (Sao Saimong 1981, 230).

To the lowland Buddhist Shan ruler, the Lawa embodied the wild, the antithesis of order. They were "base and low," in the language of the chronicle. It appears that driving the Lawa off the throne and out of the domain was an important prerequisite to any new king taking power in Jengtung.

This form of the coronation ritual involving the Lawa was last performed in 1897, after the area was made part of British Burma (Sao Saimong 1981, 284). The logic of the ritual appears to be that the order made by the previous king, his contracts with people as well as the rank order he has bestowed on individuals and settlements, was undone by placing the "base and low" non-Buddhist Lawa representatives on the throne for a meal. Driving off the Lawa, and thus driving away disorder, was the first step toward putting the new king in control of the identities and rank of people and settlements. From his coronation onward, the ruler became the source of identities and social relationships within his domain. The notion of making a domain by initially driving away the "forest people" is common among Tai groups in the region (Archaimbault 1964; Tanabe 2000). The involvement of the Lawa in the coronation ceremonies at Jengtung suggests that Lawa people may have had various relations with the court, but it is not clear whether such relations were regular or if they always implied the same villages.[3]

The spatial project of separating forests and cleared lowlands was not only about the separation of the peoples inside and outside the state. Various relations were maintained simultaneously to such separations, and there are many cases from across the region of contracts that established economic and other relations across the upland-lowland divide. Such contracts with upland peoples had a long history in the Chiangmai region. In return for agreeing to stay where they were and provide services and goods, certain Lawa populations were to be exempt from corvée and taxes: "Seventeenth-century Burmese conquerors of Chiang Mai had signed an agreement with Lawas in Chaem Tai and Ban Khon villages near Chom Thong in 1605 exempting them from supplying food to officials, carrying fodder for elephants, and performing guard services in exchange for temple servitude at Wat Wisutharam. The Burmese pact had reaffirmed an earlier agreement signed in the 1550s by Queen Mahathewi of Chiang Mai assigning the Lawas to the monastery" (Renard 1986, 237; cf. Aroonrut 2000, 143).

The scope of such agreements is not clear and is likely to have varied considerably. The term *Lawa,* like *Yao,* is a lowland term for people who had a variety of designations for themselves. It is never very clear whether contracts between states and upland peoples applied to an "ethnic group," a village-cluster, or a single village, but they are persistently stated in ethnic terms. In the Lanna area of the Chiangmai valley, now northern Thailand, the duties of peasant subjects were generally assigned in terms of villages (Calavan 1974; Bowie 1988; Ratanaporn 1989). Contracts with hinterland nonsubjects were with a leader of a larger population. One example of such a contract is an inscribed silver plate that dates from 1852. It grants Lawa exemption from corvée duties in return for tribute to the court of Chiang-mai. The grant was bestowed upon Phaya Rattana Wang Na ("Lord Jewel of the Front Palace"), the title that the Lawa leader was given, and upon the lower rankings of Khun San, Khun Konkeo, Lam Chan, and Lam Chai:

> It shall serve all of them as their staff and their golden pillar among the three million Lawa in accordance with their continuous customs, ways and traditions since the time of their ancestors. In consideration of their tribute of 220 pieces of fine silver, the equivalent of 600 shoulder loads [of rice], annually deposited in the royal treasury, we do hereby exempt and release them from all . . . duties to our government. . . . We forbid our [officials], both present and future, to impress their labor. Let them work their swiddens and gardens so that they will have tribute to fully fill our royal treasury so that it will not become depleted, empty and bare. . . . Fee for enforcing this order 50. Fee for receiving this document 100 (Kraisri 1965: 235–36).

Taken at face value, this document offered "the three million Lawa" exemption from duties to the court if they paid a given amount of silver annually. If they did not hand over the silver, they should pay in rice. The responsibility for this contract was placed with the five titled Lawa leaders. It offered protection against duties imposed by lower-ranking lowland officials and promised to deliver a curse on the Lawa chief if the Lawa population did not prosper or if he oppressed them. If the contract was respected, it would deliver blessing to the Lawa, chiefs and commoners alike. But the contract also laid out what could happen if it was not heeded; the Lawa would be made to perform corvée duties like ordinary subjects, their elephants and women would be appropriated, local lowland authorities would not show any restraint in drawing on Lawa labor, or the Lawa rulers would impose too many duties on the commoners, which might cause the Lawa to abandon their chief (see below). Importantly, the text of this contract spelled out a market in identity and protection: "Fee for enforcing this order 50. Fee for receiving this document 100." To establish the protection that the grant promised the Lawa, people had to purchase the silver plate, presumably from the Chiangmai ruler, and then to pay for each occasion that it was activated. The language of this contract suggests that identities and social relations were continually reworked within a larger social and political landscape, in part through service, tribute, and payment.

The *Jengtung State Chronicle* defined the history and practice of the state of Jengtung as informed by the success and Buddhist virtue of Queen Ja-mathewi's and King Mangrai's earlier state-making projects. Different chronicles give different dates for Jamathewi as a historical figure, one suggests the seventh and another the eleventh century (Swearer and Premchit 1998, 5). King Mangrai's conquests and his founding of many states (*müang*) are dated to the end of the thirteenth century (Wyatt and Aroonrut 1998, 32–50). While chronicles serve as important historical sources, they are also projections of particular worldviews. In Tai chronicles, the dynamics of Buddhist rulers take a central place. The *Chiangmai Chronicle* does not include the account of Jamathewi's relations with the Lawa in its short entry on her (Wyatt and Aroonrut 1998, 5). It is possible that by the time of the writing of this version in the nineteenth century, relations with Lawa were not of much concern to Chiangmai rulers and their monk-scribes or that drawing the state's boundary against the forces of wilderness was no longer particularly pressing. By implication, relations with Lawa and concerns with the state's boundaries and civilizing mission were more important in Jengtung, where Lawa representatives took part in the state-making process as late as 1897.[4]

Chronicles relate the rule of King Mangrai as informed by the precedent of Queen Jamathewi. But the extant copies of the *Laws of King Mangrai* (*Mangraithammasastra*, cf. Aroonrut and Wijeyewardene 1986) do not discuss the presence of the Lawa. A copy that dates to about 1800 CE describes the ranking of his domain, of the king, chiefs, freemen, and slaves (Kirsch 1984, 257). One notable feature of this legal code is Mangrai's distinction between Dharma Lords (*khun tham*) and Mara Lords (*khun man*, from *Mara*, the Buddha's nemesis). Dharma, the Buddha's teachings, made rulers merciful, virtuous, and compassionate, whereas "Mara Lords show no mercy or compassion to citizens (*phrai*), they extort from them, flog them, tie them up, bully and oppress them, seize their goods, cohabit with their daughters, nieces or wives" (Kirsch 1984, 256). Through this rhetoric, Mangrai established Buddhism as the only legitimate framework for kingship, which served to undermine whatever local models there had been to authority in the Chiangmai Valley. While the code did not list schemes of taxation and tribute, it addressed a related concern, the limiting of access to slavery. A lord should not accept as slaves "persons who attempt to avoid repaying their debts by becoming slaves, those who hope to gain a lord's favor in case of litigation, thieves who hope to escape punishment, and deserters from the king's service who try to avoid their obligations" (Kirsch 1984, 258).[5] The thrust of these stipulations was to keep a reliable number of citizens or freemen, and the text notes that *phrai* are "hard to find." Commoners would be "executed if caught deserting from the army" (Aroonrut 2003, 83).

The concern to procure taxable subjects is interwoven with specifications concerning rank and the infusion of Buddhist rhetoric into the dynamics of kingship and state-level inequality. In this way, Buddhism became a feature of membership in the state, which by implication defined non-Buddhist populations, such as the Lawa, as outside of society. As the Lawa did not partake of the civilized inequality of the state and the protections that it availed, they owed no duties to officials. Buddhist rulers in Tai and Burmese areas sponsored temples and monks, both to demonstrate their virtue and to integrate their domains through cosmography. Rulers channeled wealth to temples and the monkhood and kept temple lands exempt from taxation. Meanwhile, regional rulers in this tributary scheme attempted to amass their own power and wealth, thus they did not always remit much wealth to their overlords. Burmese states went through several cycles of decline and reconquest as rulers and their regional officials competed for a favorable balance in their dealings, including repeated changes in the supposedly inalienable status of farmlands donated to Buddhist temples (Lieberman 1984; Aung-Thwin 1985). "Although the percentage probably fluctuated, it has been estimated that in the mid–nineteenth century subordinate officials in Upper Burma retained two thirds of all tax collections" (Lieberman 1987, 165).

Both central and regional rulers siphoned wealth and services off peasant producers, and in Southeast Asia as well as in China the authorities repeatedly faced decline in the number of taxable subjects when people declared themselves slaves of a notable in order to escape the increasingly onerous duties of subjects (Hucker 1975, 181; Reid 1983). The list of duties from which Lawa people were exempt details what was commonly imposed on peasant subjects in the Chiangmai valley: "corvée, military conscription, serving as bearers, construction of city walls, digging moats, damming the Ping River, carrying of supplies, having their elephants and women commandeered, supplying fodder for elephants and horses. . . . We forbid our ministers, village headmen and town (*muang*) chiefs, centurions (*khun pak*) and borough heads (*nat kwaen*), village headmen and local authorities, both present and future, to impress their labor" (Kraisri 1965, 235).

It is not a given that upland populations viewed the forest from the same perspective as lowlanders—nor that they shared this state rhetoric of civility versus wilderness. But the state continually inscribed itself into particular uplanders' lives as a source of virtue and prosperity. The grant from the Chiangmai ruler to the Lawa emphasized cohesion within Lawa society as dependent on the proper observance of rank differences:

> We, the great omniscient lord of accumulated merit, who resides in the
> golden palace in the capital city of Chiangmai, whose accumulated merit

makes to live by the tenfold royal dharma (rules for kings) do hereby
graciously confer this silver-plate grant, fully sealed with our royal seal
depicting a *devata* holding Srikhargajaya Sword, upon the crown of the
head of Phya Ratna Wang Na, who is the Chief, and upon the crowns of
the heads of Khun San, Khun Konkeo, Lam (herald) Chan, and Lam
Chai. . . . Let the leaders behave as leaders should behave. Let the *lam* behave as the *lam* should behave. Let the common people behave as the
common people should behave. Let them not be disunited. The Chief
must not abandon the Lawa. The Lawa must not abandon their
Chief. . . . If the Lawa are frightened and run away from [the Chief], he
will be punished by a fine of 3300 pieces of officially minted *chieng*
money. If he causes disaster to the Lawa, let him be destroyed as easily as
a clump of banana trees; let him be annihilated like a clump of grass.
(Kraisri 1965, 236)

The fusion of the political and the natural grounded the state's designs in
places where it had only limited control. The promise of prosperity to the
nonsubject clients of the state, through their titled leaders, aligned the issue
of compliance with the state with the more local concerns of leader-
follower relations in an area that in general was beyond the state's active
reach: "If the Chief, leaders and *lams* make all Lawa respect and obey our
royal command as inscribed in this silver-plate grant, let them be prosperous and let all their business ventures succeed. Let all their wishes come
true" (Kraisri 1965, 236). The distinction between the forested highlands
and the cleared lowlands was a bifurcation of the landscape in terms of relations with the state. Being in the forest was at the same time to stand outside the protection and taxation of the state, but contracts into the hinterlands blurred these boundaries.

Some Lawa settlements lay within state orbits, while others did not.
Karen (Yang, Nyang, Kariang) settlements on the fringes of northern and
central Thai domains were sometimes specified as either *ban* ("village") or
pa ("forest"), the former being within the state's hierarchy, order, tribute
duties, and protection (Renard 2000). There were similar distinctions between "wild" and "tame" barbarians in southern China (Fiskesjö 1999).
Reading history in terms of contemporary ethnic labels obfuscates such
differences. Upland peoples could purchase protection from raids and tribute duties, and this is part of the significance of the inscribed silver-plate
grant in the village of Bo Luang.

Such contracts with the state focused on tribute payments and grounded
the prominence of local chiefs in relations with the tributary state. In the
Lawa village of Pa Pae during the early 1960s, there was a chiefly lineage

whose leader had the title *samang* and whose ancestry was traced to the Lawa ruler who reigned prior to the lowland state's takeover of the land. While this position of authority was importantly reinforced through dealings with the tributary state, Kunstadter describes it as one of local ritual prominence that was central to the annual division of village fields (1967, 656), a localization that rendered the political through practices of kinship, ritual, and farming. Kauffmann suggests that the conflation of villages and their hereditary leaders was far from general among Lawa peoples, whereas Kunstadter's informants stated that "if we did not have a samang, we would have to live like apes and monkeys in the jungle" (Kauffmann 1972, 266). The situational prominence of *samang* among the Lawa may have been specific to particular villages rather than general within the ethnic group.

There are various similarities between Lawa identity on the fringes of Lanna kingdoms and that of the Yao in relation to the Chinese Empire. The Yao case draws on a manuscript known in Mien as *Kia Shen Pong*.[6] The story's main character, Pien Hu (P'an Hu in Chinese), was a dragon dog at the court of Emperor Ping Huang. Relations between the dragon dog and the emperor were central to the making of Yao identity. Various Yao populations identify with this story, and there are published studies of numerous manuscript versions.[7]

License for Crossing the Mountains

The text of *Kia Shen Pong* states that this scroll is a grant from an emperor, modeled on an imperial decree from earlier times. Emperor Ping Huang is aiming to destroy a rival ruler, King Kao Wang. None of his ministers are willing to do this for him. Then a striped dragon dog named Pan Hu offers his services to the Emperor, and Ping Huang promises Pan Hu a lady of the court for a wife if his mission is successful. The journey takes seven days and seven nights across an ocean. After the successful mission, Emperor Ping Huang then makes Pan Hu a lord, "bestowing on [him] the rank of *gong*, [to be] passed on in the line of [his] descendants forever." Pan Hu reminds the Emperor of his promised reward, and the latter eventually agrees. Pan Hu and the lady of the court then put on elaborate clothes, he in a striped robe of five colors and she in the manner of a princess. "Each did obeisance to the other, as prescribed in the wedding rite" (Kia Shen Pong 1991, 38). After the ceremony, the couple is sent away with provisions and ordered to "stay in the wilderness always." They have twelve children, and the emperor declares each the head of a lineage and declares them Yao people:

This decree of Emperor Ping Huang shall be published in the thirteen provinces of the land [here follows a list of places of Yao residence]. . . . All of these, including the level places and wet-rice fields in the hills, shall be places where the descendants of the Yao prince may dwell and make their livelihood. They shall be exempt from taxes and military levies. . . . The descendants of the Yao prince shall be permitted to travel in search of land—not the possession of a district, a state, a province, or a town— on which to make a living. While traveling, they stall not be required to pay obeisance to anyone. They shall not be required to pay for crossing by ferry. They shall not be required to kneel when they meet lords. Their farming in the hills shall not be subject to taxation.

Then the manuscript lists individual Yao by lineage, name, and title, stating that they govern so many households (from 1,000 to 5,000) and ends by reiterating that the decree is issued for their protection, that they are to live and farm in the hills and that they stand outside the duties of state subjects (Kia Shen Pong 1991, 39–48).

Yao identity was state-sanctioned. The decree mapped the state on the lowlands and sanctioned adaptations to the forested highlands as outside the domain of taxation and other imperial duties. By stating that the Yao were to be free to take new land for cultivation in the mountains, the document implied the state's control over agriculture and settlement. This document, reissued at various times, appears to have been used by the state to control the authority of local rulers. In its statements that Yao are not to pay for crossing by ferry, that they need not bow to officials, and that their farming is not subject to taxation, the document is directed at these local rulers, through the Yao. *Kia Shen Pong* is explicitly about the Yao, but it is equally concerned with local rulers' ability to control settlement and migrations and to administer corvée and taxation.

The dates on *Kia Shen Pong* range from the Han period (before 200 CE) and until the Republic (post-1911; see Huang 1991, 108–9). The quest for a correct or original date for the document as well as for the Yao as an ethnic group (Huang 1991; Lemoine 1991) may not be particularly productive, as what is going on is a process of relational definitions of social groups, where the definition of a group and the status of its members may vary considerably over time. The reference of the document is to an imperial contract that needed to be reaffirmed with each new reign and/or in each new domain to which the Yao migrated, which makes all the dates correct and relevant at the same time as it suggest that each decree was tenuous. Analogous to the case of the Lawa in the Lanna and Shan areas, the origins and reproduction of the Yao as an ethnic category lay in the Chinese state's

Fig. 2: The color photocopy of the Kia Shen Pong scroll on display at the Mien festival in 2001.

cosmographic project of mapping out a domain of civilization within which rank and rule emanated from the center, where people would be connected through relations of tribute and services. The making of the Yao concerned the outside of the state, a process of boundary-making that joined ecological, social, political, and ethnic categories as it established the landscape of history. The state was reproduced through the distribution of rank and through the control over trade and social relations. The Yao were framed as nonsubjects in the wilderness, physically and socially separate from the civilized domain.

The narrative of a grant by the emperor in return for a major favor appears to have been shared among various *Man* ("barbarian") peoples of China's south (ter Haar 1998) and may only have become limited to Yao peoples as of their incorporation into the orbits of the Chinese state. The Yao and Lawa cases show how the reproduction of the state's classification and ranking of places, peoples, and identities resulted in a bifurcation of the natural environment into the civilized, cleared lowlands and the savage, forested hinterlands. Categorizations of people were then projected onto this regional space in terms of how people related to the courts. As people engaged with the state or averted all dealings with its agents, their identities became informed by their particular place within an ecologically and socially bifurcated region. The adaptation of highland populations was not to the natural environment as such, but to an environment that had been prefigured by the politics of identities and social relations in terms of the cultural and political economic dimensions of the state.

Kia Shen Pong depicts the hinterlands as regions of ignorance, the Yao people knowing nothing of the wisdom of emperors or wise men: "The descendants of the Yao prince are to dwell in the wilderness, to farm to make a livelihood, to live orderly lives, and to observe the law. Since they live in the forest and hills from the time they are small, they never see the writings of emperors or study the treatises of the sages so they are ignorant of cultivated usages and manners. They are thus counseled to refrain from causing disturbances; any who ignore this behest will be punished severely" (Kia Shen Pong 1991, 45).

While one may read a coherent ideology from the written statements of the state, there are reasons to suggest that the way "the state" was acted out was often less than coherent and that there were ongoing tensions between the central court and its regional satellites. A report from a judicial commissioner in what is now southern Guangdong from 1145 CE (quoted in Li Mo 1991, 150) reprimanded officials for tolerating "interrelations between the Imperial subjects and the Yao." There was no inherent agreement between what the state decreed and what local officials did. Entries in annals and gazetteers show that some Yao populations in Guangdong and Guangxi had exchange relations with local authorities (Cushman 1970, 207–8; Pan 1991, 187). The ability of the state to order things in the outlying domains appears to have been negligible. Instead, the outcome of the state's projections came down to the relations of particular groups of Yao with individual local rulers.

Copies of *Kia Shen Pong* may have been quite significant in this context, as they situated the Yao in imperial terms, categorized them as an entity in relation to sumptuary laws. The document was also important within Yao social formations, as it enabled a would-be leader to establish his prominence through agents of the state. With or without such written contracts, Yao leaders may have been able to strike deals with lowland authorities allowing them to collect land-rent or taxes from a range of settlements in terms of the Yao category. Even if the imperial categorizations specifically excluded the Yao and the forested hinterlands from the domain of state control, local authorities exercised some control over migrations and settlements involving highland people such as the Yao, and would-be Yao leaders could ground their prominence through relations with these local authorities. The Yao and the state were consolidated through their interactions.

Cushman relates that in the first millennium CE most Chinese accounts refer to upland groups in the south as *Man* ("barbarians") of one sort or another and that a shift to the current ethnic labels for these groups occurred in the eleventh and twelfth centuries in tandem with increased state control of these regions (1970, 22–73). One reason for defining the Yao as a population engaged in shifting cultivation in the highlands and free from corvée and taxation was an attempt by the rulers of the state's center to limit the reach of their regional subordinates. In this context it is worth noting that, in the increasingly bureaucratized climate of eighteenth-century China, "rigid legalistic prescriptions on behavior coexisted with expectations that circumstances varied, individual judgment was important, and exceptions to the rule could always be made. . . . As written contracts became standard practice in daily life for formalizing agreements and reducing risks, red contracts that carried the official seal were outnumbered by the more inexpensive (but apparently equally enforceable) white ones that had no official authorization" (Naquin and Rawski 1987, 229–30).

Just as such deals indicate tensions among lowland officials between the levels of center and region, they could influence the social dynamics within and among upland populations, anchoring the power of would-be leaders over their constituents, sanctioning particular identities, and centering ethnicities in particular locales. The grounding of chiefly power through ethnic identities, sometimes marked by contracts and titles, occurred in a historical context of frequent warfare and raids on unprotected settlements for manpower and provisions. People could buy their way into protection networks, and this contributed to the consolidation of highlander identities such as Yao on the fringes of lowland states. The circulation of unofficial but enforceable documents suggests the complexity of documented realities. This has some bearing on the issue of whether *Kia Shen Pong* derived from the court. Some scholars have suggested that the Yao people made it up to gain leverage in relations with agents of the Chinese state (Lemoine 1982, 11–12; Theraphan 1991, 7–8; ter Haar 1998, 3).

Contracts between the state and the Yao contributed to and created status distinctions among the latter. *Kia Shen Pong* lists individuals with titles and defines their domains as including a particular number of households that these upland leaders could tax for their own uses: "A man of the Pan clan named Qi Long is hereby appointed to the position of *zhu guo* to govern (collect the taxes of) 5,000 households, and is also appointed to the position of *teng zhou ci shi*" (Kia Shen Pong 1991, 45–46). The Yao category provided a framework for social consolidation beyond the state, such as when "the ones who are related to the aborigines are subordinated to the Yao" (Pan 1991, 185, quoting *Annals of Qu Jiang County*). In this capacity, the Yao category provided a vehicle for would-be upland chiefs to claim prominence over Yao and non-Yao populations of the hinterland, drawing simultaneously on the state and on their social and ecological separation from it. The ambiguous position of the Yao is clear from *Kia Shen Pong* in that their distinction from lowland society was only effective in terms of relations with the state.

As a discursive framework for social relations and agricultural practices, the "Yao" category was never conclusively defined by the state. Rather, it opened certain possibilities and denied others. The universalistic framework of *Kia Shen Pong* provided a model of particular relations with the state that simultaneously defined the Yao population as an entity and played up the interests of would-be upland chiefs. While there are many known copies of this document, it appears to have always been a rather rare object. The dissimilarity of *Kia Shen Pong* from other known imperial documents may indicate that the manuscript was made up by Yao peoples. But the document's apparent uniqueness may have a different explanation, which is that the social project it conveys is fundamentally different from other business of the Chinese state. Copies of *Kia Shen Pong* were not kept by Chinese authorities but were granted and reissued to particular Yao leaders. The traces of Yao styles and agendas in the text are a product of this context. The historical reality of the document lay in the deals that it could facilitate with the agents of the Chinese state who issued or ratified it. For such deals to be made, the two sides had to share a rhetorical framework of identity, difference, and relations to the emperor. The validity of the contract came down to the relationship between Pien Hung (Pan Hu, Pan Wang) and Emperor Ping Huang as a framework for defining ethnicity, forms of livelihood, areas of residence, and relations to the state. The key point of *Kia Shen Pong* as a Chinese document is that one's identity and duties to the state derive from one's contributions to the state in the person of the emperor. The emperor was the source of identity, and position on the social landscape of rank and ethnicity resulted from one's contributions to the state's mission.

Much of the Chinese writings on the Yao in imperial times concerned Yao rebellions and their suppression. "Many gazetteers devote special sections to histories of tribal rebellions and the biographies of noted civil and military officials likewise contain accounts of campaigns or, more rarely, of various kinds of particularly effective policies" (Cushman 1970, 34). In their descriptions, these accounts make history at the same time as they construct the relevant subject, which is whoever is concerned with the stability of the Chinese state. The state emerges from such histories as the guardian of order and civility.[8]

Some parts of *Kia Shen Pong* gave the state's agendas prominent emphasis: While at the court of Kao Wang, his ruler's rival, Pan Hu's "sole thought was to serve Emperor Ping Huang" (Kia Shen Pong 1991, 36); this comment was presumably meant to inspire the Yao toward a sense of duty to the state. After Pien Hung (Pan Hu) died, the Emperor instructed the Yao about proper rituals to him as an ancestor:

> When the time of this great feast arrives, the spirit of Pan Hu will watch over his descendants so that they will have good harvests and five kinds of domestic animals, with pigs in droves, many sons, and gold and silver in abundance. Those who have pigs should not sell them. In celebrating a marriage, animals should be slaughtered for feasting, relatives and friends and acquaintances should be brought together, the long drum and flute should be played, and men and women should join in song. In this way, both humans and spirits will enjoy themselves, and this will bring fertility and prosperity. (Kia Shen Pong 1991, 41–42)

The state's gift of ritual and thus of well-being came with the promise of Pan Hu's ancestral wrath to "anyone who departs from these customs, who is not faithful, or who creates dissent." This blurred whatever distinctions there may have been between local cultural practice and compliance with the state's rule and its control over trade: "he who is guilty will not be pardoned" (42). In this way, the state inserted itself into the fabric of everyday life among a population that was not within the reach of its officials for taxation, service, or respect. The Mien term for "customs" is le, from the Chinese li ("ritual," "etiquette," "correct behavior"). The local reference to the cluster of practices and ideas through which Mien people reproduce their social and cultural universe is derived from the contact zone of engagements with the Chinese state.[9]

The contracts with the Yao and Lawa reveal, through the list of exemptions, some of the duties of the state's peasant subjects. The Yao may not marry people of other "tribes" (44), and they are to be exempt from all duties and taxation, in all provinces under the emperor; "if someone violates this prohibition [against imposing fees on them, demanding their labor or obeisance] the descendants of the Yao prince should bring evidence to the government authorities, and the violator will be punished for oppressing those who are weaker, a crime carrying heavy penalties" (45). By implication, ordinary subjects of the state did not have a "license to cross the mountains," they were to pay taxes and perform military duties, to kneel when they met lords, and to pay a fee when they crossed a river by ferry or when they spent a night in a village during a journey. Considering the exemptions granted to the Lawa and Yao, upland peoples may have been better off than the various farming populations within the state by virtue of being declared out of reach for the oppression of regional overlords and other state agents.

Whether lowland populations viewed the state as oppressive is another matter. In the lowlands, order was associated with the protection of a just ruler. But Bowie's ethnohistorical work in the Chiangmai Valley indicates that peasants viewed lords as "arbitrary, capricious, petty, greedy, and even cruel figures of power and potential torment" (1988, 71). Her argument is clearly aimed against the one-sided notion that subjects shared in their rulers' self-congratulatory rhetoric of Buddhist virtue (cf. Tambiah 1976), but her summary of peasant views simply replaces a positive evaluation with a negative one. It is possible to describe kingship in the region as having had two sides; that of a benign overlord who exemplified religious virtue and that of a sovereign lord over life and death who deployed violence as an expression of his power. Ancient Cambodian inscriptions suggest this much. Inscriptions in Sanskrit, often poems, persistently "proclaim the grandeur of kings; [in contrast,] the Khmer [language] inscriptions [that are not poetic] exhibit the precision with which jurisdictional squabbles were prosecuted and slaves registered" (Chandler 1992, 31).

The *Padaeng Chronicle* from the Shan state of Jengtung contains many examples of these two sides of statecraft. Among other things, it lists the duties of monastery subjects, establishing the role of different lowland villages in the running of the monastery. It details the seniority of monks and the ranking of initiates as it specifies a protocol for the business of state and Buddhism. In specifying the contributions of subject peoples from different villages, the chronicle states that if they disobey, monastery officials shall "drag their hands" to perform the assigned duties. If this comes to nothing, "cut down their house posts, and then drive them away from [the village] because the Lord [king] is their benefactor" (Sao Saimong 1981, 133). In the context of this lingering threat of violence and settlement erasure, the chronicle specifies the procedure for ordaining the sons and grandsons of royalty into the Buddhist order, adding: "excepted are those born of slaves and low-caste Damila [the Lawa, see below]—they are not to be ordained in the great [ordination] hall of [Padaeng Temple], it is not done" (Sao Saimong 1981, 132), presumably because it would have the same effect as seating the Lawa on the throne. The sovereign's charting of rank and rights conflated society and identity as it established the king as the source of Buddhist historicity. This definition of society was done against the backdrop of internal outsiders, slaves, and external outsiders, highland and forest peoples.[10]

The emphasis on justice and virtue as emanating from the court is clear from the grants to the Yao and Lawa, in which rulers declared the restraint of officials who might otherwise demand obedience and taxes and require people to perform various services. These grants threatened punishment for disobedience, evoking the violent and destructive aspects of sovereign rule: "Let him be destroyed as easily as a clump of banana trees." Origin stories, about Emperor Ping Huang and the Yao or Queen Jamathewi and the Lawa, established a state-centered framework for historicity and identity. In relation to the Yao origins as spelled out in *Kia Shen Pong,* a combination of devoted submission to the emperor and the suppression of a rival who might have upset his rule were the twin sources of the place of the Yao on the fringes of the Chinese state. It is not particularly anomalous that Emperor Ping Huang is not a known historical figure. Service to him is service to the state since the First Emperor (r. 221–207 BCE), who unified the Chinese state and became a model for subsequent rulers to emulate. Queen Jamathewi is as historically elusive as Emperor Ping Huang, but like the First Emperor and many similar figures she set history in motion by charting a social order that both undermined a series of alternatives and provided a reference point for subsequent rulers who through their command over social life and political position came to define history and identity. King Mangrai may not have been much of a Buddhist ruler by subsequent standards (Renard 1996, 161–63), but the principle of identity, society, and history became centered on his image.

Fringes of the State

The cases of the Lawa and the Yao show that in both Chinese and Southeast Asian domains prior to the colonial era, the regulation of settlement, movement, identities, and status reached to areas beyond the state's active control (cf. Andrew Walker 1999 for Laos). State formations engendered particular structures and categorizations that informed the reproduction of social identity as either within or outside the state. This process informed the region-wide difference between "tribal" (nonsubject, upland) and "peasant" (subject, lowland) populations. These social types manifest different outcomes of relations with tributary states. Even in the absence of any active control in mountainous regions, the state was of key significance to the definition of both the environment and some of the social identities and options that upland peoples have lived with. The forested hinterlands and their inhabitants, in Southeast Asia and the adjacent regions of southern China, Bangladesh, and India (as well as in Nepal and Sri Lanka), are not residues of an archaic state of nature. Rather, the environment and imagery now associated with nature were consolidated in terms of various state projects. Historically, nature and the state were not separate, while the rhetoric of states assumed a fundamental contrast with wildness. The state's designs became a part of the natural environment; the political was naturalized through a cultural project of bifurcating civilization and savagery, most clearly through the state's frequent involvement in the definition of identities and tributary status extending into the hinterlands. The realms of identity, politics, society, culture, and nature have not been separate, and their alignment has been constitutive of social reality and historicity in ways that have reified the state and a range of ethnic identities.

Ideas of civility and control were integral to how states categorized people, and this was an important component of the ethnic landscape in history. In his analysis of Chinese material on the Yao, Cushman suggests that the effort of classification of "barbarian" groups was "dictated . . . by an emphasis on zones and directionality in the Chinese worldview" (1970, 22). The Chinese descriptions were formulated and motivated in terms of a theory of society and cosmos that defined the middle kingdom as surrounded by feudal states and barbarians (Cushman 1970, 46; cf. Dikötter 1992, 4). States were based on a universal hierarchy that was centered on a court, and the making of subject-populations connected to schemes of relating villages to one another and to their overlords (Chang 1983, 122). The state was simultaneously a mechanism for stratification and exploitation and a set of paradigmatic assumptions about how the world operated. This conceptual scheme aligned rank and identity in relation to state control, in part through the channeling of tribute payments. In general, swidden fields were outside the domain of tribute, services, and membership in the society that emanated from the state's court. Statecraft assumed various schemes that overrode localisms in social relations and village identities, making settlements legible as well as exploitable in terms of relations with the state.

The state positioned itself as the arbiter of legitimate exchange relationships, in part as an extension of its position as the source of identity and status. The Ming and Qing dynasties in China (1368–1644 and 1644–1912 CE, respectively) established various restrictions on people of "mean status," such as "menial servants in government establishments, slaves, prostitutes, entertainers, and various local outcast groups. . . . Their descendants were excluded from the civil service for at least three generations" (Hucker 1975, 335). In contrast to the "mean" peoples of the Ming and Qing eras in China whose exclusion from state-sanctioned society would expire after three generations, highlanders were to be permanently outside society. Prior to modern nation-states, ethnic identities implied political relations and legal status, based on premises that are no longer maintained. There are many examples of the state's jealous guarding of the boundaries of civility, such as an article from an early nineteenth-century Vietnamese law code that allowed Vietnamese men to settle in military colonies in the highlands but forbid them living among upland peoples: "Any Vietnamese who contracted marriage with a person 'of barbarous races' would be subject to one hundred blows with a rod" (Hickey 1982, 165–66).

The outsider status of mountain peoples can be compared with that of sub-caste peoples, who in general had no rights within states—the *Padaeng Chronicle* joined the two as unacceptable for Buddhist ordinations in the Padaeng Temple. In the historical record there are various parallels in how internal outsiders, such as India's untouchables and Japan's "special status people," and external outsiders, such as Japan's Ainu foragers and India's highland "tribal" people, were classified as beyond society proper. In stratified Japan, "the Ainu stood for wild nature where special status people stood for the negative side of animality and impurity" (Ohnuki-Tierney 1998, 48). In India, the term *Mleccha*, "meaning impure, goes back to the Vedic texts and referred to non-Sanskrit speaking people often outside the caste hierarchy or regarded as foreign and was extended to include low castes and tribals" (Thapar 1992, 78). Such identities implied occupation, residence, and outsider status, against which society proper was then defined. These outsider identities defined the limits of civility and society that were charted and reproduced in relation to the state and its hierarchy. In pre-national times, identity, residence, livelihood, and rights were entangled in processes of state and society whose ultimate reference was a sovereign ruler. The permanence of particular identities and accompanying status was varied. Some ethnic references for hinterland peoples from this premodern era are now recognized as ethnic labels, while others have lost their resonance or are seen as discriminatory categories that should be abandoned.[11]

The rhetoric and imagery of kingship in Southeast Asia drew on trade and traffic in ideas with Chinese, Indian, and Sri Lankan populations. Both the self-image of rulers and the identities that states projected on hinterland populations derived in part from this transregional contact zone. The term *Lawa* was used in reference to highland outsiders in the Lanna and Shan States. Its longer form is *Damilawa* (Sao Saimong 1981, 223) and is said to derive from the Sanskrit *Damila,* as did the Buddhist Sri Lankan ethnic term *Tamil* for their non-Buddhist others. The root of the term lay in Sinhalese chronicle accounts of the state and its dark-skinned enemies (Sao Saimong 1981, 175). Thus, along with the localization of Buddhism in mainland Southeast Asia came certain aspects of ethnic ranking and prejudice that contributed to rulers' ability to contextualize in universalistic terms their rule and the peoples that it excluded. Many Chiangmai chronicles used the term *Tamilla* for *Lawa* (Aroonrut 2000, 138). Some used the term *Milangka*. *Wilangka*, a variant on that term, was used among the Lawa in reference to their chief, who lost out to the lowland forces (Kunstadter 1967, 640; Kraisri 1965, 234). *Milangka* is derived from *Milakkha*, the Pali language equivalent to the Sanskrit *Mleccha* ("savages," Thapar 1971, 409). Pali had replaced Sanskrit as the language of sacred learning in Theravada Buddhist mainland Southeast Asia by the twelfth century (Strong 1992, 171–85).

The state's rhetoric of civility informed ritual practices and social relations, and it was in these cultural terms that ordinary lowland farming populations knew and feared the forest as the abode of evil spirits, dangerous animals, and general lawlessness. This alignment of natural and social landscapes, where forests equaled disorder, was common throughout (and beyond) premodern lowland Southeast Asia. Chandler's (1982) study of Cambodian chronicles and poetry shows that the effort to inscribe history was routinely about linking peoples to the ranking that emanated from a sovereign. Through the reproduction of hierarchy, the forests were held at bay and lowland peoples neither lapsed into sub-class servitude nor lost their court-derived identity in the jungles. In the lowland regions, social dynamics often revolved around acquiring slaves and other underlings and procuring goods and services from hinterland peoples. The quest for enhanced status in the lowlands often encouraged violence against hinterland peoples and within lowland societies: "A commoner who could kill and take an enemy head in war and bring it to the ruler would be promoted and rewarded" (Aroonrut 2003, 83). Slaves and hinterland peoples were entangled in various ways with the state-society that defined itself in opposition to both.[12]

As the 1852 contract makes clear, Lawa people in one particular settlement owed annual tribute to the state in return for their exemption from the apparently onerous duties of the state's subjects. Like among the Yao in southern China, there was considerable diversity in the social formations among the Lawa in Lanna areas and the adjacent Shan State. Yao and Lawa social dynamics must be understood in terms of internal histories as much as their shifting relations to state authorities. What the two have in common is a state-sanctioned ethnic reference that defined not only a people but also the environment to which they were confined. It is the mutual definition of ethnicity and the forested wilderness that is of fundamental relevance. Taken together, the two cases show how identity was mapped in relation to the state's project. Thus it is not as if "the state" drove the "Yao" or "Lawa" to inhospitable margins as it expanded. Rather, these identities and that of the state's subjects were generated and reproduced as the state de-fined itself and its project and as people defined their position in relation to the state. As can be seen from the repeated reissue of contracts with the Yao and Lawa by two separate state systems, this ethnic landscaping was an on-going process.

In southern China and across Southeast Asia, states would repeatedly try to expand their revenue base, and these efforts included various highland peoples on numerous occasions. In eleventh-century Vietnam, "four of the six categories of taxation . . . applied only to items of trade with the tribes-people in the mountains (salt, rhinoceros horns, elephant tusks, aromatic wood, lumber, flowers, and fruits)" (Taylor 1986, 151). In southern China, the establishment of authority over hinterland "barbarians" has a long his-tory, with policies such as "rule barbarians through barbarians" (*i-i-chih-i*) and offices such as "native chiefs" (*tusi*) (Cushman 1970, 155). Like rank, ethnicity marked people as belonging to a particular network of social rela-tions. People could move from one ethnic category to another and between upland and lowland systems of ethnicity and/or rank (Leach 1954; Moer-man 1965; Lehman 1967a). In the borderlands of Yunnan and Southeast Asia, the trappings of Chinese culture were taken on by local leaders, who could thus anchor their prominence or "legitimize claims to vast tracts of land that frequently included some Han settlers. . . . For others, a *tusi* ap-pointment, or nominal incorporation into the Chinese bureaucracy, was the only alternative to loss of land and livelihood. Lu, a Yi (*lolo*) aristocrat, [worked within] two ethnopolitical systems: the Chinese 'border bureau-cracy' and the indigenous Yi polity, a complex system based on descent and coerced tribute from subject villages" (Hill 1998, 58–59).

The making of Yao and Lawa identities in terms of relations to courts can be compared to Basque identity in the borderlands of Spanish and French domains (Greenwood 1985, 208). Basque ethnic identity developed in the context of relations with Catholic kings of Spain. The Basques were not tied dynastically to the crown, thus they were not regular subjects. They lived in a strategically important border region, an area that was generally poor but an important source of iron, which had military significance. "In return for their willingness to be part of the monarchy and to defend their territories against military attack, they were granted freedom from taxation and mili-tary conscription. . . . Basque ethnic identity developed in this context. In fighting to retain their privileges, the Basques came to define themselves as an ethnic group with special rights from time immemorial, before the monarchy. These rights included recognition of their collective nobility, freedom from conscription, and freedom from taxation" (Greenwood 1985, 209).

Greenwood's argument is not that Basque identity was invented for political purposes. Rather, he notes that they were one of many culturally identifiable groups in this region and that their identity as ethnicity was articulated in terms of their position vis-à-vis the court. This approach can be applied to the cases of Yao and Lawa. In both settings, an ethnic label became a term of engagement that defined a population as outside the state. As state control was routinized, various people may have invoked this ethnic label because it was one that the state recognized in its dealings with marginal peoples (nonsubjects). Subject populations participated in the ritual and discursive aspects of state-controlled society, which played down whatever differences there were in linguistic and cultural practice within lowland social orders.

Lowland states in China and Southeast Asia set the terms of social life across the region through the definition of rank and subject duties. The state inscribed itself as the source of identity and order, and lowland ritual practice contributed to the commensurability of peasant settlements and their political authorities. But while lowland states set the terms for the upland identities that it recognized, uplander cultural and agricultural practices were not within the state's terms. Uplander identities were to some extent incommensurable with the lowland state in pre-national times, and as such they triggered various efforts by state authorities to define them away to the forested wilderness. Uplander identities were also a reminder of the limits to the state's hegemony. It is from this perspective that the upland-lowland divide manifests a contact zone not only of state power and less powerful others but also of upland peoples and forms of social control that they did not fully accept. Upland peoples are and have been contemporaneous with the state, and both categories mask considerable social complexity.

To an outside observer like Chou Ta-Kuan in the thirteenth century, quoted at the beginning of this chapter, it was notable that the highland areas were raided for slaves. He also remarked on differences in the mountain people's involvement with the lowland society, that some spoke the lowland language and had interactions with lowlanders while others did not. There was comparable difference among lowland authorities in that the ones closest to mountain regions appeared to have relations with mountain peoples while their superiors who lived further away repeatedly insisted on maintaining separation with the peoples in the mountainous forests. The upland-lowland divide was an important principle of social relations and distinctions in the region's history, but it was not the only principle that informed identity constructions and social relations and may seldom have been absolute. As a structure, the upland-lowland divide became a principle for anchoring particular constructions of history. Its resonance for anthropology—manifest most clearly in peasant-tribal distinctions—may also have had much to do with the character of upland-lowland relations across Southeast Asia during the twentieth century, in particular the predominant understanding of ethnicity during that period.

New Ethnicities

Upland-lowland relations provided contact zones within which particular identities were routinized. The tendency to chart history in terms of ethnic groups and nations may be fundamentally inadequate to describe this social landscape—though, as Leach suggested, the telling of history is always about defining the present (1954, 74–100). The Lawa category refers to commoners who were under leaders with the titles *lam* and *khun,* and the higher-ranking *khun* were rendered in the Lawa language as *samang.* In some areas, the commoners were known as *Phai* or *Phrai,* the term for peasants and other commoners in lowland Tai areas (Kauffmann 1972, 257–78). The terminology varied among the Lanna kingdoms. In terms of rank within a tributary system, the contemporary Lawa peoples in the provinces of Maehongson and Chiangmai are analogous to the Prai of Nan Province, as descendants of formerly *Kha* or Lawa peoples whose identity referred to their commoner (and sometimes outsider) status. There is no Samang or Lam ethnic group, though this would have been equally possible given that the process of ethnicization involved the re-signification of tributary status to that of an ethnic group within a national and global context that took ethnicity as axiomatic. The identity of Prai has so far not been officially recognized in Thailand; they are instead classified as Thin, derived from *chao thin,* "local people," which implies a low-status rural population.

Thongchai's study of the forging of the national terrain of modern Thailand is based partly on a contrast with "the indigenous Southeast Asian tradition [where] a subject was bound first and foremost to his lord rather than to a state" (1994, 164). This distinction is important, but it is potentially misleading regarding the entanglements of highlander (and other) identities with lowland states. State control was in many ways about the classification of subjects and nonsubjects, and ethnic identities were reinforced in terms of tributary status. In Ayutthaya, a precursor to the Bangkok kingdom and the Thai state, "there were two main classes of Thai subjects [below royalty]: *phrai* (commoner, 'freeman') and *that* (non-free, 'slave'). There were *phrai luang* who were subject directly to the king, and *phrai som* who were under lesser royalty and nobility" (Renard 2000, 68). To be bound to a particular overlord was thus to be bound to the state, in an often intricate network of tributary relationships whose ultimate referent was a particular sovereign and thus a state.[13] Upland ethnic identities such as the Yao and Lawa were reproduced through interactions with specific states. Lowland ethnic identities were similarly entangled with individual states, where identity and political status implied a reference to specific courts. The identity of Tai Lü (Lue), for instance, drew on subject status to the now-expired court of Chiang Rung and the larger domain of Sipsongpanna, in Yunnan, China (Moerman 1968, 156).

The consolidation of nation states in a colonial context altered this previous structuring of the region. In Thailand, hinterland regions became the focus of the nation-state's mapping and border anxieties, but this does not imply a previous absence of the state's reach into highland settlements. The change involved a redefinition of identity and rights, from rank to ethnic essence. The process of undoing the practices of everyday life that reinforced tributary relations in order to routinize the national government as the arbiter of identity, order, and control involved administrative changes at many levels. Hereditary rulers of tributary Lanna kingdoms were deprived of their power and, with it, their command over tribute, services, identity, and social life. They were replaced by Bangkok-appointed officials, and the histories and identities that had been forged in relation to their courts largely lost their resonance. These changes were pervasive and included a fundamental redefinition of identity and rights. The Thai term for (individual) liberty and independence was fashioned during this process, based on a Sanskrit word that once referred to a ruler's sovereignty (Loos 1998).

As the identity and status of urban individuals was recast, so was that of rural farming population, which was classified in terms of ethnic identity. Taylor (2001) describes how Muong became an ethnic category in northern Vietnam as the French colonial authorities redefined social life in order to undermine the tributary framework of the precolonial Vietnamese state. The term Muong was derived from Black Tai term *müang*, which signified a ruler's domain; it was not a self-reference among the people later classified as such, nor did they share an "ethnic" reference. Rather, the people who became Muong were those whose leaders had the title Quan Lang. The later Muong were the commoners, who referred to themselves by village (Taylor 2001, 30–31). In French scholarship, Muong were not only consolidated as an ethnic group but were postulated as "a primitive form of Vietnamese" (Taylor 2001, 30), and they have subsequently entered postcolonial Vietnamese self-fashionings as such (Jonsson 2002).

Another example of this trend concerns the Karen in northern Thailand. In general, it is assumed that the Karen peoples entered Thai areas from

Burmese domains starting in the early nineteenth century (Keyes 1979, Pinkaew 2001 dissent from this view). This is based on various assumptions of modern state control regarding ethnic minorities and claims to territory that have often entered anthropology as facts. These particular conceptual problems aside, a more intriguing one resides in the Lanna identification of the Karen peoples as Yang. Renard (2002) suggests that the Yang peoples may have been settled in the Chiangmai Valley much earlier than the nineteenth century. The identity Yang is complicated, since the term is also used in reference to dipterocarpus trees. In the tributary Lanna states, Yang forests were known as places whence *yang* oil came, as tribute payment (Renard 2002, 75). The Yang people may thus have come about through the repeated ethnic landscaping of the tributary state as those who delivered a specific kind of tribute, and their identity then expired with administrative and political economic changes.

In more recent times, all that remains of these dynamics of identity, state control, and tribute is the botanical classification of five kinds of Yang trees. With the recasting of identity and state control through national integration in the mid– and late twentieth century, anthropologists came to take the Karen for granted as a hill tribe of shifting cultivators, and in these terms the Yang became just an old name for the Karen (Hamilton 1976, 8). "Ethnic heterogeneity was the historical reality of the subaltern. The forging of a more homogenous identity of Khon Muang [northern Thai], and later Thai, is as much the consequence of traditional practices of South East Asian statecraft as of twentieth century processes of nation-state formation" (Bowie 2000, 344). Regarding western India, Skaria notes that the clear-cut distinction between castes and tribes emerged from the social engineering of British colonial officials and that it produced new origin stories: "Tribals or aboriginals were seen as the descendants of the original inhabitants of India, whereas the upper castes were descendants of Aryan invaders" (1997, 729).

The widespread forging of ethnic terrains in the late nineteenth and early twentieth centuries was a complex process that redefined identity, social relations, legal status, and space. In colonial settings as well as in Thailand (which was not colonized), identity and status became classified in new ways. The state was still the arbiter of identity and political position, and in that sense there is significant continuity in how state formations have inserted themselves as the principle of social life. The shift that took place was from rank to ethnicity/race as the principle of identity, as tributary states were undone. This change in the parameters of social identity concerns the foundational logic of state formation. The next chapter describes some of these changes for twentieth-century Thailand, focusing on the public sphere wherein identities were recast in terms of unequal rights within the bounded and sovereign nation-state.

States chart particular moral orders as they delimit identity, society, and history, in part through control over trade, settlement, and social relations. The ultimate reference for such arrangements, which often involve ethnic landscaping, is the sovereign control over life and death that rests with the state's authorities (Fiskesjö 2003, 44–57). The consolidation of Thailand as a nation-state changed the classification of highlander identities. This classification rested on the territorially defined nation as the principle of history, identity, and rights and was in many ways a break from the past. Ideas of race became very significant to this redefinition of social life, replacing the previous emphasis on rank. But considering how individual authorities tended to inscribe themselves as the principle of identity, history, and rights in premodern settings and exercised control over settlement and movement in highland areas, there are also important continuities with so-called premodern state formations that leave various questions with the supposed uniqueness of the modern world. In addition, the racialized landscapes of the colonial era were very much about the ranking of peoples, though with the important difference of having a global, "scientific" framework that replaced the idiosyncrasies of various "local" rulers. Ethnography and anthropological theorizing contributed to the routinization of this global perspective and to its re-localization into numerous colonial and national schemes of identity, difference, rights, and disenfranchisement.[14]

CHAPTER TWO

Twentieth-Century Highlanders

> They live on the hill-tops and cannot live on the plains, be-
> cause they are accustomed to the high air. If they come down
> on the plains for too long they get fever. There is no limit to
> the area they cover, for they have no permanent abode and no
> land to cultivate. They are perpetually wandering from place to
> place. As for the cultivation of rice, if the soil is good, they
> come back to the same place, but if it is not they search for
> new land. They are stupid and rough, and they do not know
> the customs of other races. . . . Their ideas of cleanliness are
> very vague.
>
> —Nai Chan Rangsiyanan and
> Luang Bamrung Naowakarn, "The Yao"

This description is from the first Thai explorers' account specifically about Thailand's Mien (as Yao), published in the *Journal of the Siam
Society* in 1925 (vol. 19, no. 2, 83–128). In the early twentieth century, the
Siam Society, "an Orientalist club of foreign and Thai elitist scholars"
(Thongchai 2000a, 53), brought together expatriates and the Siamese upper
class with an interest in archeology and ethnography. The society's journal
was the main forum for the publication of articles on studies in epigraphy,
archaeology, and ethnography, and as such it must be viewed as an important vehicle for the consolidation of Siam as an object of knowledge, ethnographic, archaeological, historical, and otherwise.

Siam was not colonized, unlike neighboring states. This is sometimes referred to as a mark of the country's uniqueness, but Siam came under many

of the same pressures for administrative and political economic reform as did colonies (Herzfeld 2002). The process was also more complex than simply outside pressures on a particular state. Siamese authorities drew on many of the colonial-era dynamics for projects of national integration in order to undo the autonomy of various semi-autonomous or suzerain principalities within its orbit—that to some extent was circumscribed by British and French colonial rule of Burma and Indochina, respectively— and to fashion a nation-state. The language of rule, the classification of peoples and places, and the practices of integrating the state were increasingly in the name of national identity.

Over the twentieth century, this process brought a series of definitions of highland peoples that replaced the earlier ones grounded in tributary relationships. The earliest of these was *chao pa,* "forest people," which assumed a tripartite spatial and civilizational hierarchy that defined Bangkok as the pinnacle of civilization, Thai-ness, and normalcy. By midcentury, this term was replaced with *chao khao,* "mountain people," which signified unruliness, illicit practices, and a threat to the country's borders. The former suggests a deficiency in civilization and Thai-ness, while the latter suggests various obstacles to progress and threats to national integration. Both categories were a source of ethnographic writing and nation-building efforts that hinted at the manifold relations of local and global levels.

National imagery in Thailand has shed some of the Cold War anxiety that was attached to *chao khao* identity, and there has been a move to redefine highland peoples as *chao thai phu-khao,* "mountain Thai." At the same time, international cultural tourism that seeks markers of the unmodern in Thailand's "hill tribes" reinforces the production of images manifesting tribal essences, which are increasingly on display in Thailand's museum spaces. The images of highland peoples indicate various transnational contact zones, but they are simultaneously about the forging of local worlds. They manifest an important component of the making of Thailand as a nation-state. As in the case of Chinese ideas of the Yao and northern Thai notions of the Lawa, these identities provide an entry into the making of regions in a global context, in which the conflation of social and natural categories has isolated state power as the source of identity, status, and history.

Racialized Landscapes

The article on Thailand's Yao quoted above contains a photograph taken in Nan Town, showing the Mien leader Tang Tsan Khwoen (see chapter 3), another Mien man, and seven women. They are identified simply as "a group of Yao." Ideas of race, intelligence, and cleanliness informed this portrayal of a strange people in the mountains, and there was no mention of the administrative or economic links that Tang Tsan Khwoen and his followers had to Nan and potentially elsewhere. Instead, they emerged through the text and the photograph as a particular manifestation of a social type that was clearly uncivilized. This image of timeless primitives accompanied the disentangling of identities and social realities from a range of local kingdoms. The shift toward national integration brought new models of and for upland-lowland relations, though attempts at implementing these new understandings were not always successful. In 1921, several villages of Mien and Hmong in Maehongson Province on the Burmese border resisted the attempts of provincial authorities to conscript them: "Several skirmishes broke out. A leading central Thai official recommended chasing the non-Thai groups out of the country and burning their villages, but higher authorities suggested that a policy of benign neglect would be more productive" (Renard 1988, 42). While the modern state differed in many ways from its tributary precursors, the threat of violence and settlement erasure indicates significant commonalities.

The Siamese charting of the national terrain was about not only peoples but also places. Provinces, like peoples, served as fields for the establishment of a national perspective. In an account of Nan Province from the early 1930s, the author of a chapter on various ethnic groups uses the term *chonchat* ("nationalities," "ethnic groups") in reference to both highland and lowland peoples (Seri 1933). Importantly, this term does not assume any inherent difference between highland and lowland populations, nor does the related term *chat* that was later used by Bunchuai Srisawat (1950) in his description of the "thirty peoples of Chiangrai province."

These terms for "nationalities," which replaced the likes of "slave" as a reference to upland peoples, do not have an immediate relational component. That is, the terms themselves do not openly suggest a social relationship that draws on the state's control of social life. But there is another dimension to *chonchat* and *chat* that indicates a changing social landscape, even if the terms do not suggest the ethno-spatial hierarchy of forests, villages, and towns. As these terms were employed, they referred to identity as "flesh and blood and ancestry" (*lüad nüa chüa sai;* Seri 1933, 273) and corresponded to the lingering racialism in Thai nationalist ideology at the time (Streckfuss 1993).

The forging of a national terrain and hegemony was partly about defining peoples in relation to the rights and duties of citizens. The roots of the marginal status of highland people in contemporary Thailand lie in the conflation of race and citizenship that emerged in the late nineteenth century. In the account of nationalities in Nan Province mentioned earlier, the author notes that many Siamese in Bangkok view all northerners with some prejudice as "Lao" but adds that "in general, the lowland population of Nan are Thai people: they are racially true Thai" (Seri 1933, 273). Tai Lü "are of the same race as Thai, but since ancient times their blood has been much mixed with that of Lawa, and therefore they differ in many ways from the Thai." Both Thin and Khmu uplanders are described as having Khmer origins, Thin having shown "more progress" than Khmu. The Mlabri foragers known in Thai as *Phi Tong Lüang* ("yellow-leaf ghosts") "are the wildest of all races" (Seri 1933, 279–82). Mien and Hmong (as Yao and Meo) are described as having ancient origins in China. The author does not comment on Mien and Hmong in evolutionary terms, but it may be that for his readers these were all primitive or backward people unless otherwise specified. That is, the *chonchat* terminology conveys the Thai as progressed and racially of Thai space, with references to sites of ancient Thai history such as Sukhothai and Sawankalok (273). "Racially" non-Thai peoples are not of Thai national space, they are of Chinese or Khmer extraction and thus their identity refers to other national territories.

This racialized discourse of Thai proto-ethnography was in important ways formulated in an international contact zone of Western colonial-era advisors to the Siamese government and the racial classifications of French colonial authorities in Indochina (Streckfuss 1993) and the British in Burma. For an understanding of the Thai public sphere during the twentieth century, the fundamental significance of the classification of peoples lies in the nationalist appropriation of agency and identity. Non-Thai peoples were deprived of agency through the nationalization of space, identity, and history that accompanied the racialization of the Thai landscape. Notions of progress and civilization were part of this discourse. As these notions were mapped on to the ethnic landscape, the Thai were civilized and had progress while the various others lacked these attributes to a greater or lesser degree. This imagery consolidated the nation-state's authority and established its civilizing mission at the same time as it defined and differentiated the subjects of the modern nation (Thongchai 2000b; Iijima and Koizumi 2003).

The origins of Thai nationalism are commonly attributed to the nation-building agendas of King Vajiravudh (r. 1910–25, Vella 1978). Subsequent nationalist dynamics during the 1930s are often described with reference to the considerable influence of Luang Wichit Wathakan (1898–1962, see Barmé 1993). But Terwiel (1993, 136) suggests that W. Clifton Dodd's (1923) *The Tai Race,* which "stresses the importance of the existence of Tai speaking peoples in French Indochina, British Burma, and China," and

W. A. R. Wood's (1925) *History of Siam,* which "gave a prominent place to the early history of the Thais," were quite important for Thai nationalism in the late 1930s. In his preface to *The History of Siam,* Wood remarked that the topic was one of which the Siamese could be proud. Echoing the evolutionary rhetoric of the time, Wood depicted Siam as one among many nations-as-species in an evolutionary struggle where only some had been worthy of survival:

> It is the story of a collection of more or less uncultivated immigrants from southern China, who settled in the country now known as Siam, overcoming a mighty Empire, and establishing a number of free States, which became finally fused into the Siam of today. We see them humbled to dust again and again by a more powerful neighbor, yet always rising up and regaining their freedom. A hundred years ago there were dozens of independent States in South-Eastern Asia. Today there remains but one—Siam. Those who believe in the survival of the fittest will admit that the Siamese, whatever their faults, must possess some special qualities which have marked them out to maintain this unique position. (7–8)

Seen from high-society Bangkok and Chiangmai, ethnic minority highlanders in the north were dirty savages. Wood, the British consul in Chiangmai, included a chapter ("Some Exotics") on various ethnic minority highlanders in his memoir *Land of Smiles* (1935). There he relates the following tongue-in-cheek account:

> When the King and Queen of Siam visited Chiangmai in 1927, representatives of most of the hill tribes were brought in to take part in a procession in honor of their Majesties, and to give exhibitions of their own particular styles of dancing and music. After the King had seen them, he remarked to me that the Meows and Yaos [Hmong and Mien] looked very smart and clean, whereas he had always been told that they were disgustingly dirty. "But Sir," I replied, "those Meows and Yaos have been in Chiangmai for a month, and the Governor has had them scrubbed three times a day during the whole of that period, so as to make them presentable." Turning to the Governor, the King asked:—"Is this true, Your Excellency?" "No, Your Majesty," replied he, "Mr. Wood has grossly exaggerated the matter. I only had them scrubbed *twice* a day." (1935, 130)[1]

Concerns other than civilization and cleanliness informed the interest in ethnicity and highland peoples. Notions of modernity and its opposite, tradition, became increasingly important in the varied projects that consolidated the image of the modern nation. Erik Seidenfaden, an expatriate major in the Siamese military and an enthusiastic amateur ethnographer, opened an exhibit of ethnic dress in the lecture hall of the Siam Society in 1937. His idea for the exhibit was to collect

> all the costumes of the various branches of the Thai people, as well as the dresses of the non-Thai communities who are mostly domiciled in the hills on the western boundary of the kingdom in the mountainous North. My thought was really to have all these dresses executed in a size to suit models of a height not more than fifty centimeters. . . . I have noticed to my sorrow how the picturesque and time-honored national and regional costumes, nearly all over the land, are fast disappearing, to be replaced by dresses of more or less international fashion. . . . Therefore if future generations are not to be kept in ignorance as to how their ancestors clothed themselves, it is high time now to collect all the various dresses still worn by the inhabitants of this picturesque and beautiful land, and keep them carefully preserved in our museums for future information and study. It has been rightly said that the honk of the motor lorry with its load of cheap foreign textiles sounds the death knell of the national costumes, while the radio and the cinematograph are rapidly exterminating provincial dialects and ancient manners and customs. (Seidenfaden 1954, 84–85)[2]

As an expatriate whose role it was to help modernize the Siamese military, Seidenfaden sidestepped the role that he and his upper-class audience had in the changes taking place in Siamese society. Instead, he discussed the corrupting influences of movies, gramophones, and trucks carrying cheap textiles. That is, his focus was on material objects rather than the social relations that engendered the apparent disappearance of ethnic diversity. Seidenfaden's ambivalence about this transformation triggered his commissioning, collecting, and displaying of ethnic diversity through dress (see also Seidenfaden 1958). He speculated that the National Museum could establish an ethnographical branch "where all the national and tribal costumes of Siam would be exhibited on full size models, wearing the traits of the great Thai nation and of the many lesser tribes, whether of Mongolian, Mon-Khmer or Negrito stock" (1954, 84–85).

The racial distinction that Seidenfaden drew between "the great Thai nation" and the "lesser tribes" corresponds to currents in Siamese nationalism, but it is also indicative of how Western ethnography at the time engaged in charting the racial landscape of national territories in the late colonial era.[3] Some of the Thai ethnography offered a vehicle for speculation about Thai ethnic essences across time and space and suggests a prospecting for national/racial heritage based on Thai identity as ethnolinguistic. Luang Wichit Wathakan, one of the key players of Thai nationalism, wrote a preface to Bunchuai Srisawat's *30 Peoples of Chiangrai*. He wrote that the author "is of high learning and is interested in the knowledge derived from anthropology" (Luang Wichit 1950, n.p.). His hierarchical arrangement of peoples is telling; diversity implied branches of the main race, and any difference from the Central Thai was simultaneously spatial, temporal, and evolutionary. Establishing the modernity and civilization of the Siamese/Thai entailed postulating the ancientness of the peoples who came to be viewed as lesser manifestations of Thai-ness:

> The study of the background of the various peoples who live on Thai soil, such as Tai Ya, Lue, Khoen, Ngiao, and others, is of great value for the study of the history of our own Thai race, because most of these groups are branches of the Thai race. The Tai Ya, Lue, Ngiao, and Khoen are real Thai. Studying the ways, origins, and customs of these groups will greatly improve our knowledge of the ways and customs of the ancient Thai people. These [other] groups have preserved the old ways, as modern civilization has not yet entered to destroy the ancient culture. (Luang Wichit 1950)

Like Seidenfaden's exhibit, Luang Wichit's approach to ethnic diversity was informed by notions of nationality and modernity. His antiquarian interest in "other" Tai peoples assumed that the forces of modernity erased "ancient" cultures. The quest for ethnic essences was primarily a celebration of the master (Thai) race, of which the various others were merely branches. Whatever qualitative differences there were among Tai peoples— in culture, language, and social life, for instance—were rendered as quantitative on an axis of ancientness and modernity. In his preface, Luang Wichit made no mention of the various non-Tai peoples that Bunchuai's book covered. Much of *30 Peoples of Chiangrai* is in the same mold as the ethnography published in the *Journal of the Siam Society* in the early part of the century, essentially a list of traits attributed to each ethnic group—origins, language, livelihood, customs and ceremonies, and so on.

In the first ethnic entry of *30 Peoples of Chiangrai*, on "Northern people" (*chao nüa*, the lowland northern Thai of the province), Bunchuai described Chiangrai as a fertile area and well-suited to agriculture: "Before, it was forested wilderness. At that time, Lawa people owned the land. When we Thai fled from Sipsongpanna [in Yunnan, southern China], a confrontation occurred with the leader of the local people. At first he had the upper hand. Later we Thai were victorious and became owners of the land. From the beginning [we] had freedom and were not subject to the authority of anyone else. The first capital was Chiang Saen Luang" (1950, 17–18). The "northern people," the true subjects of the province, were thus fore-grounded with the historical destiny of "our" Thai conquest of the land from the earlier Lawa owners.

What the *Jengtung State Chronicle* depicted as the achievement of Queen Jamathewi had become the legacy of the Thai people/race. The account es-tablished Thai ethnicity and sovereignty as tied to a particular terrain, and the term "northerners" routinized an ethnic and regional hierarchy that as-sumed the primacy of Bangkok. The term also erased all the violence and complexity behind the nineteenth century (re-)population of the northern Thai lowlands (cf. Bowie 1996, 120–26). The nationalization of territory is evident in the brief overview of the province that precedes the ethno-graphic chapters: "Most of the population is Northerners (*chao nüa*), and aside from them there are Thai Yai, Khün, Lü, Tai Ya, Thai from Indochina, etc. There are also foreigners (*chao tang prathet*) such as Chinese, *Haw* [Yunnanese Chinese], Burmese, *Yuan* [Vietnamese], *Khek* [Indians], Kari-ang, Lawa, Westerners, and others, and Mountain Peoples (*chao khao*) such as Khamu, Khamet, Meo, Yao, *Musoe* [Lahu], *I-kaw* [Akha], *Khe-Risaw* [Lisu], Kui, etc." (Bunchuai 1950, 16).

While the term *chat* did not inherently differentiate kinds of peoples, Bunchuai Srisawat's arrangement of peoples assumed clear distinctions separating Thai-Tai peoples as those who had claims to the land; foreigners, who by definition had no such claims within Thailand; and *chao khao*. Given this scheme, one must assume that *chao khao* had no claims to the terrain and that this was the rationale for the account of winning control of the land from the Lawa peoples in ancient times. Even if many Tai peoples came from southern China and French Indochina, the conflation of race and terrain made them belong on Thai soil. For the same reasons of racial-ized landscape, the identity of the mountain people lay outside of Thailand. Whereas Siamese travel writers had earlier established the strangeness of forest people, the forging of an understanding of mountain people (the two terms implied essentially the same group) came to center on their lack of a racial connection to the national terrain.

Listing the Karen and Lawa peoples as foreigners is a clear manifestation of these dynamics, where identity and historicity were based on a particular relationship between ethnicity and territory. Since both ethnic categories subsequently indexed hill tribes, the classification of them as foreigners may have related to their then-numerous lowland settlements. Of other foreigners, only *Haw* were included in the book, possibly since they lived in the mountainous countryside—ethnography was primarily about rural populations. The entries on the various highland peoples start by stating their foreign origins: "Yao originally lived (*doem asai yu*) in the mountains of Yunnan Province, China" (Bunchuai 1950, 462). "I-kaw or Aka are a tribe that originally lived in the highlands of southwest China" (485). The entry on Yao described, among other aspects, where they built their villages and what their houses looked like; that they grew opium, rice, corn, and tobacco; how they dressed; characteristics of the language; ceremonies; courtship; and bride price, a loosely organized assembly of facts that defined "a people." The Yao people are described as "hospitable and generous, they love orderliness and peace and quiet" (476).

Bunchuai's tendency to upgrade the peoples of Chiangrai Province for his presentation to a national audience is evident in the term *Khe-Risaw* for Lisu. The prefix *khe* is a reference to China, hence the term means "Chinese Lisu." But *Risaw* was not a local pronunciation. Instead, Bunchuai had "corrected" the *l* consonant to an *r* in terms of the stratification of Thai dialects. In a hegemonic linguistic environment, the various regional languages that were related to Bangkok Thai were viewed as inferior dialects (Diller 1993). This matches the ethnic ranking of Tai groups as inferior or more backward versions of Thai people proper. *R* is not a consonant in northern Thai, the language of Bunchuai's Chiangrai Province, and the Siamese terms that have an *r* are pronounced with an *l*. *Rot*, "vehicle," becomes *lot*, for instance. The same sound change also takes place within Siamese among lower-class speakers. Bunchuai's modification of Lisu was an attempt to erase what to an upper-class Thai reader are markers of lower-class incorrectness. Assuming that both the uneducated lower class and the rustics in the countryside got it wrong, any *l* correctly was an *r*.

The same unconscious upgrading is apparent in Bunchuai's glossary of Mien terms, where his corrections match those between Shan and Bangkok Thai but do not make sense for Mien, which is not a Tai language.[4] Like the twice-daily bathing of Meow and Yao prior to the king's visit to Chiangmai, these linguistic modifications concerned the indexing of difference as deficiency. Through a national framework for what was proper and thus presentable in public, difference was variously erased, as in the case of linguistic variation, defined as of the past, as in Luang Wichit's notion of various Tai cultures as manifestations of what Siamese used to be like, or projected to the outside of the country, as with the identity of the mountain peoples. What remained, though it was often left implicit, was the contemporary hegemony of national life through notions of race and language.[5]

As the Thai nation was being charted through notions of civility during the first half of the twentieth century, in important ways through descriptions of the nation's outsiders in the northern highlands, it was also being defined in terms of its patrimony—race, sovereignty, and territory. The various Tai groups within and beyond Thailand had not "progressed" as much as the Siamese, but in their supposed ancientness they revealed some of the Thai racial heritage, in culture, social life, and so on. Ethnography provided a site for articulating and reifying Thai-ness. As such, it contributed to the selective appropriation of cultural diversity for the project of nation-building through the distinction between hill tribes and peasants. This effort was based on racial distinctions, the conflation of race and national territory, and on modernity as an index of state control.

Bunchuai Srisawat's *30 Peoples of Chiangrai* reflected as well as contributed to the racialization of this landscape and the insertion of national parameters for identity. His book was simultaneously an attempt to bring investment and tourism to the region. He began the book with an overview of economic prosperity: Chiangrai ranked fifth of all provinces in terms of rice production, there was still "empty" land, the forest had many large trees (1950, 27). Like Seri (1933) in the account of Nan Province, Bunchuai insisted that the identity of the lowland peoples of Chiangrai was that of "real Thai. There has been no mixing of blood from elsewhere. . . . They are unhappy to be called Lao, and call themselves lowland peoples (*khon müang*). They have progress, they are not peoples of the forest" (32). At the end of his account of the thirty peoples, Bunchuai provided information for prospective travelers from Bangkok, who would go by plane or train to Lampang and take a car from there, including a list of the available accommodations in the city of Chiangrai.

There was considerable demand for the book. It had been reprinted six times by the time Bunchuai wrote a new version of the material, this time focusing only on the non-Thai hill peoples. This subsequent book, *Mountain Peoples in Thailand* (*Chao Khao Nai Thai*, Bunchuai 1963) covered not only the north, it also included chapters on the hunter-gatherers of the southern borders with Malaysia. The shift in focus suggests how national modernity was being charted through its opposites—all the "primitives" of the national terrain made a coherent set. By implication, all Thai "had progress" and were outside the concerns of ethnography. In the assembly of the nation's outsiders in the mountains, the book reinforced the paradigmatic status of progress and its conflation with race and the national terrain.

At the end of *Mountain Peoples in Thailand*, where *30 Peoples* had information for tourists, Bunchuai classified the various mountain peoples by race and suggested conditions of lack: "There are over 260,000 forest people and mountain people in Thailand. There still are no facilities for education or health care, but the Border Patrol Police (BPP) has set up some schools to teach Thai language for the betterment of future generations of forest people and mountain people. A budget is needed for the welfare of this group of forest people and mountain people" (609–10). Thus, along with classifying forest and mountain people by race, which was simultaneously about defining the Thai "race" as civilized, Bunchuai charted a landscape of lack. The state needed a budget for "the welfare of this group of forest people and mountain people." Behind the improvement of life in the hinterlands, which was only being addressed to a limited extent by the BPP, lay an image of the rural and urban lowlands as advanced. Thai society had progressed, but the highland societies were far behind. More had to be done. From encouraging domestic tourism and investment in *30 Peoples,* Bunchuai had shifted his focus toward national development projects, and this changing ethnographic orientation belonged squarely within the national and international context of Thailand's national development plans during the late 1950s (see Thak 1979, 226–72; Demaine 1986).

The imagery of national integration and development provided a model for recasting the issues of race and civilization, and this informed the ethnographic gaze. In his entry on Yao, Bunchuai described the elderly leader Thao La as the fifth generation of *kamnan* (sub-district headman); he was in fact the second generation Mien leader in Thailand and the first to attain the position of *kamnan.* He also wrote that he and his sons had changed their family name to Srisombat. "This shows that these Yao have received much progress. He [Thao La] has sent his sons and grandsons to study in the capital." Then Bunchuai provided a list of the headmen of the five officially recognized villages in Phachangnoi *tambol* (1963, 432–33). This imagery cast markers of national integration as a measure of progress, something the *chao khao* had to some extent "received" in their supposedly remote locations, measured by incorporation into provincial administration and the use of Thai names. In this formulation, progress measured the legibility of subject populations, where the comprehensibility of *chao khao* names to a Thai audience was analogous to their entanglements with governmental structures.

Mountain peoples had emerged as a national category, and during the 1950s they were increasingly viewed in terms of border security, settlement migration, and the related issues of orderliness and progress, often seen as lacking. In many ways, the subsequent ethnographic work through the Tribal Research Center (later Institute) was a direct continuation of these trends, increasingly focused on the parameters of national integration and state control. The largely structural-functionalist work of the Westerners affiliated with the Center never merged with the governmentality of this national research agency. But the two shared the emphasis on a fundamental divide between highland and lowland populations, one that rested on the classification of ethnic groups in relation to Thai identity, a twentieth-century conflation of race, language, and unequal rights.

Forging Mountain Peoples

The hill tribes of Thailand were discovered as such in the 1950s, as mountain peoples who were a problem population and an object of government policy. The definition of *chao khao* was simultaneously a cultural and a political economic project, concerning the consolidation of national space within a particular Cold War global order. The initial government-sponsored research on highland peoples in the 1950s concerned ways to stop opium cultivation and to halt settlement migration, and it was with this research that *chao khao* became a particular object of Thai knowledge. The 1962 *Report on the Socio-Economic Survey of the Hill Tribes in Northern Thailand* defined shifting cultivation as the root of all the problems with highland peoples: "Slash and burn agriculture is the economic foundation of the hill tribes under discussion. Without any exception they have not yet advanced to stabilized farming. As it will be seen that almost all the problems which the hill tribes constitute in this country—such as destruction of forests, opium growing, border insecurity, difficulties in administration and control—derive from this very fact. An immense progress would be made if the hill people would learn and practice cultivation in permanent fields" (Department of Public Welfare 1962, 17).

When the Committee for National Tribal Welfare was established in 1959, the government's stated aim was "to speed the assimilation of tribal people by settling them in the fashion of Thai lowlanders on some single tract of land that would provide a living. As the uplanders 'became Thai' they would no longer grow dry rice or opium, and thus the forests would be saved and these non-Thai would be absorbed" (Hanks and Hanks 2001, 128). The implied boundaries of Thai-ness were thus involved in the definition of highland peoples as a problem, and they concerned farming methods as much as allegiance to the markers of nationhood.

The efforts to bring shifting cultivation to an end didn't just bring the territorial sovereignty of the Thai state to highland villages. At the same time, these efforts also involved the projection of a national view, within which highlanders' farming was seen as a threat to national well-being. The motivation to eliminate shifting cultivation was predicated on images of national resources and the nation's water supply: "Swidden cultivation is . . . regarded by law as very harmful to the economy of the nation and is indirectly prohibited. It is the government's policy to keep half of its territory as forest. It is believed that the destruction of forest will cause a shortage of natural water supply during the dry season. This will result in losses to the agriculture and economy of the nation" (Sophon 1978, 48). This is an example of what Scott aptly calls "seeing like a state" (1998); the highlander practices of livelihood were "regarded by law as very harmful to the economy."

"Clearly, *chao khao* lack knowledge regarding soil protection" (Khajadphai 1985, 17). Farming practices were also viewed as somewhat analogous to the highlanders' perpetuation of cultural, religious, and linguistic difference from mainstream Thai society as harboring a threat that could be alleviated to the extent to that *chao khao* "entered society" (*khao sangkhom*). "Their society is firmly attached to their customs. They have not been willing to change in any way along the lines of wider society. Because of this, many problems arise, for example forest destruction, security problems, and a drug problem" (Saimuang 1986, 48). According to the Tribal Research Institute (TRI; 1995): "There are many hill tribe problems as identified by Thai authorities. Most of these problems are related to some aspects of the hill tribes way of life which are [sic] considered to be inappropriate to the present socio-economic and political situation of the country" (2).

As a mode of livelihood largely apart from state control, shifting cultivation was important to the reproduction of identity and agency in upland communities. The ban on shifting cultivation and various official campaigns against uplanders' practices of difference show the nation-state's refusal to accommodate upland formulations of agency, as well as the state's power to eliminate the economic basis of such difference. The warfare against uplanders and units of the Communist Party of Thailand (CPT) from the late 1960s until the 1980s was about "national loyalty" (Bowie 1997); in most cases it is difficult to determine whether the reason for attack was swidden fields, opium cultivation, uplander ethnicity (Hmong in particular), the presence of CPT units, or the nervous but violent consolidation of Thai society through attacks on its supposed enemies. This violence faded significantly when CPT members were granted amnesty in 1982, but attacks on upland ethnic minority settlements continued, variously because of swidden cultivation, lack of citizenship papers, or the ongoing consolidation of Thailand.

The cluster of ideas about *chao khao* is pervasive, and it is a major component in the relations between highland peoples and various Thai agents. The contemporary contact zone, which defines Thai people and uplanders (as *chao khao*) in and from their interrelations, is in many ways conditioned by the ideology of the modern nation-state (Pinkaew 2002). Thongchai has described how Thailand as a bounded nation-state, a "geo-body," became a powerful metaphor for society in the twentieth century. The borders of Thailand were conveyed as analogous to the boundaries of a national essence, Thai-ness. The Border Patrol Police was established in 1959 to fight communism in rural areas. "The border" was both literal and figurative—and firmly political: "This police force can be found operating anywhere from the border areas, among the minorities (to teach them the Central Thai language and introduce them to the Thai flag, a Buddha image, and pictures of the king and queen), in a village of Thai peasants well inside Thai territory (to organize a counterinsurgency unit), to an urban center like Chiangmai" (Thongchai 1994, 170).

Some of the concern with the borderlands was informed by anxieties regarding the civil war in Burma and warfare in Laos and Vietnam, which in the Cold War climate had both local and international dimensions. Communism was a major cause of the anxieties of the Thai authorities, and it was viewed as an external threat, stemming from China, Vietnam, Laos, and Cambodia. Because some highland peoples in Laos fought on the side of the communist and nationalist Pathet Lao (many also fought with the royalists, and still others with neutralists), it became a widespread notion in Thailand that the Meo (Hmong) were communist sympathizers (Moerman 1967; Tapp 1989; Smalley, Vang, and Yang 1990).

In 1965, the mother of the Thai king had sponsored the building of a school that used Border Patrol Police officers as teachers. This act of royal generosity was to win the allegiance of the *chao khao* to the Thai nation. The school was in the Hmong village of Ban Meo Maw (*Ban Meo* means "Meo village") in Chiangrai Province, near the opium fields of the Mien people of Phulangka village (who are the focus of chapter 3). Among the rural police force, the intimidation of opium growers had for some time served as a source of income. Unlicensed growers were continually at risk of arrest and fines. In late 1967, the Hmong in Meo Maw had already been taxed for their illegal fields by one police force when another unit of the police came demanding money and arrested some villagers after they refused to pay a second time. The villagers, upset at this, retaliated by burning the bridge that led to the school donated by the king's mother. The police then fired their guns at the Hmong, who fired back. The villagers fled, and the army dropped bombs on sites in the forest where they thought the Hmong were in hiding. This and related incidents became known in Thailand as *kabot meo daeng,* "the Red ["Communist"] Meo revolt," which contributed to the major mobilization of military forces against highlanders. At this time, units of the CPT had taken to the forest, and some highland peoples joined their forces in response to the increasingly frequent attacks. The Hmong in particular were singled out for attack, many of their villages were burned down, and some were bombed (see Race 1974).

What might have otherwise been an isolated incident of fighting between a police unit and a Hmong village was viewed as a sure sign of subversive communist activity. The national fear of communist infiltration became an important lens on highland people as they were brought into national consciousness during the 1960s and 1970s. While members of the Communist Party of Thailand were Thai people concerned with achieving more equity, such as improving the situation of lowland farmers impoverished by high rents on farmland, the party was characterized as foreign and a threat to the nation's borders. During the 1960s and 1970s, all cases of rural discontent were viewed as "simply regional outbreaks of the same communist insurgency that threatens the nation's security and interests" and were violently suppressed (Chairat 1988, 188).

Mien from Phulangka village had fled into the lowlands during the fighting and lived for two years in temporary shelters. They recalled having often gone without food during this time. Thai military forces burned down the villagers' shelters at least once. Subsequently the Mien built more permanent houses in a small valley that does not allow for wet-rice fields. This was the beginning of the village of Pangkha. When U.S. Navy "Seabees" built a road through the area, from Chiangkham to northern Nan Province, Pangkha people moved their houses next to the road. The fighting was even more intense in another district of Chiangrai Province, Thoeng. As in the Phulangka area and in Nan Province, the highland areas were declared free fire zones. "Accessible villages were ordered to be evacuated and then were bombed and strafed by the Thai Air Force. . . . Anyone found in the hills after this warning was considered a communist" (Hanks and Hanks 2001, 195).

Highlanders' ethnic clothing was often viewed with suspicion. One teenager from Phulangka was on a bus to Chiangmai City in early 1968 when the police at a roadblock told him to "go back to the hills where he belonged." Near the town of Chiangkham, downhill from Phulangka, two men were stopped by military forces as they walked to another Mien village for a visit. The men were promptly arrested when the soldiers found handwritten manuscripts in Chinese in their pockets. These were Mien ritual manuals, but anything written in Chinese was automatically suspect as communist subversion—in Chiangkham, some ethnically Chinese Christians were arrested when police found a Chinese-language Bible in their car. Subsequent to the arrest of the two Mien men, who were in prison for a full year, Mien people became anxious about their copies of ritual chants and other texts in Chinese characters, such as genealogies. Many burned their texts to avoid imprisonment. One man from Thoeng District who eventually moved to the resettlement of Rom Yen near Chiangkham burned his copy of *Kia Shen Pong,* one of only three that Mien people had brought to Thailand.

The intensity of nationalist anxieties during this time is ably described in Bowie's analysis of the village scout movement. While the movement has now faded in significance, in its heyday it was a major organization: "Since its founding in 1971, about five million people have been initiated into its ranks, approximately one-fifth of Thailand's adult population" (1997, 1–2). Bowie describes the movement's five-day initiation ritual, which combined anxiety, theatrics, and hope for the future in terms of the twin principles of national survival as threatened by foreign forces and national identity as based on the union of nation, religion, and king (183–232). In the twentieth century, Thai identity was repeatedly consolidated through the use of external threats (Irvine 1982; cf. Reynolds 1993).

In the Thai definition of *chao khao,* national time (history and destiny) and space (the landmass and the borders) are under threat, and this is what creates agency and defines the acting subject. The notion of *chao khao* facilitated the imagination of the national Thai subject defending its terrain and destiny, and this construction consolidated the state as an actor, as much through the military defense of its national border as through the agencies mobilized to classify the *chao khao* and to subordinate them to the control of the government's administrative, agricultural, educational, and military apparatus.

One element of the construction of *chao khao* in relation to national space (the "geo-body") is a map that shows where each "tribe" entered Thailand (Young 1962, x; Lewis and Lewis 1984, 8; Khajadphai 1985, n.p.). Reducing the complexity of individual and usually small-scale migrations to ethnic moves, such maps define each of the ethnic groups in relation to the border. Several of the museums in northern Thailand feature such maps of "immigration routes." Through the idea of the border, highlander identity is construed as standing in a problematic relationship to the Thai nation. But as a discursive practice, the idea of the border can be viewed as constructing both the (settled) Thai nation and the migrating *chao khao.* This contrast between the Thai and their internal outsiders also constructs the agency of the Thai state to define and control the social landscape through violence and other means.

The Thai government's efforts at national integration created the notion of the country's "hill tribe problem" (Pinkaew 2001, 2002). The process, while local and national in its repercussions, indicates how an international post–World War II contact zone reinforced particular projects of national integration (cf. Kelly and Kaplan 2001). The Department of Public Welfare, under the Ministry of the Interior and with international funding from the Asia Society and the United Nations, contracted Austrian anthropologist Hans Manndorff to lead a research team in a survey of "opium-growing tribes" during 1961 and 1962 (Department of Welfare 1962; Manndorff 1967; Tannenbaum 2001, xiv–xv). This effort led to the establishment of the Tribal Research Center in Chiangmai in 1964. The Tribal Research Center had a Thai director and Australian anthropologist William R. Geddes as its advisor. "A national research scheme was proposed involving socio-economic studies of the six main tribes, each to take two years" (Geddes 1983, 5).

This mandate effectively defined the social landscape of the hills of northern Thailand as consisting of Akha, Hmong, Lahu, Lisu, Mien, and Karen (Geddes 1967; Hinton 1983). Lawa, while highland swidden farmers, were not on this list, as they were not viewed as a "problem population"; they did not grow opium, and migration was less common among them than among other highland peoples. Foreign anthropologists were invited to conduct research with a Thai counterpart, so that Thai scholars could gradually learn the relevant research methods and take over the research on tribal peoples. Each Western anthropologist (American, Australian, British) conducted an in-depth study, largely in a single settlement, from which the structures of society, culture, and agriculture were to be extracted. This ethnographic work projected a particular timelessness on highland social formations. One of the official studies collected and assembled statistics to show the migratory tendency of each hill tribe. This survey, undertaken in 1965, stated that over a ten-year period, migration among the hill tribes ranged from 25 percent to over 90 percent, systemically varied by ethnic group—lowest among the Karen and highest among the Hmong (Geddes 1976, 42).[6]

Miles (1972a, b, 1974) described Mien household formations in terms of competition over available laborers. Larger dwelling groups, which could include many households, "literally pay to gain and maintain control over the productive capacities of more families than their smaller counterparts" (1972b, 194). "The Yao regard labor as the scarce factor of production in their economy. Outlays for weddings and bridewealth constitute the linchpin of a mechanism whereby dwelling groups compete for manpower. The most successful corporations acquire exclusive control over a large portion of the workers in the village" (1974, 416). The village that Miles studied, Phulangka, had 244 inhabitants in 19 dwelling groups, 107 of them in households of 15 or fewer people, and 137 in larger units, the largest having

57 people in 10 apartments. The local residents grew rice, corn, and opium in their swidden fields. According to Miles, scheduling conflicts among the three crops meant that only households with abundant laborers could take full advantage of this three-crop system, and this is what led to the inflationary pressures in household size and the attempts to monopolize the labor of a settlement.

Other uplanders such as Akha, Hmong, Lisu, and Lahu were similarly engaged in farming that combined these three crops, but there is no indication that they made comparable attempts to establish multiple households. But it is unlikely that the pattern Miles found in Phulangka was very general even among the Mien in Thailand. Writing in the 1970s and drawing on the surveys of the Tribal Research Center, Kunstadter gives average household size among uplanders as ranging from between five and six persons among Lua and Karen to between seven and eight persons among Hmong and Mien (1983, 19). Kandre's (1967, 1971, 1976, Kandre and Lej 1965) generalizations for Mien society from household formations in the Phale area suggest the opposite of Miles's Phulangka case:

> The Iu Mien have a tendency to spread out into small hamlets, sometimes comprising only a few households. This is to some extent symptomatic of the concept of individual enterprise which is favored in their society. Individuals are always on the move searching for better opportunities, better soils, or a more convenient social climate. . . . [Mien household heads] always refer to disciplinary problems [as limiting household expansion]. A frequent opinion is that if it were not so difficult, they would like to have as many working hands as possible, 'to make it big, have large fields, and be strong.' (Kandre 1967, 611, 601)

While Mien tended to achieve increases in household production through purchase adoptions and extended households (see chapter 3), other upland villagers took advantage of increasing poverty in the uplands in a different way. Hmong and Lisu farmers, for instance, hired impoverished Karen to do some of the more onerous tasks of field preparation for low wages (Keen 1973, 40; Cooper 1984, 107–10). Both purchase adoptions and hired labor established household prominence by taking advantage of poverty and marginalization within the region. What the ethnography rendered as the structures of individual ethnic groups drew on a selection of patterns that were very much of a specific historical moment and might as easily have been interpreted as a manifestation of systemic inequalities within and among upland settlements in a regional, political economic context.

The various studies by Western anthropologists of the highland peoples of Thailand—intensive research in settlements that were made to stand for ethnic groups—exaggerated ethnicity in terms of the somewhat arbitrarily defined structures of traditional society.[7] The explanation for this trend lies partly in the way research was structured at the Tribal Research Center. It was the task of the anthropologists to define the structure of ethnic groups. In general, they became quite knowledgeable about the local histories of highland peoples. But they tended to portray highland social or other dynamics as matters of ethnic structures that were (implicitly at least) out of time. Among the reasons may be ambivalence about modernity among ethnographers and a general lack of models for dealing with history; the two may be strongly connected. Studies that focused on ethnic groups tended to reinforce the notion of an ethnically defined society. The next section describes trends in the display and contextualization of ethnic minority highlander identities in the Thai public sphere between 1960 and 2000. These images variously elaborate or recast some of the Thai projects of self- and other-fashioning described above, and the continued use of ethnographic materials for reflecting on the nation shows various continuities with the early twentieth century.

Museum Imagery

Various violent aspects of national integration brought upland peoples into the national fold as of the 1960s. The process is ongoing, in part because the Thai notion of uplanders as lacking some essential attributes of membership motivates efforts to remedy this situation. Upland formulations of agency and identity through cultural as much as agricultural practices came to be viewed as unacceptable by agents of the Thai state, and this is part of the context for the Western anthropologists' exaggeration of ethnic structures and their arguments for the inherent rationality of upland farming practices. One remnant of the heyday of Western anthropological work in the hills of northern Thailand is a museum-like exhibit in the library building of the Tribal Research Center. The exhibit consisted of mannequins showing each of the six officially recognized tribes in their ethnic outfits—children at play, people eating dinner, women embroidering, and so on. The exhibit conveyed ethnic groups as bounded units, each with its own dress and other particulars that were described on text captions. The exhibit did not suggest any links to national space or the reality of national integration. Thus, it embodied some of the theoretical emphases of the Westerners at the center and their ambivalence about national integration.

Fig. 3: The fountain statue at the Tribal Research Center in Chiangmai, depicting the domesticated mountain peoples.

The Thai counterpart to advisor William Geddes insisted (to Geddes' dismay)[8] on an outdoor display that consisted of two water fountains, each with a sculpture of a Hmong man and woman pouring water into the fountain. The fountain sculptures are unusual for Thailand, where statues tend to be limited to Buddhist monuments and those commemorating kings and other national heroes. The fountain does not appear to commemorate any contribution to the nation or the Buddhist religion. As an art object and a source of pleasure, the Hmong fountain stands as a peculiar historical monument, particularly given that it was constructed during the height of state-sponsored violence against the Hmong and other highlanders. The fountain has a possible analogy in the imagery of Buddhist temples. Temple walls and gates tend to feature serpents, lions, giants, and other creatures of the wild who, overtaken by the loving kindness of the Buddha and his disciples, have turned their ferocity toward guarding the religion and its practitioners. The old Tribal Research Center buildings on the campus of Chiangmai University are not a temple complex, and the Hmong couple are not portrayed as ferocious guardians. But the (desired) domestication of the Hmong portrayed in the two fountains suggests that the politically subversive mountain people have been swayed by the government agency's mission into providing the gentle pleasure of a water fountain. This sculpture is a manifestation of a historically specific image of the Thai state's internal outsiders and thus of the Thai state as an agent of history and identity at a particular moment in upland-lowland relations.

In her study of the National Museum in Bangkok, Cary has described the pervasiveness of the trope "nation, religion, king" as the constituting elements of Thailand. She extracts the multiple links drawn between monarchy and Buddhism and investigates the genealogies of the Bangkok-based polity: "If elite Bangkok culture has come to be identified with the traditional, with patrimony, with the greatness of Thailand's past, the museum participates in that identification. Each section reinforces a sense of past greatness as identified with the royal court. Buddhist images, weaponry, costumes, ceramics are all framed by royal patronage. The emphasis on the continuity of a tradition mediated by the present royal family reinforces the space of the museum as the territory of monarchy" (1994, 382).

The ethnographic display from the Tribal Research Institute was moved to a new Tribal Museum that opened in 1997. This is an elaborate building compared with the previous annex-style library and museum at the previous location of the Tribal Research Center. The earlier displays are largely the same, but more groups are now represented—displays of Lawa, Palong, Padong, Khmu, and Mlabri have been added. But the major change from the old to the new museum is the narrative context of the display, which manifests a reworking of the Westerners' imagery of ethnic groups as independent of the national reality. There are three floors to the new museum exhibit, and the three levels are important indications of hierarchy (higher status being matched by museum elevation) as much as historicity. As in the previous museum, the highland ethnic groups are still defined as traditional. Defining its subject, the museum declares: "The hilltribes are mostly farmers. In older days, they were doing subsistent farming, but now they begin to grow cash crops. They are still using the slash and burn method. And move to another place when the soil is depleted. This is called 'swidden cultivation.' Some are practicing rotate and terrace farming. These methods of land use are out of date."

Another text panel in the new museum, "Hill tribe development," says much about the official reality of the TRI. It states that highlanders' farming methods result "in the increasing destruction and depletion of forest, soil, water, and other natural resources." Further, most of the highland people "are non-literate and live in sub-standard and unsanitary conditions with poor health and low income." To respond to this condition, "a program has been operating since 1959 to deal with the problems associated with the hilltribes, welfare and development." Describing the government's development efforts as a success, the text panel concludes with the following: "From these continued development activities and from technological knowledge introduced by the Department of Public Welfare personnel, there have also been successes in environmental conservation. Therefore, the Department received awards from the Thai Association of Soil and Water Conservation in 1989, and from the International Erosion Control Association. The Department received the International Merit Award in 1995. The present General Director, Elawat Chandraprasert, went to America to receive the award."

Accompanying this text is a photo of the DPW director receiving his award in the United States. The choice of a photograph to go with the text panel is a significant indication of what is commemorated in the new museum. "Tribal lifestyles" deplete and destroy the nation's forests, soil, water, and other natural resources. Most of the upland peoples are illiterate and live in sub-standard conditions. "Mountain people," in other words, contribute only problems to Thai society. As such they also present many opportunities for intervention. That is, they engender the state and nation as forces of improvement. The Tribal Museum commemorates the government's effort to bring "occupational, social, educational, and moral development" to what appear to be backwards and ecologically destructive peoples and, with it, the consolidation of Thai society as modern and committed to progress.

The notion that hill tribes are inveterate migrants shines through the text: "The implementation of hill tribe development at present is satisfactory. Most hill tribes in the care of the Department of Public Welfare have settled down permanently." Making the hill tribes of Thailand settle down, ending the supposedly pathological tendency of people to move about, is presented as a manifestation of development. Hill tribes have been swayed from their destructive ways though the "care of the Department of Public Welfare." This imagery is very much in line with the depiction of the Hmong in the water fountain sculpture from the late 1960s.

On the second floor, the Tribal Museum's assembling of Thailand is taken a step further. The exhibit space is devoted to development efforts, in particular Buddhist missionary activities in the hills. This missionary project, Dhammajarik (see Keyes 1971; Sanit 1988), is said to benefit "all three parties involved: the government, the Phradhammajarik [monks], and the highlanders. . . . After more than thirty years, there has been gradual progress, and an augmentation of activities. The goal has been to facilitate and utilize this education and training in order for them [highlanders] to become self-reliant, responsible members of their societies, the nation, and Buddhism." In the absence of the civilizing influence of Thai society through Buddhist monks and national development projects, highlanders have by implication not been "self-reliant, responsible members of their [own] societies, the nation, [or] Buddhism." Highlanders have been brought into the national imagination as problem peoples who are recognizable as members of the nation only to the extent that they are recipients of the care of government agencies. But they can "improve" by committing themselves to becoming responsible modern citizens, as ethnics, nationals, and Buddhists.

"His Majesty the King and Highland Development" is the title of the third-floor exhibit. One wall is taken up with a large painting showing the king riding a horse past a highland village, accompanied by military men and male highland villagers in ethnic dress. The king's entourage is all walking, preserving the parallel between social standing and physical elevation, as he towers above them on the horse. There are many photos of members of the royal family, including one in which the king in military uniform stands with two princesses wearing Hmong skirts; it most likely dates to about 1970. Various text panels communicate a clear message about the loving kindness of the royal family and the importance of the king's leadership in bringing peace and prosperity to the highlands: "His Majesty the King began travelling in the northern hills in 1964 to see the difficulties the hilltribe people faced and the problems caused by opium cultivation. He called for 'the contentedness and security of the Kingdom's people' and established the Royal Development Project to solve the hill-tribes' problems through their own ability and industriousness."

This text panel declares "many successes" of the Royal Project that draw on the king's leadership "with the assistance of the entire royal family, government agencies, and the private sector in both Thailand and other countries." As evidence of how the Royal Project has improved life in the hills, the ethnographic display on this floor consists of glass cases in the center of the room containing dried fruit and flowers, canned fruit, honey, and packaged coffee, as well as embroidered crafts aimed at a souvenir market. The products of the Royal Project are proof that highland peoples have been transformed into presentable members of the nation through their marketable produce. Highland ethnic minority participation in global capitalist markets, no matter how marginal, is an entry to a national stage of "contemporary" peoples, and this implicit international dimension is an important component of the national contact zone. There are no markers of the "traditional" highland cultures on the two upper floors. Tradition, while important for tourism and thus a draw for the museum, is the negative against which Thai modernity and the state's civilizing influence are measured.

The Tribal Museum's spatial hierarchy of the royal family, Buddhism, and the ethnic minorities is a variation on the nationalist linking of nation, religion, and king as the constitutive elements of Thai identity. The generally non-Buddhist highland peoples are not "the nation." But the logic of this three-floor exhibit, the combination of spatial organization and the text panels, is that the non-Thai ethnic minorities are would-be nationals through their subjection to the king and Buddhism and potentially on par with the nation through participation in global capitalism. By physically placing the ethnics under religion and king, the Tribal Research Institute has created an image of the domestication of the highland ethnic minorities. *Chao khao* have thus become a kind of Thai-in-waiting, a phantasm for envisioning Thailand in terms of the benefits of modernization and national integration.

Most of the museums in Thailand's north date to the 1980s, when warfare against the CPT had come to an end. More peaceful conditions, combined with growth in tourism and the decline of the communist threat, played a part in the proliferation of museums. The spread of museums in Thailand's north during the 1980s must be seen as part of the refashioning of the national public sphere. International tourism, while important, does not explain this process. Bangkok hegemony is very central to the displays and text captions, to the point that the identity of any of the Lanna kingdoms-turned-provinces is depicted as deriving from their subordinate position to the national capital, which precludes the articulation of identity or historicity outside the framework of national history (Thongchai 1994, 1995, 2002; Jonsson 2002). All of the national museums are under the government's Fine Arts Department.

The "greatness as identified with the royal court" that is central to the display in many of Thailand's museums (Cary 1994, 382) is apparent in the National Museums in Chiangmai, Lamphun, Nan, and Chiangsaen. In the Nan museum, housed in the former palace of the last king of Nan, Buddhism and royalty are placed upstairs and the "peoples" of Nan are on the ground floor. The "peoples" are spatially divided into two sections, the Tai "ethnic majority" and the "minorities" (Fine Arts Department 1987). In the display of the material culture of the majority Tai peasants, there is no reference to their ethnicity on the accompanying labels. The various Others are always marked ethnically. Among the Others are a Tai-speaking group, Tai Lü, who in social and cultural terms are quite similar to the Tai of Nan. Non-Tai Others are Khmu, T'in, Phi Tong Lüang (Mlabri), Hmong, and Mien. Each of these ethnic groups is presented in the abstract manner of ethnographic summaries. The Mien panel declares that they originated in Central China, that some migrated to Nan over a century ago, that at present there are over 8,000 Mien in the province, that they tend to settle at over 3,000 feet above sea level, and that their houses are similar to those of the Hmong. All the ethnic minorities, as well as the majority Tai peasant population, are described in the timeless fashion of key characteristics (age in province, altitude of settlement, appearance of villages, and dress). History belongs upstairs, with royalty, Buddhism, and relations to the nation's authorities in Bangkok.

In the entry hall of the National Museum in Chiangmai, there is a large photograph showing the Thai king cutting the ribbon at the museum's opening ceremony in 1973. The text panel accompanying this photo makes further links to the king in declaring that renovations in progress were initiated "on the occasion of the celebration of the Golden Jubilee of His Majesty the King's Accession to the Throne, and the 700th Anniversary of the establishment of Chiangmai in 1996."[9] Images of contemporary royalty at the entry to museums evoke sacred space where the coordinates of national heritage are fused with the parameters of identity, rights, and sovereignty. They also evoke sacred time in relating the anniversaries of the city of Chiangmai and the reigning monarch. In the translocal public sphere of national museums, violent histories are transformed into celebratory renderings of the principles of unity and belonging. In the Thai public sphere, the consolidation of identity and tradition, the definition of difference, and the commemoration of the monarchy go hand in hand.

There is not an analogous museum in the city of Chiangrai, but there is a temporary exhibit of similar pretension and scope in the city hall. In the entry hall of the exhibit, there is a big photo montage showing the princess mother with the king and queen. The exhibit in this hall concerns royal compassion and development projects in Chiangrai Province. Significantly, one text panel in this entry hall concerns highland ethnic minorities as a national problem. Of equal significance is the conclusion to this text, which describes the aftermath of the Thai military's successful actions against "communist" unrest among highland peoples: "On February 27, 1983, Their Majesties, together with Princess Maha Chakri Sirindhorn and Princess Soamsawali paid a visit to the base of the [Thai military] battalion on Doi Yao, Thoeng District, Chiangrai Province. There, upon request, His Majesty graciously agreed to the battalion commander to make two sets of the imprint of his feet. One set is retained by the commander and the other is installed in the Footprint Pavilion in the headquarters of the battalion which is located in Fort Mangrai Maharaj." This is where history takes place, in battles to defend the Thai nation against "foreign" enemies such as communists and their highlander sympathizers. The conclusion of the struggle is the making of a royal relic, imprints of the king's feet, and the division of the two sets of the relic to the leading commander and to the army division's main fort. This fusion of history and territory establishes the parameters of identity and society as derived from royal guidance and benevolence in combination with the military defense of the nation's borders. State violence and royal, Buddhist compassion have the same reference, Thai-ness, and they are fused with the national terrain and the classification of enemies through the making of the king's footprints.[10]

In this context it is instructive that sometime during the 1980s, the Thai king initiated a move to dissociate highland peoples from the connotations of *chao khao* by referring to them as *chao thai phu-khao*, "mountain Thai" or "Thai mountain peoples." The proposed insertion of national identity is ambiguous, and the term has not firmly replaced its precursor—during the early 1990s the two terms were used interchangeably in Chiangmai newspapers. There are many parallels to this nationalization of difference, such as in nearby Laos, where the country's various peoples are increasingly known as nationals-by-altitude—Lao *Sung*, Lao *Thoeng*, and Lao *Lum*, or Highland, Midslope, and Lowland Lao (Vatthana 2002, 180). During nationalist reconstruction in 1930s Turkey, Kurds were for some time called "Mountain Turks" (Kirisci 1998, 239). The Thai-ness of "Mountain Thai" can be viewed as an attempt to erase social and cultural difference through the paradigmatic status of national identity. At the same time, the image of *chao khao* continues to inform constructions of national identity through oppositional logic.

Public Spheres

Much like the construction of Chinese national identity through the imagery of highland minorities,[11] the Thai notion of hill tribes informs a forging of Thai-ness. It combines racialism, state control over the parameters of everyday life, and military violence, all based on the fusion of nation and terrain where royalty and Buddhism are the coordinates of identity and history. The Tribal Museum displays some dimensions of this relationship of inequality between the nation-state and its *chao khao*. The state's care for their mountain peoples is the duty of the Department of Public Welfare. The Tribal Museum can be viewed as a temple to hill tribe problems and their solutions, commemorating the state's agency and the nation's unity and progress. On the first floor are the unreformed ethnics, whose culture and livelihood are dangerous and out of date. Above this site of intervention, on the second floor, are the projects to replace previous forms of agriculture and religion, ones that conserve the environment and turn *chao khao* into nationals and Buddhists. On top are the displays of royal interest and compassion, and the glass cases that show how the Royal Project has made *chao khao* presentable through the making and marketing of souvenirs and consumer goods.

The Tribal Museum's collection of *chao khao* traditional culture, now also on video recordings in addition to the earlier displays of dress and tools, informs the forging of the un-modern that interests foreign tourists but is incompatible with modern Thailand. By superimposing celebratory renderings of transformations—the active insertion of the parameters of state control and national belonging—on the ethnic display, the Tribal Museum stands as a monument to state control over identity, cultural practice, livelihood, and social life. This may not be what foreign tourists want to see in the museum. In a recent guidebook, *The Extraordinary Museums of Southeast Asia,* Kelly states that the Tribal Museum "provides a compact, succinct, and comprehensible introduction to the rich cultures and practices of the hill tribes of northern Thailand and the Golden Triangle, both for those who plan to trek through the area to visit the tribal villages and those who just plan to shop in the Night Bazaar in Chiangmai." Of the display in the new museum, she writes, "It is the first floor that is of greatest interest to the visitor" (2001, 149). With separate aims, international tourists, anthropologists, and the Thai government have sought markers of the un-modern among the hill tribes, for enjoyment and consumption, for study and analysis, and for elimination and transformation. The three projects systemically identify modernity with aspects of state control and regulated economic transactions (cf. Jonsson 2004).

From indexing unruliness and threats to the nation's borders, *chao khao* have become part of the un-modern national heritage that is guarded by the state's institutions. With government approval in the 1960s, the original hill tribe museum display was to have two components: an exhibition room with "tribal costumes and jewelry" and, outdoors, "actual houses of the six main tribes. . . . Together these houses will form a small composite tribal village in natural surroundings. The houses may also be used on occasion to accommodate tribespeople visiting the Centre" (Geddes 1967, 574–75). The planned outdoor component came to nothing, but recollections vary as to why that was. Peter Hinton (personal communication, January 2003) stated that three or four houses were built, but since there was no budget for maintenance the houses "just rotted to the ground." John McKinnon (personal communication, January 2003), who arrived later at the TRC, suggested that for the Thai director (Wanat Bhruksasri), the museum would primarily serve as a place for visiting dignitaries—not for tourists—which might explain the emphasis on the "spiffy" fountain. "For many years before the branch of the National Museum was built and there was only one small bookshop in Chiangmai, the TRC was the center of information. Royalty, leading government officers, and ambassadors called. When I first went there the walls were lined with photos of all the important people who had made a visit." McKinnon added that the TRC had a hard time finding people to live in the houses that had been built for display and that "the University didn't like the idea of a bunch of hill tribe people living on their land."

The idea for an outdoor museum was later picked up by the banker and scholar Kraisri Nimmanhaeminda, who established a museum and performance center on the road to the Chiangmai airport during the 1970s. This later became the Old Chiangmai Cultural Center, which offers "traditional" northern Thai *kantoke* dinner in the main room. The following description draws on a visit I made in 2000. During dinner, professional dancers went through a repertoire of classical dances that were all identified as Tai/Thai.[12] The exhibit of mountain people's dances followed the national/regional dinner and display. In sharp contrast to the air-conditioned dining room where people sat on pillows around small tables, the hill tribe display was in a roofed but open-air room with hard benches in a semicircle around the concrete floor. But while the outdoor display was announced as a hill tribe show, it started with a "northern Thai victory dance" featuring drummers and one dancer. Given the history of Thai-highlander interactions during the twentieth century, this lowlander victory dance plays like an unconscious celebration of the virtues of national incorporation through military force.

After this peculiar introductory act, troupes representing each of the six tribes performed very short dances. The announcer's commentary summarized each group's ethnic traits: "Next, Lahu or Musser, Tibeto-Burman language family, live at 1,100 meters above sea level, wear black clothes with silver buttons; Hmong, Meo-Yao language family, arrived in 1850, live at 5,000 feet above sea level. Women practice the art of making batik; Mien, Meo-Yao language family, live at 3,500 feet above sea level. They don't have many dances; Lisu, Tibeto-Burman language family, live at 5,000 feet above sea level. Their silver decorations can weigh up to two kilograms." The Lisu ended their dance show with a *wai,* paying deferential respect to the audience in the Thai manner.

Through a traditional dinner and dance show, engagements with international tourism sustain the ethnological and state-driven separation between Thai peoples and the non-Thai mountain peoples, the latter bracketed by the Thai victory dance and the internalized Thai gesture of deference and respect. Mountain peoples are exotic and unfit for dinner entertainment, but they have at least learned the basics of what Thai society considers manners, which, not unsurprisingly, also signals the civilization of Thai society and its ongoing civilizing mission among the ethnically non-Thai highland peoples. Mountain peoples or hill tribes have thus earned a place in the public sphere as safely un-modern, as they serve to emphasize the modernity and civility of the Thai nation.[13]

During the 1980s and thus contemporaneous with the proliferation of museums in northern Thailand, children in a number of highland villages were given T-shirts that had the Thai flag and the legend *nu rak müang thai:* "little-I love Thailand." The implied love in this statement rests on a desired conversion; in contrast to the widely assumed disloyalty of *chao khao,* the next generation in the hills has come to be loyal to the nation. Love in this context suggests submission and reciprocity, for the little *chao khao* (*nu* literally means "mouse") will subserviently obey the country (*müang thai,* the geo-body of Thailand, implies nation, religion, and the monarchy). The intended embodiment of love-of-nation suggests a transformation analogous to the fountain statues at the Tribal Research Center, where the unruly Hmong provided calm and gentle pleasure (through their submission to the state) as their statue-images channeled water into fountains. It appears that the more recent transformation can be measured statistically, a little like the migratory tendencies that had been attributed to *chao khao* some decades earlier: As a Thai guide to Western tourists on a van excursion to the hills of Chiangrai put it, "Now 93 percent of the Akha love the Queen" (Heather Montgomery, personal communication, 1993).

CHAPTER THREE

From Strongmen to Farmers

The chief was a grand old man, known and respected among all the Yao of Indochina. He was almost like a king over the Yao villages in this area. It was only a few years ago that he had led guerrilla warfare against the French, and he was known all over Indochina as among the boldest of raiders and smugglers. But then he got older and got a few clocks as decoration, and also a fine, white, uniform-style jacket with a couple of medals, and then he turned very friendly toward the French. In the back of his house he had a room that he valued highly. There he kept a collection of clocks which he proudly showed me. The clocks had originally been set for different time-zones so they told various times. Like others in this area, he relied on the sun for knowing the time of day. The clocks were more a decoration and a marker of wealth and power, much like bronze drums among the Lamet.

—Karl Gustav Izikowitz, *Över Dimmornas Berg*

The social organization that ethnographers described for highland ethnic groups in the 1960s and 1970s was in many ways influenced by a larger historical and regional context. Notions of prominence had shifted from chiefly control and uniqueness toward more equality in feasting and farming. This is the context for the household centrality that was of key importance to anthropological descriptions. This dynamic was not within everyone's reach, and ethnography privileged the voices and agendas of better-off people. The elaborations of culture and identity in relation to households served to silence both poorer people and those of chiefly ambitions. Because situations of chiefly control expired along with the tributary states to which they were connected, it is important to establish their relevance for culture and social life in the period prior to the twentieth century.

During the latter half of the nineteenth century, the social landscape across the south China borderlands was in considerable upheaval. The Opium Wars, various rebellions, and a rise in warlordism contributed to the conditions within which the Mien moved as they came to settle in northern Thailand. Lowland peoples in this region, such as Tai Lü (Thai Lue), were also moving southward from southern China (Moerman 1975, 152), and there was also some degree of forced movement. The kingdom of Chiangmai had sent armies to raid the surrounding domains for subjects, and the Bangkok polity had the populations of the northern Lao areas rounded up and moved away from the sphere of influence of the Vietnamese court (Renard 1980; Breazeale and Sanit 1988; Grabowsky 1999). This wider context of movement, upheavals, warlordism, and forced migrations is relevant for two reasons. One is that the Mien migration of the late nineteenth century was not an isolated incident, and it was not a move in a peaceful setting where everyone else was firmly in place. The other is that the ongoing threat of violent confrontations had an immediate bearing on the social and cultural orientations among Mien and other highland peoples during this period.

Chiefly Control and Lowland Connections

Around the turn of the twentieth century, high-level Mien chiefs were known for their military prowess, and some had titles from lowland authorities. These chiefs articulated their prominence in terms of unique ritual connections, titles, and prestige items that set them off from the commoner population. In the Mien village of Phale in Thailand's Chiangrai Province, Kandre's (1967, 1976) informants mentioned that in earlier times, when they lived in the borderlands of Laos and China, the Mien had sometimes raided other upland villages and that from these raids they acquired children whom they then adopted (1976, 187). The most prominent Mien leader in northern Laos at the time, Tsew Wuen Tzo, had authority over more than a hundred villages of various ethnic affiliations. He appears to have had a long career of leading raids and undercover trade before receiving a Phaya title and placing himself within the colonial state (Izikowitz 1944, 71–73). As Kandre describes high-level headmen among the Mien in northern Laos earlier in the twentieth century, these were generally men who "started as wealthy and respected village headmen and gradually secured their reputations by skillful mediation of conflicts in the mountains. In some cases they finally established themselves as semi-feudal princes over huge collections of villages with a wide range of distinct socio-economic-ritual systems [e.g., Mien, Lanten, Akha, Khamu, Meo, Lahu, and Kato]" (1967, 615–16).

These positions of prominence related to connections with lowland authorities, which in Laos at the time was the French colonial administration. Kandre does not discuss what relations there might have been between Mien social dynamics and such colonial or pre-colonial frameworks, but he emphasizes the role of dispute mediation, wealth, and expensive rituals in the rise of such men to power. The authority of Tsew Wuen Tzo (Tseu Uen Tsoe) "was recognized by more than a hundred villages [of various ethnic affiliations] located in the Mung Phon-Mung Mang area of Yunnan and the Mung Sing-Nam Tha area of Laos" (616–17)—that is, into areas that now belong to China. As Kandre describes Wuen Tzo from the recollections of his informants, "He was intelligent and rich, had a 'good heart,' and helped the hill people and the French government. . . . Uen Tsoe spoke for the hill people [to the colonial authorities], and he also helped the French defeat the Akha, who did not obey the government (619–20). Kandre does not follow up on the contradiction that while Wuen Tzo was a spokesman for the highlanders to the colonial rulers, he also aided the French in suppressing noncompliant upland peoples.

Further information on Wuen Tzo comes from Izikowitz, who visited his village in 1936 during his research among the Lamet and is quoted at the beginning of this chapter. Wuen Tzo's collection of clocks was a museum like display of this chief's unique connection to the contours of power and privilege, a one-man show of prominence. The collection and display of wealth and power constructed and reflected the prominence of an upland leader who had a title from the lowland authorities. Tsew Wuen Tzo had the title "Phaya Luang," and his sons later had the titles "Chao Mai" and "Chao La." Phaya Luang's sons reproduced their prominence in terms of military prowess, organizational skills, and connections to the lowland government, and Chao La was later a major in Vang Pao's CIA-supported army in the 1960s (see McCoy 1991; Westermeyer 1982).

The population that Kandre studied in Phale village in northern Thailand had left northern Laos starting in the 1940s. One of the subsequent leaders of that group, Le Tsan Kwe, told me later that the reason for their move was that farming was very strenuous because of the ongoing warfare. The move can be seen as a reaction against conditions of warfare, which made farming difficult (Kandre 1967, 635). But the move may also have had to do with internal politics. It may have been a form of resistance to the monopoly on prominence and wealth that high-level Mien leaders had in this colonial setting. Some support for that assertion comes from the manifest ambivalence about wealthy people that the Mien of Phale expressed to Kandre in the 1960s (598, 604).

Miles's (1967–68, 1974) description of the Mien in Phulangka does not indicate any ambivalence about wealthy people. This difference is interesting, and while it is somewhat questionable it does suggest the importance of local histories for the articulation of a worldview. In the 1880s, the king of Nan denied a large group of Mien and Hmong people permission to cross the Mekong River and enter his domain. He only allowed them entry after being paid in silver, rhinoceros horns, and/or elephant tusks—there is no documentation of this payment, and recollections in the early 1990s varied. The initial refusal by the king may have been a way to press for benefits from the group. It resonates with the notion of a market for identity and rights in tributary states, and it indicates lowland rulers' command over hinterland areas. In contrast to the common "centrist" image of premodern Southeast Asia, where concern with borders was absent and rule was concerned with retaining lowland subjects, there has been considerable continuity in state control regarding borders, rights, and identity that included highland regions (cf. Andrew Walker 1999, 25–41).

As the group of Mien and Hmong settled in the mountainous areas of Nan, a Mien leader named Tang Tsan Khwoen and two other men received Phaya titles from the king of Nan. Among the three, Tsan Khwoen ranked the highest. He was made responsible for tribute collection among the highlanders and was the commander of the highlanders' reserve army for the king. Tsan Khwoen had the title Phaya Khiri (or Inthakhiri) and received from the king a sword and some spears and gongs. His collection of tribute was not limited to his Mien and Hmong followers, it also extended to other highland peoples within the Nan king's domain (Jonsson 1999). The king of Nan did more than give out titles. He allowed the Mien to grow opium for the royal opium monopoly as of 1907.[1] This was confined to the mountain where the Mien were centered, since that time known as Doi Suan Ya Luang ("Mt. Royal Opium Field"; in Mien known as *tawm in te*, "big opium field"), and officials came annually to inspect the fields and assess the tax. Mien and Hmong uplanders were growing opium at the time, and people outside the official framework were continually at risk of arrest. Reginald le May, who went through this area in 1913, witnessed an aspect of this control of cultivation and trade in the arrest of "picturesque ruffians [caught] smuggling illicit opium" (le May 1926, 229). This incident involved Hmong farmers outside the monopolized trade.

It is likely that both the King of Nan and the Mien leader benefited considerably from this controlled trade in opium, but while the trade was within the royal opium monopoly, it appears to have been unknown to the Bangkok authorities (cf. Ministry of Finance 1938, 20; McCoy 1991, 103). According to Western missionary accounts, Phaya Khiri made frequent visits to Nan City (Park 1907, 100) and he "was said to have 100,000 ticals laid by" (Callender 1915, 85). His house was the only one in the Mien area to have an elevated floor (82). Tsan Khwoen's architectural separation from the rest of the population, his quite considerable wealth, his unique ritual contract (described below), his supreme ritual rank, his prestige items, his title from the Nan king, and his trade relations with the opium monopoly all indicate his unique standing and how he acted on it. As tribute from his followers, Tsan Khwoen received a basket of rice from each household every year. Tsan Khwoen's prominence, like that of Tsew Wuen Tzo, was a one-man show; his markers of power were not within the reach of his followers.[2]

This group of Mien and Hmong settled in Nan around the time that the northern principalities were losing their autonomy and tribute-base to the centralizing Bangkok polity (see Calavan 1974; Bowie 1988; Rattanaporn 1989). Unlike other formerly autonomous rulers in Siam's north, the Nan king was allowed to hold onto some of his royal prerogatives for as long as he lived (Wyatt 1994, 128). He died in the 1920s, having bestowed the follow-up title "Thao La" on the third of Tsan Khwoen's sons (for the titles, see Rattanaporn 1989, 6). Establishing rank by giving out titles was part of what gave a king power. To some extent one can view the Nan king as attempting to retain his prominence by bestowing titles in the hinterland while he had lost his prerogatives, such as the ability to demand services and tribute, in the lowlands—the king had also lost almost half his domain as Siam and France negotiated the borders of French Indochina in 1893 and 1904 (Davis 1984, 33).

Lowland Nan provided the Mien population with a market for their opium and rice. The market for rice was in part due to national integration, as Bangkok had undone the tributary base of the Nan kingdom. Bangkok authorities posted a number of soldiers along the border with Laos, and the Mien sold their rice to the garrisons (le May 1926, 172–73). It is possible that with the rice tribute undone, lowland farmers lowered their yields correspondingly, which may be why the Mien were able to sell their rice. In contrast to the marginalization of upland rice production since the early twentieth century, uplanders marketed their rice in the lowlands, particularly in Lao domains before French colonial road networks made cheaper rice available over long distances (Izikowitz 1951, 310–11). Around and after the turn of the twentieth century in northern Laos, regulatory strategies encouraged upland agricultural production and a focus on handicrafts and trade in lowland settlements (Andrew Walker 1999, 39).

The integration of highlanders into lowland administrative orbits continued past the initial Mien leader. Wuen Lin, Tsan Khwoen's son who received the Thao La title, was subsequently made a *kamnan* (*tambol* headman) when the area was brought into the official Thai provincial administration around 1940. He had moved his household to Phulangka after his father's death, in about 1927. There he was the center of an extensive trade in locally produced opium for provincial and national agencies. After Thao La had established his house in Phulangka, he received as a gift a grandfather clock from Bangkok-based opium merchants, which indicates some of his importance.

The change in settlements was also a change in official connections from Nan to Chiangrai Province. The highland area was brought into the national administration as Phachangnoi *tambol*; aside from Phulangka itself, the subdistrict included the villages of Phachangnoi, Suanyaluang, Namkat, and Phadaeng. After this change in administrative status, government officials visited Thao La and took away a letter of authorization. This was in the early 1940s, and the letter (now long lost) was presumably a grant from the Nan king about privileges that were no longer respected by the state. Prior to Thao La's new settlement, the people under his and his father's command had been brought into a new scheme of taxation, from taxes in kind to a payment of one to two Baht per household. When Thao La moved to Phulangka, he delivered the tax to the district authorities in Pong. This taxation is of significance, not only as it relates to the incorporation of highland peoples into administrative frameworks well before the 1960s but also for an understanding of the dynamics of farming, settlement, and local inequalities.

Migration, Spirits, and Prominence

Tang Tsan Khwoen was renowned for his military prowess before the migration, which probably contributed to his ability to inspire a following. His prowess related to his connections into the spirit world, in which he had the highest level of ritual rank (*ja tze*, the third-level ordination in the ranked scheme of Daoist rituals). Before he took off, he had purchased from another Mien man a *Kia Shen Pong* scroll. With his various markers of leadership and his success in inspiring a following, Tsan Khwoen set off into the unknown. The migration constituted the social unity of the participants as well as the leadership of Tsan Khwoen; the subject of action shifted from that of separate householders or villagers to that of a multi-village migration group centered on its leader.

Some of the Mien people told Western missionaries that "in their former home in China they farmed valley land as well as hills" (Callender 1915, 81). This shift in livelihood is one reason for questioning generalizations in twentieth-century ethnographies about the traditional features the agricultural adaptation, social organization, and worldview of highland peoples. The migration itself was socially constitutive—it made the group a social unit through their leader and his relations with a particular spirit. The list of domains that the people stayed in during their migration is preserved in ritual chants to the King's Spirit, which is a spirit specific to this migration group. In annual chants that maintain the relationship with this spirit, the medium lists the domains with whose rulers the population has had relations: Müang Long, Müang Siang, Müang Khwa, Müang Tsan, Müang Lai, Müang La, Müang Hun, Müang Nan.[3]

The migration is remembered in terms of relations with spirits, in particular how spirits preserved the well-being of their people. These accounts tell of two important confrontations: one in which ancestors advised the people to leave a domain whose lowland inhabitants were attacking them and the other in which a royal spirit made the leader invulnerable during an attack by Chinese warlords.[4] The two kinds of spirits, royal and ancestral, point to two important dimensions of social identity—as a unified migration group and as separate householders. The episode with the King's Spirit made the leader of the migration into a founder of the group, in ways that correspond to Mien origin stories and ritual practice.

The group had learned of an imminent attack by an army of Chinese people. Tsan Khwoen then made an offering to the spirit of the king of the domain. When the attack came, it was clear that the spirit had made Tsan Khwoen invulnerable. Whenever the Chinese aimed their guns at him, he was immediately transported to another location. They would re-aim, only to find that Tsan Khwoen had disappeared again. The highlanders successfully fended off the attack. This episode most likely occurred during the "Haw raids" in the northern regions of Laos and Vietnam between 1869 and 1874 (Breazeale and Sanit 1988, 47–49). These raids, and Bangkok's attempts at suppressing them, continued into the 1880s, but published accounts do not provide information that would help to date the Mien episode.

This event established the relationship between Tsan Khwoen and the spirit of the king of the domain. He had to renew this relationship annually to avoid losing this connection with the spirit world. Tsan Khwoen proved himself to his followers in the episode in which he successfully made a deal with the King's Spirit. The ability to make such a contract confirmed the relationship between the leader and the ruler/spirit and between the leader and the rest of the migration group. A contract of this sort assumes a social entity. If the spirits and leaders do not take good care of them, the Mien people will abandon one of them (or both) and enter into another contract elsewhere. The underlying assumption about contracts with both spirits and rulers is that things are all right as long as each side meets its obligations. If one side does not live up to its part of the deal, then the deal can be revoked.

As well as establishing a connection to the royal spirit, Tsan Khwoen made relationships with lowland rulers. One such relationship took an unfortunate turn. After the Mien had lived for some time in the Tai domain of Muang Lai, some lowlanders placed the body of a dead Tai man against the door of a Mien house and accused the Mien of having killed him. The Mien made an offering to the household's ancestors and asked what offering could cancel the offense. The spirits replied that nothing would do and advised the people to leave immediately. After the Miens' rapid departure, the lowlanders destroyed everything they could find. Mien stories about the event suggest that the root of the offense was a Tai man's romantic interest in a Mien woman. She would have none of his attentions, and the Tai took revenge with a dead body and an accusation of murder.

Mien accounts suggest structural parallels in their relations with spirits and lowland rulers. Mien people engage with spirits for prosperity and protection. There is an important spatial distinction between domestic and extra-domestic spirits. If people are not, in their own estimation, properly taken care of, they conduct an offering on the assumption that offerings oblige spirits to grant well-being to the people concerned. If the offerings come to nothing, people tend to assume that "wild" (*hia*) spirits have entered the household. A medium then conducts a ritual where such invading wild spirits are gathered and sent away, with violent threats if they dare to re-enter. But if the cause for an accident or the lack of expected prosperity is not wild spirits, then people discern that their guardian spirits are not taking good care of them. In that case, usually after several attempts at improving a relationship with the relevant spirits, the common reaction is to relocate. People then move to another household if the cause is ancestor spirits, to another village if it is the cadastral spirit, and so on.

Mien people struck a contract with spirits for mutual benefits, except for wild spirits who did not belong anywhere and needed to be driven off if they entered a household or a village. The same structure applied to relations with lowlanders. If they caused trouble in the uplands, people would drive them off only if they were not local ("wild"); otherwise the Mien uplanders would relocate and either stay out of the reach of lowland rulers or enter a more beneficial contract elsewhere. This interpretation—that is, my abstraction of the way some Mien episodes past and present cohere—suggests the Mien as a "free agent" that would not be stuck in a difficult or oppressive situation. The implication of the interpretation, that the Mien, as householders, villagers, and multi-village units, would only settle in a favorable situation, does not describe the historical record of Mien settlements or the conditions of Mien people's lives; it is an ideal.

This ideal contributes to an understanding of the different Mien reactions to the two incidents, the fight with the Chinese and the escape from the Tai. The attack by the army was in the same structural category as an illness caused by wild spirits. It was a misfortune from an entity with which the population had no relations. This justified or even called for firm and violent reaction. The attack from the Tai was in the same structural category as an illness caused by ancestor spirits, misfortune caused by an entity to which the people were in a subordinate position. Thus, because they presumably owed allegiance to the ruler of the Tai people who were attacking them, the Mien were nonconfrontational. They escaped and moved elsewhere.

Mien highlanders recognized the power of lowland rulers and occasionally attempted to domesticate it for their own purposes. This surfaces for instance in relation to cadastral spirits. When the Mien would "open the forest" (*khoi kem*) to establish a new village, they asked around (if the area was new to them) who had been the most powerful ruler in the nearest domain and then proceeded to make an offering to establish a contract with his spirit as the guardian spirit of the village. In Thailand, Mien villages have a lowland ruler or official for a cadastral spirit, which can be seen as a domestication of relations with the state. The King's Spirit is a similar domestication of lowland royal power for Mien purposes, but the difference is one of scale; with a settled village, a local official is adequate, but with a migration in trouble, only a royal spirit will do.

Tsan Khwoen himself was not a farmer; he did not work in his fields. But like chiefs in other upland situations he received tribute, a basket of rice from each household under him. Tsan Khwoen's relationship with the King's Spirit stayed at the level of the migration group, it did not become a ritual framework that could be activated by individual villages. Only the leader and then one descendant in each generation after him could maintain the relationship with the spirit. The relationship to the spirit is unique, and its social reference is simultaneously the migration group and its leader. The dimensions of the King's Spirit cult were shaped in important ways by the place of these uplanders within the larger social landscape. Its perpetuation was not the result of the routine replication of Mien ritual tradition. The continuity of this cult has drawn on motivated action. It has relied on the leaders' immediate descendants being invested in accounts of his prominence and drawn on the institutionalization of their prominence through titles and other links to lowland authorities. This initially included the Thai government's royal opium monopoly and later the provincial administration and other such agencies of national integration.

Both Tang Tsan Khwoen (Phaya Khiri) and Tang Wuen Lin (Thao La) are remembered as having had complete control (*kun zeng*) in the highlands and as having kept the area peaceful and safe. As with leaders in other situations of chiefly control in the uplands, they brought order by enforcing customs, in particular against thieving. Mien people varied in how they remembered Thao La's rule. Some said he actively made the area peaceful and safe; others that he just sat in his house and mediated disputes that people brought to him; still others that he maintained a reign of terror, arbitrarily punishing people he did not like.[5]

Among other things that people recalled about Thao La was that his enforcement of order within his domain drew to some degree on his relationship to the King's Spirit. Thao La had sometimes decided on cases involving theft by lining up the suspects. Facing them, he would hold the spear from the king of Nan in front of him. With the help of the King's Spirit, the spear would then point to the culprit of the crime in question. In this way, the King's Spirit has contributed to the prominence of the leader outside of situations involving military confrontation.

This ritual contract with a king's spirit was a novelty, and it does not have any parallels among other Mien groups. But it is possible to view it as belonging to a continuum of ritual contracts that varied in scope and reach by the social unit involved. Households were formed and maintained through ritual contracts with ancestors; villages implied a founder who invited the spirit of the most powerful local lowland ruler to become its guardian. The supra-village unit of the migration group made a link to a still higher spirit. The King's Spirit cult collapsed ritual and social frameworks on the leader, but it did not erode the household as a structural pose. It is reasonable to assume that whenever the group settled, which they did several times before the arrival to Nan, people mobilized their labor, resources, and ritual attentions toward household goals at the cost of the migration group as an acting unit. The migration is remembered primarily in ways that reinforce the prominence of the leader, and the cult of the King's Spirit is an important component in the reproduction of this memory. But the episode from Müang La (when the Mien fled the attacking Tai) points to the continued importance of households as the subjects of action and ex-

Fig. 4: Photos of Tang Tsan Khwoen, Wuen Lin, and Fu Tsan, three generations of Mien leaders, in the home of Fu Tsan's son Tsoi Fong. The photos of ancestors are on the level of the shelf for ancestor spirits, and above them are photos of kings of the current Chakri dynasty. The arrangement of the photographs of royalty and ancestors replicates the Mien distinction between big and small spirits.

perience, in this case through relations involving ancestor spirits. Warfare in northern Laos and the promise of a more peaceful situation within the Nan kingdom may have contributed to the group's eventual choice of settlement location. Tsan Khwoen's leadership benefited from the tributary relations that Nan availed, as he struck a deal with the lowland king that anchored his prominence among his followers.

Tsan Khwoen had bought a copy of *Kia Shen Pong* from another Mien man "to move to a new land" (*ming siang ta-pung*), as is written on a transfer note attached to the scroll. It does not appear that Tsan Khwoen used the scroll in his dealings with the Nan king, most likely because the king of Nan stood outside the conceptual framework of the Chinese Empire. But his contract has many parallels in relations such as those of the Lawa with the court of Chiangmai. In each case, one or more highland leaders received titles, and they were obliged to pay annual tribute to the court in return for protection and exemption from particular duties. The highlanders under the titled leader were free to farm in the hills. In both cases, there were economic benefits for the lowland rulers. The Nan king is likely to have benefited from the highland people's tribute as well as from the opium trade. In Chiangmai, the court received iron that the Lawa worked from mines in their area. In both cases there was a central settlement where a titled highland leader lived, and in both cases there were numerous subordinate highland villages with which the lowland ruler had no contracts and over which highland leaders probably had uneven control. Le May's account of the arrest of Hmong "ruffians" mentioned above suggests the control over opium production and trade at the time. Such control, the lingering threat of state violence, is likely to have made highland peoples disinclined to strike out on their own and thus more willing to place themselves under tributary leaders like Tsan Khwoen.

Intermittent warfare was a rather constant feature of the landscape of precolonial Southeast Asia. Rulers raided one another's domains for subjects, and unprotected settlements were fair game for marching armies. Such raids for people and resources often reached into the hinterlands. In this context, upland cultures are likely to have been articulated to some extent in terms of warfare. This is the background for Tsan Khwoen's leadership and his ability to attract followers, and it is also an important component of the remembered features of the migration. But the account of the two attacks points to separate dimensions of the Mien identity. One is as followers of a leader who had great military prowess and links to high-level spirits, and the other is as householders who relied on their relations to ancestor spirits. These two aspects of Mien identity related to migration in separate ways. The former, focused on a leader and his ability to deal with spirits, rulers, and armies, contributed to the effort to take off into a new land.

The identity of Mien as householders has not been directly concerned with rulers and high-level spirits. In structural terms, it has been anchored at a lower level and centered on the well-being of farming households. Households maintain relations with a set of ancestor spirits, and they may have a relationship with the leader of a village or a larger unit. But as components of highland society, they never merged structurally with that of their leaders, and this is one reason the notion of highland society, ethnically or otherwise, is descriptively and analytically problematic. As a generalization for social dynamics in the region over time, highland society or an ethnic category such as "the Yao" glosses over the divergent agendas of chiefs and their followers in this tributary setting.

This case suggests various entanglements between highland and lowland worlds, and it offers some support for Leach's assertion regarding Burma that it was only in the colonial period, as a result of deliberate policies by the British colonial administration, that highland and lowland populations became firmly separated (1954, 244). In Thailand, this severance of long-standing upland-lowland relations occurred in the absence of direct colonial intervention. There, the deciding factor was national integration and political economic change in a colonial-era context (cf. Hong 1984; Renard 2000; Thongchai 1994). The most significant factor was the undoing of the multiple lowland kingdoms, such as Nan and Chiangmai, that had maintained relations with upland peoples. Economic changes shifted trade from forest products, most of which highland peoples had supplied, to bulk items such as logs and rice. The timber trade made forests into a resource, and this context redefined highlanders as an obstacle or a menace, after having been an important source of valuable produce for international trade and local, royal wealth.

The consolidation of nation-states also did away with the need for highlanders as border scouts between rival domains (Renard 1986), and local armies of small kingdoms were replaced with units of national armies, such as the soldiers posted in Nan on the relatively new border between Siam and French Laos. The major consequence of this change for the dynamics of migration and other aspects of highland social life was that lowland courts were no longer interested in striking deals with highlanders. With the kings of small states gone, there was no longer a party willing to grant titles to highland leaders. Titled highland leaders became a feature of the past, and the focus of later highland migrations and social life more generally shifted from leaders to householders. But the case of Tang Wuen Lin, Tsan Khwoen's successor son, is instructive about both continuities in relations with lowland authorities and important revisions in articulations of prominence. Thao La was the only upland leader in this area to receive a title after the integration of Nan into the nation-state. It is very likely that his title was in recognition of the wealth he brought the authorities through taxes on farmland and on opium cultivation.

Toward Household Centrality

The history of the population that eventually settled in Phulangka indicates that the extended households that Miles found symptomatic of Mien social dynamics were particular to the twentieth century. Miles's account of a household of fifty-seven people is quite striking, given the average household size in the uplands during the 1960s and 1970s, which was between five and eight people. But the precursor to this large household of the 1960s had almost ninety people in the 1910s, and one hundred and twenty people in the early 1940s. These dynamics were historically specific to a particular group of people, and they concern equally ritual practice and political economy.

These patterns were not only particular to the Phulangka area, they were also played out unevenly in terms of the connections that this Mien population had with a trade monopoly and administrative integration. These uneven connections to the region's political economy resulted in a bifurcation in household and settlement formations within this area. The inflationary pressures on household production are not manifest among the previous generation of Mien leaders, such as Phaya Luang and Phaya Khiri. These leaders, who stood in occasional and sometimes longstanding tribute relations with lowland rulers, had the means to expand their households through the incorporation of outsiders but apparently did not. They articulated their prominence in ways that set them apart from the general population.

One aspect of the changes that took place can be gleaned from a missionary's description of the difference between the household of Phaya Khiri and that of his sons: "Their [Mien] houses are long, shed-like structures with wild palm-leaf roofing. Most of the houses have no board floor, but the Chief's is an exception, being raised from the ground. Most of them contain more than one fireplace, each fireplace representing one family. The long house next to the Chief's in which his children and grandchildren live has 12 fireplaces and 86 occupants" (Callender 1915, 82). If the quest for an extended, large household was a common goal among this Mien population and came down to all the wealth a household could muster, then Tsan Khwoen's uniquely wealthy household would have been the most visible sign of this pattern. The available evidence points in another direction, but it shows that extended households were emerging among the subsequent generation. Phaya Khiri's sons established a large multiple household. The elements of his leadership were not accessible to his sons, and their multi-unit household can be viewed as an attempt to retain prominence in new circumstances. These changes concern the relations between lowland polities and upland populations as much as the relations between chiefs and commoners in the uplands.

The monopolized opium trade required that growers and their fields were registered with a buyer and that the yield be estimated at registration. The agents would not bother with small-scale cultivators, and the result was that only larger households could take advantage of the officially protected monopoly trade. The social outcome was that extended households were a common feature in the five villages that were registered settlements, where people benefited from the state-monitored cultivation and trade. There were some smaller households in each of these villages. More significantly, each village was surrounded by a handful of satellite settlements of smaller households that stood outside the legitimate trade and were continually at risk of arrest for illegal cultivation.[6]

Larger households in these registered villages could become wealthier through monopolized farming and trade. Thao La collected tax from each household for the district governor. Without the means to pay this tax, people presumably had to locate themselves outside the registered villages and outside the inflationary pressures of extended households. The social outcome for the Mien in this area was a bifurcation into poorer, smaller households in transient settlements and better-off households attempting to outdo one another in farming and ritual in the registered villages. People recalled a general condition of poverty and minimal ritual life in the marginal settlements. No ritual ordinations took place, and there was little ritual activity. "People barely had one set of usable clothes," remarked a woman who had grown up in one such settlement during the 1930s.

One indication of the shift toward articulating prominence through farming is that while Thao La received tribute like his father, his took the form of one day's labor from each household in his following. Neither he—at least after he became the chief—nor his father physically engaged in farming themselves. This suggests that both modeled their notions of prominence partly on lowland rulers. But Thao La was not architecturally separate from the rest of the population in the way that his father had been. He received tribute from his own fields, rather than from the fields of his followers, so his fields must have been larger than those of his father's household. While the absorption of rice and labor are both markers of power, in this case they have different social and agricultural correlates. Thao La's tribute in labor belonged to a time of heightened emphasis on farming, for householding, trade, and rituals. Phaya Khiri's tribute in rice came during a time when farming was played down relative to military organizational skills and a leader's link to lowland rulers and ruler spirits.

There is some indication that all the opium that Mien sold to the monopoly passed through Thao La's hands. The Chiangrai politician and writer Bunchuai Srisawat visited the area in the late 1940s. He referred to Thao La as "Phaya," conflating his title with that of his father as some contemporary Mien villagers do, and he stated that "all the Yao in the [Phulangka] area are subjects of the Phaya. Any one of them who grows opium must bring it to the Phaya, as he is the agent" (1950, 463–64). At least once in the early 1950s, Thao La's relatives and assistants collected opium from all over Chiangrai Province and took it on a truck to Lampang, where it was sent on to Bangkok by train. During this time, Phulangka people told visitor John Blofeld that in one year the police had come thirty-seven times to check on the cultivation and to collect the tax (1960, 151). In the 1940s, affluent Mien from the Phulangka region would peddle consumer goods such as ceramic bowls among highlanders in Laos in exchange for opium. They then sold the opium in Thailand for a better price than highlanders were able to get in Laos.

The widespread quest for household prominence drew on inflation in household production goals, which had come about when upland chiefs lost their prominence after tributary states had been erased. That is, changes in regional political economy and state structures were an important part of the historical context for the patterns from which anthropologists generalized. Equally, these dynamics concerned a revision of uplanders' articulations of their farming and feasting that took place in this new context. Douglas Miles's argument about the quest for extended households assumes that these were coordinated production units. This holds for the prominent households in Phulangka at the time, but subsequent recollections indicate that this was not generally the case. Extended households were always units in ritual, in relations with spirits, but each unit often went its own way when it came to farming.

The shift in Mien cultural orientations from military prowess toward success in farming and trade went along with the transition from situations of chiefly control to the subsequent period of greater household autonomy. This shift can be seen from the practices of acquiring children for adoptions among the Mien population in Phale. During the 1960s, this was always through purchase and was thus a direct indication of the productivity of a household. Kandre's informants indicated that in earlier times, other settlements had sometimes been raided for children. So in that time the ability to incorporate outsiders was at least in part a measure of military prowess. As Yoshino describes *kwa-tang* rituals, one of their implications is that ordained men are committed to a set of ancestors and thus cannot become ritually incorporated elsewhere as out-marrying husbands (1995, 271–72). These expensive ordinations imply that only better-off households could ensure that male heirs of the household stayed linked to a given set of ancestors. The ability to hold onto household members and to acquire others for incorporation was very unevenly distributed. The concern to keep household members and increase their number was strongly related to the new centrality of farming in cultural and social dynamics.

The household (*pyao*) has been a key component of Mien social life, agriculture, rituals, and exchange relations, but it also implies a normative framework of social and economic life that poorer people cannot always afford. As a central element of social life among Mien in twentieth-century

Thailand, the term suggests social and ethnic continuity through a basic unit, but this assumption obscures both systemic social inequality and variety and fundamental changes in household composition during the twentieth century. Mien people conceptualize the household as intimately connected to ancestor spirits. When a household is established, the members invite their ancestor spirits to look after the household members and their fields. Any major life cycle transition includes a ritual to the ancestors, in which they are informed about the arrival of an in-marrying spouse, the birth of a child, or the death of a household member.

Central to each household's relationship with its ancestor spirits is the renewal of its ritual contract, which takes place at the New Year. Such rituals require an offering of a chicken as well as locally stamped spirit money, incense, and liquor. After the ritual, the chicken is cooked and the medium and household members eat it. Guests are invited, as the occasion of renewing a relationship with the ancestors is also one of making and maintaining social ties within a village. The number of guests is to an important degree a measure of the prosperity of the household and thus of its relationships with the spirit world, as spirits bring blessing in the form of good health and good harvest. The spirit medium and household members may inspect the chicken's liver, skull bones, and the shape of its cooked feet for signs of the future of the household, and they exchange blessings and toasts before the meal. During the meal, after some time spent drinking, eating, and chatting, cooked rice is brought to the table.

Only adults can engage in the exchange of blessings, and one becomes an adult by establishing a household unit through taking a spouse and initiating relations with a set of ancestor spirits. The imagery of the ritual chants suggests some of the priorities of Mien ritual and social life, where the prosperity and well-being of household members is a measure of their relations to their spirits (see Conclusions). Religion is not a domain separate from everyday life; spirits are taken for granted as one of the world's components. People assume that they themselves will become spirits in the afterlife and that they will be in a relationship of mutual dependency with their offspring. One older man remarked, "In the old days a couple would want to have five or six children, and even adopt a few more, because when you die you want to make certain that you will be fed. Now people take medicine [birth control] to have no more than two children." This reference to children assumes not just a set of intergenerational obligations within the household but also the continuity of these obligations with those between household members and the spirits of their ancestors. The assumptions are that life goes on in the spirit world and that the spirits depend for their well-being on their descendants making offerings to them.

Fig. 5: A spirit medium chants, renewing a household's relationship with the ancestor spirits.

An annual offering to the ancestors has been the minimal requirement for a household to maintain face in Mien social relations. People who do not maintain a relationship to ancestor spirits are looked down upon as dishonest, since they do not take the minimal step toward prosperity and respectability. Such people, usually destitute and sometimes opium addicts, fall below the minimal requirements of Mien society and cannot engage in the exchange of blessings at feasts. If they are present at feasting after a ritual, it tends to be in a servant role, helping out in the kitchen. They may be given a token payment for their assistance as a way to help them out, but they are not within the orbits of normative Mien social life.

Mien people characterize ancestors as "small spirits." The spirits they refer to as "big" include the King's Spirit and various Daoist divinities.[7] Access to such spirits is limited by wealth and ambition. The most common way to access these larger spirits is by ordination. The lowest level of ordination is *kwa-tang*, the second is *to-sai*, and the third is *ja-tze*. There is some variation among the Mien as to whether a man undergoes a ritual to reach *ja-tze* rank or whether he is automatically promoted to this status when all his sons have reached the rank of *to-sai*. *Kwa-tang* ordinations take three days and require three "big" spirit mediums, *to-sai* twelve, and *ja-tze* eighteen mediums. This graded ritual hierarchy affects men's status in the afterlife; they become spirits of rank rather than just ordinary ancestor spirits. Importantly, while women are barred from such ordinations and other dealings with spirits, the wife of a man who has ritual rank also acquires ritual status.[8]

The differentiation in Mien ritual life that is apparent from these contrasts between ancestor worship and Daoist rituals has parallels in Mien weddings, which can either be small or large. A small wedding is a one-day affair. A large wedding, on the other hand, takes three days, and it involves more people as guests and more pigs, both as an offering and to feed the guests properly. Some of the big weddings that people recall from the 1960s and earlier required thirteen adult pigs to feed all the guests. In the number of pigs killed, there is considerable parallel with *kwa-tang* rituals. Without wealth, a household could not hold on to its members or acquire new ones. Among Thailand's Mien, this was not simply a matter of bride price and ritual ordinations. Mien also purchased non-Mien children for adoption in order to increase the size of their households. The changing dynamics of the Mien household in twentieth-century Thailand are evident from both ritual life and the practice of adoptions.

Ethnographic accounts from the 1960s suggest that 10–15 percent of the adult Mien population had been purchased from other ethnic groups in the region, both upland and lowland (Jonsson 2001a). The people were purchased as children and were incorporated through rituals into Mien households. While the process was one of coercive incorporation, the adoptees had the same rights and obligations as other household members once they grew up and got married.[9] By the 1990s, Thailand's Mien no longer practiced such purchases of non-Mien people for adoption. They appear to have come to an end in the late 1960s. The halt to this incorporation of non-Mien into Mien society is only one aspect of the social changes that relate to the Thai government's somewhat abrupt takeover of the highlands along the northern border.

A Mien spirit medium in Pangkha village made an equation between adoptees and the other children of a couple. He couched this in terms of the obligations that the couple built up with their children, who then took care of them in the spirit world through offerings. Kandre and Lej (1965, 131, 139–40) make much the same observation, that adoptions concerned ritual connections with ancestor spirits, parents built up obligations from their children for their old age and afterlife. Miles (1972b) suggests strong connections among adoptions, matrifiliations, and marriages as transfers between households regarding the rights to people as residents and laborers. This ability to incorporate non-Mien outsiders was thus of a similar order as the incorporation of Mien spouses and children into a household as an economic and ritual unit. The practice appears to set Mien/Yao apart from the other upland groups in this area in terms of how they defined the household as a bundle of relationships.

Practices of adoption and fosterage are common in Southeast Asia, island and mainland, upland and lowland (Schrauwers 1999). Diverse cases from across the region support the notion that kinship is constantly being created, and family ties come no more "naturally" than other social relations (cf. Carsten 1997; Hanks 1972). In his case about the highlands of Central Sulawesi, Schrauwers shows that "negotiations [of parent-child relations] are on-going and always subject to review and failure" (1999, 320). The Mien case, similar to what Schrauwers describes, shows clearly the strategic uses of kinship in the context of regional inequalities, better-off Mien absorbing children from indebted or impoverished non-Mien households.

The centrality of households for uplanders' constructions of identity and social life has been described as an indication of egalitarianism as the structure of society. If so, one may propose a shift from relatively hierarchical arrangements in the nineteenth century to relatively egalitarian ones by the mid-twentieth. Such generalizations may obfuscate the complexity of social life. The Mien case, for instance, suggests that the autonomous household was very unevenly distributed and took different forms, coming about after the dissociation of highland social dynamics from lowland tributary systems in the early twentieth century. The roots of the supposed traditional structures in the highlands lay in entanglements with the nation-state and a regional/global political economy.

Thao La was the undisputed champion of the inflation in household size, with his household of 120 people in Phulangka. With his first and second wives, he had six sons and two daughters, and he adopted one son that his third wife brought up—she did not have children herself. Each of his children brought a spouse into the household, and the high number of people includes three generations. The prominence of Thao La within this region can be gleaned for instance from Blofeld's notion that he was "the king of Yao" (1960, chap. 7). The first reduction in household size came when his fourth son left with his wife and their thirteen children. The household fragmented further at Thao La's death in either 1964 or 1965, a year or two before Douglas Miles started his research. Some people still recall signs of Thao La's prowess and links to the spirit world. One example is that soon after he died and before he was cremated, there was a solar eclipse. "While humans travel in daylight, spirits travel in the dark. By making it dark, the spirits were speeding up the arrival of Thao La's soul in the spirit world."

The way administrative integration and the opium monopoly played up the interests of large and stable households in the five officially registered villages literally spells out which households in the Phulangka area had the means to purchase children for adoption. The Phale village was situated outside the framework of the opium monopoly and is thus more representative of the general condition of northern Thailand's upland population engaged in opium production. But like the Mien in Phulangka, they incorporated outsiders through purchase adoptions into their households. Given the comparable rate of adoptions between the two settings and the divergent social outcomes in terms of household formation, it is significant that while Phulangka Mien appeared to take wealth and a large household as paradigmatic for their assessment of success, Kandre's Phale informants were decidedly uneasy about the wealthy.

The historical background of the two populations is quite similar, and the difference between the two cases indicates how the dominant voices in each setting turned contingent outcomes of engagements with a regional political economy into a matter of local society and culture. There were some extended households in the Phale area as late as 1990. It is possible that men's general failure to establish extended households lay as much with their wives as their children, that articulations of gender and intergenerational relations and inequalities gave the latter a greater voice than was the case in well-off households in Phachangnoi *tambol*. This is speculation, but the point concerns the potentially varied sources of agency behind the articulation of the culture and social relations of a settlement or an ethnic group in time and place.

Mien social life in about the 1940s privileged the agency of men over women. Affluent Mien men would engage in trade, leaving farm labor to wife (or if wealthy enough, wives) and children. One woman in her fifties recalled: "I was eighteen when I married and moved house. We later had nine children, so I was always busy at home or in the fields. My father-in-law did not do any work in the fields. Things were really difficult, there never was any rest." In contrast, many men of the same generation spoke with some nostalgia about their many travels, the places they went and the friendships they made while on the move. The difference in the mobility of men and women around the middle of the twentieth century came up in various conversations with Mien people, such as in the following, triggered by my questions about access to salt in the old days. Mien men from the Phulangka area went to Bo Luang and Bo Yop near Laos,[10] and the journey took ten days:

> Women never went anywhere, they helped [their parents] at home, then some male would come who would like her and try to get her for a wife. It is not like nowadays, when women go to be *kali* (Thai: prostitute) or

meban (Thai: maid). In those days males, some fifteen years old, some twenty, would go off courting together to other villages. Sleeping together? [*my question*] Yes, people did that sometimes. Young men would dress up nicely and put on a skull-cap, and then go to villages like Rom-Yen, where the young women knew their names. If we were not invited to stay overnight, we'd return home, sometimes we were asked to stay. When parents decided that a daughter was visitable, marriageable, they would tie a red cloth around her tied-up hair and wrap an embroidered black [indigo] cloth over that. This meant she was now visitable. Some villages had maybe two or three young women, others fifteen women. We would visit a house and chat, sometimes walk around with the women. Some women already had a child when they married. With two people leaving the household, the price was thirty *lung* for the woman and twenty *lung* for the extra person [her child], this was *ong-ku-nyan*; grandparents' money or silver. These were the customs in the old days; a descendant "exits the door" (*thsuat keng*) and takes a husband [a woman marries out], and the grandparents cannot leave with that person. Therefore, money must be given to the grandparents to provide for them and compensate for the loss of the person who married off.

Ethnography's Representative Villagers

The pervasive migration that characterized the highland areas of northern Thailand in the 1950s and 1960s occurred after the tributary framework had largely been undone. The major exception to frequent settlement mobility was the Phulangka area, where officially licensed opium production and trade continued until about 1958. These deals with agents of the state contributed to settlement stability, and the likelihood of arrests for noncompliance served to encourage relations of subordination to highland leaders. Such cases blur the assumed separation between highlanders and lowlanders, and they highlight the arbitrariness of the notion of highlanders in Thailand as a product of adaptations to the natural environment. The upland-lowland divide was a component of how people placed themselves within a landscape as social as it was natural, but highland populations had various relations with lowland states. Furthermore, their links to regional political economic structures had local consequences through ritual practice, trade, and patterns in village and household formations, migration, and farming.

The characterizations of Mien social structure through the dynamics of household formation can be viewed in this light as a product of a particular historical moment, when anthropologists studied what they assumed were ethnic societies on the brink of a major change that would undo their traditional structures. Both Kandre and Miles paid attention to the entanglements of Mien village life with regional and historical forces in relation to the opium trade and the practice of adoptions. Still, both conveyed a stable and traditional society in which the changes that had taken place prior to active national integration in the 1960s were cast as belonging a traditional Mien order. The varied repercussions of Mien engagements with tributary states and a regional political economy thus were internalized by ethnography as they had been by many Mien people, as features of local culture.

Mien practices of purchase adoptions and the changing dynamics of their household formations are best known for better-off Mien people. Poorer households and settlements were not prominent in these studies. They could not purchase new members, and they were either absorbed into more affluent households or lived in marginal settlements that were not always recognized as villages. When poorer people established a new household, it was commonly done without a wedding ceremony, as they did not have the means (silver, pigs, rice, liquor) to feast a group of people and thus claim face in society. As in the normative framework of Mien ritual life and exchange relations, some poorer people fell outside of what anthropology recognized as Mien society. Only wealthier people actively engaged in defining the parameters of Mien culture and their ability to lend a particular shape to the social setting made them exemplary within their society. In their positions of considerable local power, they also contributed to the anthropological understanding of ethnically bounded cultures and societies. It is important to note that it is not only the poor that are marginalized in this fashion. Studies of the Lisu that emphasized their egalitarianism portrayed ambitious headmen as an aberration, as something that did not fit their society. But Lisu leaders sometimes forged links with lowland authorities, including one man who received the title Samphaya and successfully controlled and taxed a number of settlements from the 1920s to the 1940s for the district officer in Mae Chan of Chiangrai Province (Hanks and Hanks 2001, 84–89). Subsequent attempts by "assertive headmen" to establish their prominence may have drawn on similar ambitions, or they may have been akin to Wuen Lin's extended household.

Among Lisu, a new couple had to pay compensation if they did not initially reside with the bride's father or in his village. In some cases, such clusters of sisters and their husbands were the basis for 'allegiance groups,' though this was not uniform. Durrenberger notes that in the area of his research most couples paid the compensation and set up a household elsewhere (1975a, 303–4). Without resources, a new couple would then have to reside with the bride's father and contribute to the success of his household.

Among Mien, postmarital residence depended largely on household resources. While there was a normative preference for patrilocal residence, Thao La sponsored the marriages of all his sons and daughters, and each of his children brought a spouse to live in the extended household, which for some time around 1940 had one hundred and twenty inhabitants. Without the means to pay for either bride or groom, a Mien couple had no claims on their married children's labor.

This suggests a perspective on the stories that Lisu told among themselves and to their anthropologists about killed headmen (Durrenberger 1983, 217–18). These Lisu stories may have been about real events, but they also charted the social landscape in particular ways and routinized a specific subject of action, as did the stories of Phaya Khiri's prowess and of Thao La's benevolent rule. Lisu stories revolved around household autonomy, while the Mien stories concerned the social cohesion of a migration group and the prominence of their leader. In both settings, there were various alternatives to what the stories proclaimed. Successful headmen may have been somewhat common among the Lisu prior to the mid-1960s, but the stories about their assassination made them a remote possibility. While the stories concerned assassinated headmen, they may have been prompted by the more immediate possibility of older men's command over their married daughters' households. The memory of assassinated Lisu headmen was thus involved in the construction of the household as a particular subject of action. That is, such stories reinforced a particular perspective on social life that concerned household prominence and were aimed against ambitions toward consolidated or extended households. In this, Lisu stories have considerable affinity to the "disciplinary problems" that Mien household heads in Phale reported to Peter Kandre.

The inflation of Mien household goals in the Phulangka area that bifurcated Mien households into large and small lasted until the hills became a zone of fighting between the Thai military and units of the Communist Party of Thailand in 1967. In early 1968, the village of Phulangka was abandoned when "shooting, bombing, and land mines [had] made it impossible for sociological research [and everyday life, one might add] to continue in the sub-district of Pha Chang Noi" (Miles 1967–68, 8: 2). The violence of this period contributed to a reworking of internal, social, and cultural dynamics in the highlands, and it also reshaped the settings wherein lowland authorities, anthropologists, highland farmers and their leaders, and others defined the parameters of highlanders' identity within the national public sphere.[11]

In the ethnography of northern Thailand's hill tribes, household dynamics provided a central element for generalizations about the social structure of ethnic groups. This strategy involved a radical simplification of the historical dimension of social formations in the area, particularly in the case of Phulangka Mien, where the exemplary extended household was the manifestation of particular cultural dynamics specific not only to a narrow time period but also to a political economic setting that was both unique to a small region and very unevenly distributed. There is every indication that Miles learned the same things about the past of the Phulangka population as I did later. In his dissertation, he discussed their integration into administrative and political economic networks during the early twentieth century. He stated that given this information, "Phulangka must have been one of the most prosperous opium communities in Thailand prior to World War II" (1974, 50). That he described Phulangka as typical of Yao in his other work (1972a, b, 1973, 1990) may reveal as much about what the anthropological community considered a case as it does about the conventional steps from a village to an ethnic group in ethnographic writing (Thornton 1988). Both administrative relations and the organization of the opium trade contributed to social dynamics in the hinterlands, but given the uneven outcomes of these engagements it is descriptively inadequate to portray the Mien or other uplanders as simply adjuncts to global processes (Wolf 1982; cf. Tsing 2000).

The articulation of household dynamics in the poorer satellite settlements around the five villages that had formal links to the opium monopoly did not result in lasting forms of ritual or remembrance. Poorer people are systemically silenced when it comes to statements about culture and identity. This silencing derives in part from the normative framework of Mien culture, which assumes certain basic resources to sustain claims to autonomy and prominence. The position of poorer people in this setting can potentially be compared to that of unmarried members of a Mien household who could not engage in the exchange of blessings at the feasts that follow offerings to spirits. In many cases, when poorer people established a new household, this was done without a wedding ceremony (which they could not afford), and in the early 1990s some of the poorer households did not maintain any relations with ancestor spirits. It is difficult to ascertain the absence of basic ritual contracts among poorer households earlier in the century because of the emphasis on forgetting among people who cannot sustain the normative practices of wealthier households. Ritual contracts, ceremonies, weddings, and soul callings activate connections to spirits at the same time that they motivate economic activity and make claims to identity and honor in society through exchange relationships. These practices are already normative statements about Mien ways, independent of ethnography.

Unlike the Lisu, who embodied the memory of killing assertive headmen as they sustained the prominence of small households, poor highland farmers could not claim agency and thus never emerged as the kind of subject of action that established identity or historicity in social life. Instead, like the impoverished Karen, who did heavy labor in the fields of Hmong and Lisu farmers, they have occasionally contributed to more affluent farmers' claims to prominence and their articulations of what is involved in being Mien, Lisu, Lawa, and so on. The household and the ethnic group assume particular subjects, and ethnography has contributed to the silencing of a number of voices that did not match the expectations regarding identity and culture that have been forged at the intersections of anthropology and its informants. The varied interests of Western anthropologists, the Thai state and its Tribal Research Institute, a range of prominent upland peoples who have constituted the dominant voices in village affairs, these have come together in a particular image of social life in the hills of northern Thailand. Through notions of the ethnic landscape, the Thai state, anthropologists, and prominent uplanders have also constructed their own identity and agency. In these triangular dynamics, the notion of hill tribes and individual ethnic groups has been significant in a range of settings within and beyond the ethnic minority settlements.

CHAPTER FOUR

Village People

> When administrators talk of the hill tribes as Thai citizens,
> they are generally impressed by the way highlanders adopt the
> Thai way of behavior, e.g. simple greetings such as sawasdee
> (respectful Thai greeting). Officials are even more impressed
> when they see that highlanders combine Thai and other ethnic
> customs into their own ritual practice. This way performances
> like that presented in the competition [for Model Develop-
> ment Village] in Phattana satisfy both officials and villagers. Of-
> ficials are convinced that the people have become Thai and the
> villagers are reassured that they are accepted as Thai citizens.
> —Chupinit Kesmanee, "The Masque of Progress"

The village of Pangkha is the administrative center of Phachangnoi *tambol*, in Pong District of Phayao Province. As the administrative center, it is better connected to national realities than other villages in the area. The village has a primary and secondary school, a post office, and a *tambol* meeting hall, which are all markers of the state's presence in the village. In 1994, it was still the only village in the *tambol* that had electricity, to the envy of people in the other villages. Various markers of prosperity indicated that the village "had progress" (Thai: *mi khwam jaroen*). Several house-holds owned rice cookers, refrigerators, and television sets. These conveniences of modern life in Thailand are at the same time markers of wealth, and television provides a link to the national and international world of news, entertainment, and cultural trends. In the village, three sundry stores and a noodle shop indicated disposable income.

The village lies on both sides of a hard surface road and has the general appearance of a poor, lowland Thai village, in terms of the housing styles, official buildings, stores, TV antennas, and clothes. There is nothing specifically Mien about the look of the village or its people. Its population is a little over four hundred people, living in eighty-five households. Villagers grow primarily cash crops, such as ginger, cotton, corn, mangoes, and litchi, and they buy their rice from the town of Chiangkham, roughly thirty kilometers away. Villagers have usufruct papers (*S.T.K., sitthi tham kin,* "right to livelihood") to their plots, which they have used since about 1970 and which require herbicides, fertilizer, and/or tractor plowing to sustain yields.

The annual household cost for rice was usually in the range of 3,000 to 6,000 Baht ($120–240), but rice was costlier for poorer people who could not afford to buy it in bulk and instead bought about a kilogram at a time from one of the local stores in the village.[1] Some of the poor people formed a distinct underclass. They held no land and thus did not farm, and they made a living from occasional day labor and help for wealthier people, making maybe 10 to 30 Baht in a day. The most abject would sometimes beg for food or money in the village. Farmers' annual income in Pangkha ranged from about nothing to about 100,000 Baht ($4,000); most was in the range of 7,000 to 30,000 Baht ($280–1,200). This income for crops was balanced by the growing cost for fertilizer, herbicide, and insecticide for those who could afford it. One household that made about 30,000 Baht from cotton, litchi, and mangoes had spent about 20,000 Baht in the same year to treat their fields and orchards.

The marginality of upland populations has been actively brought about by laws about land use and citizenship, laws that have made swidden farming illegal and made it difficult for ethnically non-Thai uplanders to acquire the citizenship papers necessary to own land (Anan 1997, 2000). In the Pangkha area, people had generally abandoned swidden farming around 1970 and were growing corn, cotton, and ginger in permanent fields and gardens for which they had usufruct rights. In 1993, about thirty people from Pangkha and nearby villages went to a meeting with the Forestry Department for Phayao Province in the district center of Pong, where the topic was use of forest land. Most of the meeting was taken up with the concerns of the lowland villagers about the classification of fields. Mien upland farmers, who were both vocal and articulate about their need for permanent claims to land, were met with outright and repeated dismissal.

The head of the Forestry Department stated that the usufruct land rights that they had were only intended for an eight-year transitional period while the people switched to lowland farming. There was no land available for the expansion of lowland farming in this area. People had already been using their upland fields for over twenty years. In an attempt to sustain cultivation in these fields, most people had resorted to tractor-plowing, which was illegal in terms of how their land was classified. At this meeting, a further dismissal of uplanders' needs came from an MP for the province, Ms. Laddawan Wongsriwong, who had entered politics after a successful career as a TV reporter known for her concern over environmental issues. Some of the uplanders, both ordinary farmers and those with official positions, pressed her on the need for a reworking of the land classification to accommodate upland people living in the area. She replied that uplanders were so numerically insignificant—barely one percent of the nation's population—that there was no reason to modify the national law. She hinted that if authorities were to give in to the demands of such a minuscule portion of the nation's population, the precedent thereby set would bring about absolute chaos.

State hegemony is in certain non-negotiable ways a fundamental feature of the social landscape of upland populations, and to the extent that it visibly is not such a feature, the assumed disconnection serves as grounds for the erasure of settlements. By the end of 1992, five villages in Phachangnoi *tambol* had been declared illegal settlements according to a new official "Master Plan on the Environment," and the villagers had been told to leave the area. The initial number of villages was six, but one was dropped off the list because it had a school donated by H.R.H. the Princess Mother and staffed by the BPP. This Master Plan was introduced to Mien villagers with a slick video presentation that the coordinator of one of the two rival umbrella organizations for rural development NGOs in northern Thailand brought to Pangkha in early 1993. Villagers questioned him on the plan and criticized its construction of reality, specifically the classification of villages and land use that justified the planned erasure of several settlements. He responded by stating that he was only asking for villagers to cooperate with the government in protecting the environment.

When this did not silence the villagers' criticisms, the man responded by asking them how well they really knew the situation—could they, say, give the accurate number of Mien people and Mien settlements in Thailand? This gave him some control over the discussion, which is itself instructive about the strands of governmentality in this area (the man is ostensibly working with and for non-governmental organizations). The "accurate" numbers of people and settlements, which he teased villagers for not knowing, were from a 1988 survey. The social fact of this encounter is that government statistics, no matter how questionable or outdated, define local realities. Forced relocation of uplanders has continued for longer than the military attacks, lately in the name of watershed and forest protection (see McKinnon 1989; Thawin 1997).

Both local people and the officials from the government's Tribal Research Institute (TRI) stated that the villagers had agreed to relocate but were still waiting for word on where they could resettle. The discursive framework of this Master Plan shows how current notions of national space leave no areas outside the state's reach. The "problem" villages ("type 3") were defined as illegal because they were not by a hard-surface road and did not have a state school or an agricultural project. Only through connections to national space via a road, a school, or some other official presence or to an agricultural or other project could villages remain in place.

Because of the limits that state control had put on livelihood in the area, many people had gone elsewhere for work; to Thai cities and abroad to Singapore, Cambodia, Taiwan, Hong Kong, and Japan. The Thai government had contracts with the authorities in Taiwan and Hong Kong, and Thai labor gangs went there legally. Several Mien men had gone to work as translators with such work groups, having an easier time with the Chinese language than their Thai co-workers. Mien women mostly went to Hong Kong as maids. The conditions for overseas work have changed over time. In about 1980, workers from Thailand were recruited for construction in the Middle East, and some of the Mien men who left at that time had all their expenses taken care of. In the early 1990s, people had to pay for their passport, visa, work contract, and travel cost, and in the Pangkha area the outlet for these expenses ranged from 20,000 to 86,000 Thai Baht ($800–3,440). In some exceptional cases people were able to wire home about 10,000 Baht ($400) per month, and one man returned home from two years away with about 700,000 Baht ($28,000). In comparison, the work available in Thai towns rarely paid more than 1,600 Baht ($64) per month, and often less. Most of this would be spent on food, housing, clothes, and the occasional entertainment, with very little left over to save.

The word about the salary one could make abroad spread rapidly. The increased local cost of living, coupled with often disappointing yields from farm work, made many people desperate about their finances, and most had to borrow money for the initial cost of going abroad for work. While this was sometimes successful, the interest was in several cases close to 50 percent per year. I heard stories of people who became stranded abroad, having been sold a fraudulent guarantee for a work contract and having no means of finding work to repay the loan. In despair, some had killed themselves. Others had more luck and eventually found work through networks of kinship and other relations among Mien or Thai people already there. In Japan, people arrived on a short-term tourist visa and then slipped away into menial tasks that local people found unrewarding. The implicit danger of taking a loan and going abroad was in some cases no greater than that of trying to earn a living locally from farming. Wealth made the greatest difference for mobility regarding wage work during the early 1990s. Only a few people could afford to place themselves in a position of potentially earning good money from wage work abroad. Because most Mien people did not have college educations, their options of wage work in Thailand unambiguously situated them as lower-class within a national political economy, and the wages they stood to earn from work within the country reproduced their position as lower-class.

Villages are increasingly entangled with national and international markets for produce, labor, and consumer goods. At the same time, state regulation and monitoring has eroded villagers' control over their local livelihood. Rural villagers are increasingly involved in national and global networks. Given this trend, the growing importance of the village as the focus of ritual, identity work, and socializing among Thailand's Mien is somewhat unexpected. Three examples of this village focus are discussed below. They vary in scale; one concerns a single village, another a *tambol*, and a third all the Mien villages within Thailand. In each case the social universe is an abstraction and excludes a range of possible participants.

The first event recast Mien ritual imagery in terms of the Village Committee and the village's Housewives' Group, both of which are aspects of the state's modernizing agenda in the countryside. The second, which revolved around sports contests among elementary school students at school grounds, routinized schools and official village registration as the criteria for membership in Mien social dynamics whose universe was the *tambol* of Phachangnoi. Both of these cases took place in 1993, whereas the third, in 2001, assumed a social universe of all of Thailand's Mien settlements. This last event was a combination of sports contests and cultural programs, and among its effects was an embodiment of Thailand's Mien as a social entity. These efforts, in ritual, sports contests, and the like are performative expressions of identity and social life. Each of these projects not only engenders particular social visions, it is important to note that they also silence a range of alternative perspectives as they redraw the parameters of identity. These events are motivated public alignments with nation and state that serve to redefine Mien identity and society as they forge links with national structures.

Recasting the Village

Annual Mien offerings to the village guardian spirit do not have a leader. In Pangkha, they are conducted by five mediums who chant simultaneously to a range of spirits. These offerings run on voluntary contributions from each of the households in a village, thus implying that the village is a voluntary assembly of equal households. The annual offering to the village owner spirit is the only occasion where all the households in the village cooperate in ritual, and it is as significant that they contribute voluntarily as it is that very few households (15 of about 85) sent a contribution or a participant to it in 1993. One novel village-level ritual from that year exemplifies some of the creative configurations of national and local realities that are increasingly common among Thailand's mountain people. While it was not repeated in the following year, this ritual is an important indication of how basic social units are defined through embodied practices (cf. Hayami 2004, 91–138).

Around four in the morning on January 23, many villagers were at the house of Tang Tsoi Kwin. A band was playing, and the air outside was thick with the smoke and smell of firecrackers. There were flowers and fruit on the ancestor shelf in the kitchen, and incense and two candles burned. The spirit-shelf in this house has a house-like structure on it, and for the New Year the householders had strung a red banner above the altar, and four silver flowers were pinned on the banner. One man sat at a table and chanted, but the large kitchen was alive with various activities: rice was already cooked; tables were set with bottles, cups, and glasses; rice porridge was ready a little before 5 a.m. and poured into a bowl and cups and glasses. People were still arriving, some with sheets of spirit money or boats folded from gold and silver paper to use in the offering. They came to the tables to drink what was served, and the medium, increasing the speed of his chanting, started letting the divining sticks fall. He had them fall four times, and then he declared that the spirits wanted the assembled group to head north.

The band led the procession, and, as there is no door on the north wall of the kitchen, the group went out of the door facing west and then headed north. They continued, heading not north but rather around the house and then out to the hard-surfaced road that bisects the village, and they walked following the band for approximately a hundred meters westward. There the group left the road and headed for a flowering tree near someone's house. The aim of the trip was to get flowers to offer to the spirits and also to get pebbles for good luck. The pebbles were gathered on the way back to the house. Once back, people stuck the flowers in vases on the shelf or in cracks in the wall, but they kept the stones in their pockets for posterity. They might turn into wealth.

The assembled people were all given sheets of spirit money, and a medium led them in bowing while he chanted to send off misfortune (*fung kwang*), facing the door they had used earlier. The chant was over within fifteen minutes, and the spirit money and gold paper boats were taken outside, where they were burned. The band was playing again, and now the assembled all got a new batch of spirit money and gold paper boats, and they bowed in the direction of the altar, led by three mediums. Then that offering was burned in a big wok in front of the altar, and the kitchen filled with smoke. As this fire went out, about twenty-five men assembled and went through the same bowing gestures as the larger group had before. These were all men with ritual rank (*kwa-tang* or *to-sai*), and they were paying respect to their lineage of teachers. Their bowing was over in about ten minutes, and then the whole group, led by the band, proceeded to the *kamnan*'s house. People had picked flowers off of trees along the way, and now they put them on the altar and in the wall behind it. Then the air filled with the sounds of firecrackers right outside the house, a medium let divining sticks fall, and the assembled group went through the double bowing again, first facing the door out (away from the altar) and then facing the altar, with the offering money burnt at the end of each sequence. This was over a little past 6:30 a.m. By then it was almost daylight outside. The woman of the house brought out a tray of red-dyed eggs, which some people ate right away. The eggs are a form of blessing, and are common at the New Year.

At the *kamnan*'s house there was an amplifier wired to the village PA system, and after one of the men had sung for the village in the archaic song-language, the *kamnan* and the headmaster each took turns telling people what was in store for the day. The headmaster, who spoke in both Mien and Thai, encouraged people to wear Mien clothes during this particular day in order to "preserve Mien culture" and to "show that this is not a village of lowlanders." People were then fed a rice drink and sweets made from pounded sticky rice with sesame seeds, wrapped in banana leaves and lightly roasted, a treat that every household is expected to make for the New Year. With the announcements over, the *kamnan* played Chinese pop music over the PA system. Firecrackers went off here and there in the village, but the parade had dissolved for the time being.

Guests sat around and chatted, but the people of the house were beginning to set tables for a festive meal, with many meat curries and store-bought liquor and soda. There were about thirty guests, mostly men, who drank, ate, and sang, and the band from the parade played music. Most were Pangkha people, including a Thai man from the *tambol* health station, but there were also relatives from other villages. This meal went on for about an hour, but then the parade came together again and followed the band to the house next door. People took flowers off a tree by the *kamnan*'s house and brought them to the adjacent house, where they were received with a small cup of liquor at the door and given sheets of spirit money. As before, people bowed toward the door to send off misfortune, the spirit money was collected and burned outside, and they then bowed, new bills in hand, toward the altar. By 1 p.m., the group had arrived at the eighth and final house of this parade through the village, and there was little variation from one reception to the next. Then everyone was invited to lunch in a *tambol* agricultural and handicrafts center, a building that was seldom used. There is a *tambol* meeting hall at one end of the village, and it was used for meetings and as a classroom for the Pangkha school. The agricultural center was used when the meeting hall was occupied.

In the agricultural center, there was an announcement in Thai and Chinese on the blackboard that this was a "ceremony of paying obeisance to the lord and respect to elders." The assembled people made five lines, two of women on the left and three of men on the right, all facing the elders. The elders sat at a table at the end of the hall, below the blackboard. As the crowd was forming lines, food was brought to the tables. The table servants, who had also done the cooking, were members of the village Housewives' Group. Most, though not all, of the elders at the head of the table, five men and four women, were in the grandparent category. They were also not all local people. They were elders by being descendants of Thao La (Tang Wuen Lin), the founder of Phulangka. Seven of the nine were actual third-generation descendants, and the other two were spouses of descendants, one in the place of her husband, the other accompanying hers.

The band played in front of the lines of "young" people, and then Tang Jiem Hin, one of the leaders of the parade since early morning, led a speech to the elders. During his speech, women in the two lines held red eggs in front of them, and the elders at the table chanted blessings. Then the *kamnan* thanked the assembled on behalf of the other elders, the headmaster took the microphone, and Jiem Hin placed a red egg on a string around the *kamnan*'s neck. Then other people came and draped eggs on the elders, and then everyone was seated and fed lunch, largely meat curries but also vegetables and rice, and served tea and liquor. After lunch, some of the people went home, but many stayed on, and something of a singing contest emerged, though this time the songs were not in the Mien song language but in Central and Northern Thai.

This village-level event drew on existing patterns in Mien culture, but they had been reworked in important ways. Mien tradition includes practices of paying respect to ancestors, which people do as members of particular households and lineages. In this new, village-level ritual, the paying of respect had been moved from the lineage level to that of the village and from spirits to living villagers and other relatives. The parade through the village with a reception in a household has a close parallel in Mien wedding ceremonies. At weddings there are only two parties, the bride's kin and groom's kin. At the village ritual, the village has been divided into several components. One of them is generalized villagers, who come and pay respect, contribute flowers and a crowd as an offering to household ancestors and are received honorably by the individual households. Another is the stationary households, selected by the Village Committee as wealthy enough to receive the crowd of up to a hundred people. Five of eight households that the parade visited were descendants of Tang Wuen Lin (Thao La), the founder of Phulangka, who is the grandfather of the *kamnan*, Tsoi Fong, and of Tsoi Kwin, the headmaster's father, at whose house the event started.

The prominence of the founder lineage was most apparent in the "paying respect to the lord and obeisance to elders," where the descendants of Wuen Lin had become village elders. Village Elders constitute one component of the ritually assembled village as designed by the Village Committee. Yet another component of the village that this ritual defined was women as cooks and table servants as members of the village's Housewives' Group. Both the Village Committee and the Housewives' Group are products of the modern nation; they are frameworks that national authorities have provided for village-level organization.

There is no precursor for recognizing village elders, and the Mien have no custom of paying respect to seniors or elders like the lowland Yuan (northern Thai) *dam hua* or the Tai Long (Shan) *khan taw* (Davis 1984, 132–40; Tannenbaum 1995, 72–75). The notion came from the headmaster, and his imagery and notions of propriety are very clearly informed by national Thai culture. He also had children pay respect to their mothers on Mother's Day in August 1993 in the *tambol* agricultural and crafts center, in a way that was unambiguously Thai in all respects and had no previous grounding in Mien interaction patterns (for the Lisu, cf. Gillogly 2004, 127). But while the headmaster was instrumental in arranging some very Thai events, he simultaneously asked people to don their Mien clothes for these events, to preserve Mien culture and to show any passerby that this was not a village of lowlanders.

These dynamics draw on an emerging reworking of culture and identity, one informed by engagements with the modern nation-state. But these engagements with the nation-state's framework are grounded in specific local concerns. In particular, the creation of a founder lineage draws on the previous prominence of Thao La in local life, but what gives it significance is the headmaster's ability to influence the social landscape. He is a great-grandson of Thao La, and like some of his close relatives he draws on his ancestor's prominence to project his own centrality onto the life of the village. The novel mobilization of the village through ritual constructed the prominence of the founder lineage and mapped it onto the social landscape in a particular and unprecedented way. The rest of the village became subordinates who drew on the blessing of their seniors. The event also constructed a village where there never has been one before—in feasting. All rituals, soul-callings, offerings to ancestors or other spirits, weddings, and ordinations are accompanied or followed by a feast. These feasts are always in, for, and about particular households, and they concern the prosperity and face of household members. The exchange of blessings is between members of the two sides, hosts and guests, and the food offered is from the resources of that particular household.

In this village-level New Year's celebration, there was no household behind the feast; it was held in the *tambol* agricultural center, and the food was paid for by money that the better-off households in the village had been taxed by the Village Committee and cooked by members of the village Housewives' Group. The exchange of blessings was not between hosts and guests but between founder-lineage elders and the rest of the population, with a clear ranking between the two sides. Several of the participants said that this was the first time they had celebrated the New Year in this way. This particular ritual was just another of the headmaster's whims, they said, and not the way they usually did things. But even if this particular ritual construction of the village was a one-time event and was dismissed by some of the participants, it is indicative of a broader trend wherein the units of Mien social and ritual life are being reworked through engagements with the administrative and conceptual framework of the nation-state.

Ethnic Fun

In the middle of the Mien New Year festivities in late January 1993, there was a two-day event held at the grounds of the school in Pangkha, one that to some extent constituted a *tambol*-level celebration of minority identity. A banner strung over the highway declared in Thai to anyone passing through:

> SANUK AGAIN, PHULANGKA FUN-FAIR 36 [2536 Buddhist Era (1993)], JANUARY 19–20. EVENINGS. DISCO, DANCE WITH BEAUTIFUL YAO AND HMONG GIRLS. TWO EXCITING MOVIES PER NIGHT. SHOWS BY YAO AND HMONG SCHOOLKIDS.[2]

The banner suggests engagements with national society through a rural funscape of festivals with movies, pretty dancing girls, and displays of local culture. "Thai society" appears on the highway. Some of the rhetoric of village festivals is clearly aimed at a male culture of drinking and flirtation, while other parts cater to a consumption of local culture in the countryside (O'Connor 1989; Fordham 1995, 2004). The whole event was expressly about fun. While the banner clearly declared minority ethnic identity, both with the beautiful girls as dance partners and with the students' displays, it employed the common and official label "Yao" for the Mien, but it did not use the equivalent term "Meo" for the Hmong. This divergence in ethnic labels is a part of a more common trend in northern Thailand, one that concerns the dissociation of Hmong people from the subversive connotations of *meo daeng* and ethnic minorities collectively from the Other-ness of *chao khao*. The ethnic label *Yao* does not carry connotations of insurgency.

The two-day fair provided various manifestations of national order. It started with a parade to the school grounds by groups of students in sports outfits. Each group carried a banner indicating the village-school it represented and, in cases where a school had several teams, also a number indicating the division. The parade was led by a marching band of students in elaborate Hmong clothes and the schoolteachers in jogging suits or uniforms indicating membership of the government bureaucracy. The Mien headmaster of the Pangkha school was an exception to this trend of extralocal dress in that he wore an embroidered Mien jacket. Bringing up the rear of the parade were about two dozen adult villagers, all Mien, wearing Mien clothes. A marching band of students performed as the procession entered the field and formed lines in front of the roofed structure where the event's special guest, Mr. Witthaya Srijan, a Democracy Party MP for Phayao Province, was seated.

Teachers from the Pangkha school then took their positions in front of the lines of people. Facing the MP under the roofed structure with a Thai flag hoisted on top, the teachers led the students and "ethnics" in singing the King's Anthem. The lines of people then dissolved, and a group of about thirty students in red T-shirts, boys wearing shorts and girls embroidered Mien women's pants, performed a dance to the music of a Mien band. After this ethnic dance, the MP opened the event with a speech, in which he told people not to destroy the forest with slash-and-burn farming techniques. Most of his speech concerned the importance of democracy and development and voiced many of the issues that commonly appear in the Thai media about the upland ethnic minorities "entering society."

In multiple ways, the opening events of this two-day fair constituted a ritualized act of allegiance to the modern nation-state. Through the banner-invitation and the range of events, the fair placed ethnic minority culture and identity inside national society. The parade and the line-up of participants and ethnics displayed orderliness and hierarchy. This production of order was framed as Thai by the national flag and, further, the participants engaged in a national communion through the King's Anthem. The link to national society was strengthened through the presence of the national-level politician, and he acted his part through an edifying speech about a progressive and democratic national society. He also charted some of the contours of membership in the national society with his discussion of how swidden farming destroyed the nation's forests, all of which served to render *chao khao* as antithetical to the nation. When he was finished, the *kamnan* placed a red-dyed egg on a string around his neck as a Mien form of blessing and good wishes.

The presence of the politician was a sign of the success of the denizens of this minority area in linking themselves to the nation. They were in and of national space not only through the Thai flag and the King's Anthem: the *sanuk* events catered to members of the nation who would otherwise pass through the village on the highway and barely notice it. Uplanders' presentable culture took the form of ethnic dress and dance in a rural village, precisely what modern Thai would expect about tradition, community, and culture (O'Connor 1989). The visiting politician not only embodied and represented the nation's authorities—more importantly, his presence and his speech were indications of official attention to the inhabitants of the sub-district. The Mien and Hmong in Phachangnoi *tambol* conveyed themselves as good Thai citizens, albeit ethnic minorities. They were orderly, nationalist, presentable to a generalized Thai audience, and fun to visit—the opposite of the Thai stereotype of disorderly and destructive *chao khao.*

Most of the daytime activities were taken up with sports competitions, and during the first evening there were displays of song and dance by both students and older villagers. The students' races and dances were contests, with awards to the winners in each category. For the races, the fastest three in each group stepped on a podium by position, and each was awarded an imitation medal, as if this were a national or international sporting event. For the dances, the winning team in each category received an education-oriented prize of pencils and notebooks. Both sets of awards drew on social distinctions between the contestants and the event officials. At the daytime races, the politician, the *kamnan,* and I (the foreign anthropologist) were asked to award the medals. At the evening dances, after the politician had left, the headman, some schoolteachers, and I gave out the awards.[3]

In bringing together the inhabitants of the sub-district, the fair not only constructed a social statement externally regarding the ethnic minorities as

Fig. 6: A rare moment of royal attention in the ethnic minority area: H.R.H. Princess Maha Chakri Sirindhorn, flanked by Border Patrol Police, in Phachangnoi *tambol* in 1993. On her visit she opened a library at a school run by the BPP. The ethnic minority people expressed disappointment that the visit was not about them and that they were not even visible in the television coverage of the event. Note the soldier on the left instructing the *chao khao* to pay respect properly.

in and of the Thai nation; the event's social statement was also aimed inward as a self-fashioning of the sub-district as a social entity. There are important divisions among those who fashioned the "account": those who acted it out, those who were on the sidelines, and the collectivity it was about.[4] As an event, the fair manifested the ability of schoolteachers to objectify particular visions of society and to mobilize people as performers and audience. To compete in the dances and the races, the kids had to belong to a school, and this already passed over a sizable segment of the sub-district population. There were seven registered villages in the sub-district and various unregistered settlements that ranged from about two to twenty households. Five of the seven registered villages have a school; of these, Pangkha is the central school and the others are its branches. A village with a school is an artifact of the modern nation-state, but in terms of who could compete at the fair, this administrative fact became a local criterion for social membership. Literally, people who did not belong to a village with a school could not compete and thus were effectively not of the society that the fair was celebrating. In this capacity, the fair reinforced the nation-state's definition of society and localized it through the contests among the students.[5]

Mien people do not respond to Thailand's national integration collectively. Particular actors, primarily those taking on a school or a village as the subject of action, have achieved prominence because of the character of contemporary entanglements with the state. These entanglements concern agricultural production, hegemonic portrayals of uplander culture, and the currently predominant ways of mobilizing labor, resources, and attention. Household agency has been undermined through laws concerning land use and settlement stability. It has been further decentered with the widespread notion that uplanders' "traditional" cultural, agricultural, and social practices are antithetical to national well-being, which serves to predetermine any form of resistance as subversion. Meanwhile, schools and sports have pulled the Mien and other uplanders into a range of networks of the modern nation-state, where they compete with other members of the national community. In this way, schools and sports teams carry similar implications as do Buddhist temples within lowland Thai society. As contact zones, they set up commitments to exchanges with comparable social units and thus draw communities into a particular hierarchically ordered universe of culture, society, and politics whose ultimate reference is state control and hierarchy that emanate from the capital, Bangkok.

These social commitments imply financial contributions that may be beyond the means of villagers. This can provide an opportunity for powerful outsiders to impress their generosity on local communities, which is a further analogue with the role of Buddhist temples in linking villages to larger worlds. In 1992, the school in Pangkha received a major gift of sports equipment from the politician who had given the opening speech at the fair. A native of the nearby town of Chiangkham, he was actively courting votes in this area. Such displays of generosity may be particularly common just prior to elections, and other ways of acquiring the necessary funds to maintain social membership are more common.

A Mien village in Chiangrai Province, Khun Pong, held a one-evening fair to raise funds for their sports team in 1993. Many Mien people, including some from Pangkha, visited to lend their support. This was the ninth consecutive year of their fair, and it consisted largely of selling food and alcoholic drinks. These were served mainly by young women accompanied by Thai pop-music from a cassette player. As with the disco at the Phulangka Fair, this was an enticement to young men who cruise around with disposable income to drink and flirt and spend their money. In her account of the village scout movement, Bowie describes dancing girls for hire as a new feature of village fund-raising in the northern Thai lowlands during the 1970s (1997, 173–78). At that time, the dance partners were nonlocal young women brought in whenever fairs were held. The difference in the mobilization of labor and resources for women dancers since the 1970s is instructive as to the changing role of villages within the nation. Increasingly, local villagers are mobilized to generate the funds needed to maintain their membership in the nation-state. While this new trend contrasts with dynamics from the mid–twentieth century, it resonates with the position of villages in tributary states, which is to say that characterizing "change" depends on the temporal and spatial frameworks implicit in the analysis.

Whether the social reference of contemporary cultural dynamics in these minority areas is the normative gaze of the nation state or the more fun-driven quest of northern Thai male culture, the social outcome tends to reinforce the village as the relevant subject of action. Another aspect of this change is the emphasis on village beautification, as with the collective cleanup in Pangkha village on a major Buddhist holiday (Jonsson 2001c, 164–65). One dimension of the beautiful countryside is competition among villages for official recognition, sometimes with the hope of an award or the appearance on national TV. Chuphinit (1992) has described one aspect of these contemporary cultural dynamics in his account of a Hmong village in Nan Province that was nominated by local government officials for recognition as a model development and defense village. The villagers acted their part, entertaining the officials with a dance show by students and a blessing ceremony for the benefit of the officials and, on later visits, by entertaining the officials with food and alcohol. His material parallels the Mien case in the increasing ability of people who assume the position of village leaders to mobilize their constituents for displays of village-level action for the purposes of official recognition. In part, these efforts are motivated by the concern to prove that upland populations are not *chao khao* or *meo daeng*. Given Thai national anxieties about the upland ethnic minorities, such displays of order are a prerequisite for benign official and other recognition.

Contemporary cultural dynamics in upland areas display hegemonic processes that draw on two separate strands of social life. One concerns the national gaze on uplander culture and social life as backwards and threatening to national well being. This motivates various displays of order, compliance, and presentability by upland villagers as collectivities. The other, which conjures up such collective action, draws on changes in the avenues of social action. It concerns the ability of schoolteachers, headmen, and others to assume leadership positions and mobilize the villagers' labor

and attention for sports, fun, development, beautification, and environmental protection. These processes come together in the shift from households to villages as the main sites of social action, as people in minority
areas place themselves within a national public sphere. The Phulangka
"Fun-Fair" presented the Mien and Hmong as within Thai society, without
implying that the population had shed their previous ethnic identity and
"become Thai." National integration does currently not require ethnic
change, while the way people manifested their ethnic identity at the fair was
very clearly in terms of modern Thai society. But this ethnic display was
not a collective effort. The fair was a motivated statement about the people
of this sub-district that was fashioned by the schoolteachers. It employed
the students to act out this social rendering through competing in races,
volleyball, and dance. The fair involved the adult population of the sub-
district largely as an audience to these statements about the administrative
collectivity. The event rendered people in marginal settlements, those that
either were not officially recognized or did not have a school, as off the social map.

The frustrated agency of people assuming household primacy in social
life came up in various conversations concerning the contemporary situation of national integration, with many of the young people away from the
village: "Nowadays, kids don't help their parents, they are off somewhere
else for school and work. Nowadays [they] do not help with work, they do
not have the customs of the old days. Children are lazy, they don't want to
work, they like to *ming dzyao*, 'visit, cruise about.' For those who work [at
home], life is very difficult. Children do not love their parents, they do not
give [money], are not honest."

The notion that children do not love their parents anymore is tied to notions of intergenerational obligations and dependency within households.[6]
Care-taking moves down the generations and generates obligations in the
opposite direction. This assumes the same notions as the scheme for bride
price for a person who is moving out and who would otherwise take care of
her grandparents. The household must be compensated to cover for this
loss, to cancel the obligations that the person who is leaving would otherwise continue to honor. Younger people, entangled as they are in contemporary Thai realities of work, leisure, and identity, do not necessarily take
the primacy of this intergenerational obligation scheme for granted.

National Minority Ethnicity

In the early 1990s there was a growing concern among Mien people,
both villagers and those in the city of Chiangmai, that many cultural prac-

tices were in danger of fading away. This sense of a cultural crisis was a clear indication of a generational shift. Older people, who were adults prior to the widespread collapse of swidden farming in the late 1960s and early 1970s, were concerned that the next generation was not showing much knowledge or interest in their culture. The shift can be contextualized in relation to local and national political economy. As the state has made shifting cultivation illegal, Mien households cannot engage in competitive farming and feasting to make and maintain face to the extent that they did during the mid–twentieth century. At the same time, farming has come to require capital input for plowing, fertilizer, and herbicides, whereas prior to the 1970s the inputs in farming were all in the form of labor. This shift from labor- to capital-focused farming contributes to the redefinition of the household and has changed the implications of having children. As children go to school at an early age, they are not only removed from the household labor force, but their schooling also has to be paid for. Further, as farming went from rice (for the household), corn (for pigs and chicken), and poppy (for cash, used for household goods and for acquiring new members) to cash crops such as corn (a commercial variety for human consumption), cotton, and ginger, people buy their rice in lowland towns. As mouths to feed, children are thus increasingly costly, and this cost is increased when they are sent to school. When the children later go away for work, the parents expect them to send their salaries home.

In many cases, the Mien youth did not send much money home. They needed the money to keep up with their peers in clothing style and entertainment as they fit themselves into various forms of the urban Thai lifestyle.[7] For many of them it is important that their city peers do not know that they are Yao, because the notion of *chao khao* marks them as inferior or defective people in Thai society. One Mien man in his late twenties spent several years studying in Bangkok. He shared a flat with other students at a college, never once revealing that he was Mien or Yao. Occasionally he would talk to his parents or other Mien relatives on the telephone. To his roommates he said the language was Chinese, that his father was Chinese and his mother Thai.

In everyday life, Mien people do not accentuate their difference from Thai society. Rather, they try to blend in, and in part this is a product of the widespread stigmatization of *chao khao* identities. Some younger parents use only Thai in speaking with their children, drilling them repeatedly in Thai manners such as the *wai* greeting. *Sawat-di kha/khrap* (the polite form of the Thai greeting; *kha* and *khrap* indicate the gender of the speaker), they tell them, as they urge them to greet a visitor properly. This general emphasis on being within Thai society contributes to what many older people feel is a looming cultural crisis, one that comes down to the disconnection of the young from Mien culture and identity.

In October 1992, a meeting was held in Pangkha to establish an association for the purpose of preserving and sustaining Mien culture. It was followed with a second meeting in Phale village of Chiangrai Province in early 1993. The two meetings expressed the widespread Mien concern with the impending loss of their culture and identity, and they crystallized two sets of opinions regarding what the problems were and how to respond to them. The meetings were organized in collaboration with IMPECT, a nongovernmental organization staffed with ethnic minority people and concerned with education, culture, and development among Thailand's ethnic minorities. At the initial meeting in Pangkha, the generation gap between the older villagers and the younger and Thai-educated component was clear. Some of the younger women, for instance, insisted that for Mien culture to be practiced in the future, it was necessary to allow women to become spirit mediums. They argued that gender inequality belonged to the past.

One of the older men answered this challenge by relating an old story that concerned a Mien couple. They were poor, and while the man was stupid the woman was very clever. She told him to dig up coals and store them in their granary. Unbeknownst to him, the spirits then changed the coals to gold, and they were rich thereafter. As the man finished the story, he said that the lesson of it was that Mien culture does grant an important place to women. But women and men do separate things. Women cannot become spirit mediums, that is the domain of men only. Women and men can cooperate in running a household, and with the help of spirits they can be very successful. In this and many other stories that older Mien people told, the emphasis was repeatedly on household prosperity, which depended on proper relations with spirits. Some of the spirit mediums at the meeting in Pangkha explained various "big" spirits, and in some cases they wrote in Chinese characters on a blackboard in the meeting hall to illustrate their material.

In contrast to the voices of predominantly older people and their emphasis on household prosperity at the initial meeting, the follow-up meeting was largely in the hands of the younger and Thai-educated members of the emerging association. They were concerned to locate "resource persons" from whom to get information to compile a manual of Mien culture. With such a manual, they reasoned, younger people can know their culture and identity even if they are away from Mien village life, living in a town or a city where they work or go to school. The participants at this meeting, this

Fig. 7: The first meeting of the emerging Mien Association, in Pangkha village in late 1992. The *tambol* meeting hall displays the national signifiers of the flag, Buddha, and the king and queen above the blackboard, which references nation, religion, and king as the pillars of Thai identity.

one much smaller than the initial one in Pangkha, then located the association within a larger world. They needed a name and an acronym for the association in both Thai and English, and they decided on *Samakhom Iu Mien Haeng Prathet Thai* (Thai Iu Mien Association), T.I.M.A. Then they worked out how the association would connect to other non-governmental organizations, such as those concerned with indigenous peoples in Thailand and internationally and those concerned with development in Thailand's north. The meeting was well-organized and efficient, and Mien identity and culture were becoming matters of bureaucratic decisions and management within a network of organizations. But while the association took shape fairly rapidly, there was no public activity until almost a decade later. In late March of 2001, Thailand's Mien assembled for their first ethnic festival (see Jonsson 2003b, c).[8]

In 2001, the Mien Fair was held at the village school in Pangkhwai in Chiangmai Province. It started with a parade to the school grounds, the ceremonial raising of the Thai flag, and the playing of the Thai national anthem over loudspeakers. Soccer was central to the four days of the fair. It was played on the large central field in front of the school, and Thai school-teachers served as referees. Under a canopy by the soccer field, rows of chairs seated special guests, referees, and the commentators, whose on-going description of the game was broadcast through five-foot-tall loud-speakers. On a table under the canopy, the cups to be awarded for each sport were lined up. Simultaneous to the soccer, teams competed in other sports on fields behind the school and further away from the main event. The sports were gendered. Only men played soccer and *takraw*; both women and men played volleyball, basketball, and ping pong; and only women played handball and *betong* (pétanque, bocce). The gender division is the same as in Thai school sports more generally.

The social units activated for the partially gendered Mien sports competition were villages. The event implies competence in national sports activities as the criterion for social engagement, and, further, that it is through schools that units of Mien society are linked. Seventeen villages competed, about 10 percent of the Mien villages in Thailand. Exclusion was thus built into the event. In part, such exclusion had to do with relative prosperity, as only a large village has enough young men to field a soccer team, for instance. Additionally, villagers have to raise funds to buy sports outfits. The host village, Pangkhwai, was visibly prosperous, and this was as evident from the shoes and sports clothes of their athletes as from their ability to host the competition. There were about 500 visitors, athletes and others, and the village had come up with 250,000 Baht—the equivalent of over $5,000—to stage the event. The cost involved building new facilities at the school; buying food, drink, cups, and other prizes for contestants; paying the referees; and so on. The sponsors as well as many visitors indicated that no other Mien village in Thailand could have raised that much money for a fair. As such, the event set a new standard for social position, one beyond the reach of other villages. One man boasted about the wealth in the village, saying that while one might find a couple of vehicles in an average Mien village, there were three hundred vehicles in Pangkhwai.

An MP from Chiangmai Province had donated the money to buy the trophies. His poster was displayed on many walls in the village, and his name and the logo of his Thai-Rak-Thai party were on some of the cups. Sports align the Mien with the nation in many ways, through the imagery of a national ceremony, through the social framework of national schools, and through the manifestation of official presence in the form of the politician's reminders. There was a further link to the nation and the state in that the organizers in Pangkhwai had an official permit for their games from the District Office. The permit, complete with the Garuda insignia of the Thai state, was reproduced in the mimeographed booklet that contained the event's program (Sujibatr 2001).

There is no stipulation to get an official permit for a village festival of this sort. The inclusion of the permit serves to demonstrate Pangkhwai village's links to the state through the District Office. The program stated on the cover that the event was the "thirteenth Iu Mien Games." The games have no precursor as a Mien-wide competition, and "Mien-wide" is a significant exaggeration considering the exclusion inherent to the event, but Pangkhwai had invited Mien villages from Chiangrai Province for sports contests on twelve previous occasions. By having the event written into the official permit as the "thirteenth" Iu Mien Games, Pangkhwai had drawn on its own, more local past and rewritten it through the District Office in a way that claimed their prominence within the now-national world of Mien sports events and ethnic culture.

A further dimension to Pangkhwai's refashioning concerns its change in name. The signs at the village entry still refer to it as Pangkhwai ("Buffalo Pen"). But in the sports program only the new village name, Jao Mae Luang, was used. Jao Mae Luang ("Royal Mother") is a reference to H.R.H. the Princess Mother, the late mother of the current Thai king, who was actively involved in hill tribe development, particularly on nearby Doi Tung Mountain in Chiangrai Province. During the sports contests, fans on the sidelines chanted "Jao Mae" with enthusiasm when their team played—but no one chanted "Pangkhwai." The village thus not only staged a demonstration of its wealth through this expensive fair, the village also broadcast its upgraded identity through the fans' chants on the sidelines.

The program routinized the host village's new identity and projected its local past of sports contests onto the emerging Mien-wide social field. It also served as a vehicle for an aspect of state control and monitoring, providing a detailed chart of the referees and the other officials serving at the games, the sequence of participants in the opening parade, and a stipulation that contestants provide identification (name and photograph) in order to qualify for the sports. I did not see any sign of this "official" monitoring of identity during the games. Still, the clause in the program indicates that this officially endorsed Mien fair was not only about the host village's link to the official reality and a sanction of Mien-ness within the national landscape of sports competitions. It is equally about the state's reach and about formal Mien compliance with the state's practices of control.

The pan-ethnic event of 2001 is a novelty, as is the staging of Mien culture for a Mien audience. The emerging emphasis on Mien ethnic identity contributes to a reworking of social relations. Social action at the village level has played up the agency of village headmen and school headmasters. These recently prominent actors can mobilize people for collective concerns, which have primarily been manifest in projects that concern the village within the nation, through schools, sports, development, and the quest for official favors. When the leaders of the Mien Association met during the event, there was talk of the need to have funds for the organization so that they could operate like the country's Chinese associations. Suggestions about how to raise the funds ranged from a membership fee in the association to a tax on the harvests of individual farmers. There was no resolution on this issue.[9]

Some participants complained that the association was not democratic, that there was no mechanism for keeping the general Mien public up to date on activities, and that, as it stood, it was only serving a few of Thailand's Mien villages. This ostensible criticism of the association also seemed to apply to the sports and culture fair as accommodating and celebrating only a small number of the Mien villages in the country. This critique, while it went no further, is interesting for how it drew on the modern and national language of democratic representation. The Mien Association's leadership and its critics draw on national imagery to position themselves. More local agendas, such as those voiced by older villagers at the initial meetings of the association about a decade earlier, are silenced in this context. Agency at the household level has been firmly marginalized, and there is an increasingly shared sense of Mien having to act as an ethnic group.

The president of the association suggested that the Mien adopt a greeting. His idea was to use the Thai greeting (*wai*, with hands clasped together) and the *farang* (westerner) handshake but with the difference of saying a Mien phrase with each gesture, *peng awn* ("peace") with the Thai gesture and *yiem long nye sa* ("how are you?") with the handshake. He called for a vote on the issue, and it was approved. The issue of a Mien greeting is a good example of the reworking of local culture through national and international contexts, where Mien are viewed in terms of Thai and western customs and proposed changes in Mien culture are modeled explicitly on these other cultures. An additional dimension to the "issue" of a lack of a Mien greeting is the Thai sense that *chao khao* have no manners. It may be because the association's president lives primarily within a Thai cultural framework in his daily life, being the headmaster of a Thai school and married to a Thai woman, that he is so concerned with the matter. Following the meeting, all the participants had lunch at the Pangkhwai headman's house, which was cooked and served by members of the village Housewives' Group.

Pangkha village did not compete in sports, but much of the evening events, including all the displays of Mien culture, were from that village. The current president of the Mien Association, the headmaster of the Pangkha school, had brought a full-size color photocopy of the *Kia Shen Pong* illustrated manuscript that belongs to his uncle, and it was displayed as a piece of cultural heritage that belongs to the Mien collectively. This is a significant reworking of the object's meaning, as it had previously defined Mien vis-à-vis outsiders and had been a rare item of power and prestige with which Mien leaders could strike deals with lowland rulers. I had heard stories of such objects causing calamity for their commoner owners, that in order to have it one must have powerful connections in the spirit world. Now the object, albeit a photocopy of the actual item, is beginning to define the Mien to themselves, through the Mien Association. Other features of the cultural events proposed a similar reality of a collective cultural heritage through the reworking of practices that used to link households in exchange relationships that reflected and constructed the honor of individual households or lineages. One display from Pangkha was the march and music of a band during a wedding reception, where the players walked around and through two lines of wedding guests, beginning and ending with mutual bowing. Then older men from Pangkha performed a plate dance. Later, a group of young women performed a plate dance. People said that this was a traditional component of wedding ceremonies in Pangkha Village.[10]

The features of the cultural program were like a showcase of the cultural agendas of the Mien Association's president; his home village had emerged as representative of traditional Mien culture. Judging from the Mien case, being an "ethnic group" and having a "culture," aimed as it is at a largely national context, implies a division of labor that mutes a number of local voices (for example, in the exclusion of 90 percent of Thailand's Mien villages from the competition). The cultural program played up one segment of the population, those from Pangkha village who displayed their music and dance for others to emulate, as the bearers of the classical Mien cultural heritage. The event rendered segments of the population in a servant role, particularly in the way it structured women through the Housewives' Group as cooks and table servants at the association's lunch. The fair constituted Thailand's Mien as a social entity through the constellation of organizers, performers, contestants, staff, and audience, and this achievement is of course the main point. The organizers and participants took the Mien for granted as a category, and they came together for a celebration of their identity and for the preservation of their culture, but the event can equally be viewed as having created Thailand's Mien as an acting subject for the first time.

The cultural display was received well by the Mien audience, and this indicates a consensus on what forms of Mien culture are considered presentable. The practices of music and dance that were displayed were significantly different from those previously practiced in the host village of Pangkhwai. One of the older men from that village remarked: "This was really interesting. I liked seeing how this is done. See, here in Pangkhwai we are far from other Mien villages. Most of our neighbors have been *jan-khe*, ethnically [Yunnanese] Chinese. Over time, we have borrowed the Chinese forms of ritual presentations at weddings, and it is really important for us to see the Mien way of conducting a wedding ceremony."

A banner that was stretched across the canopy above the evening stage is suggestive about the nonlocal character of the effort to display Mien culture. It was written in Thai and Chinese in black on red cloth, and the Thai stated: *Sübsan Watthanatham Thai-Yao* ("extending [into the future] the culture of Thai-Yao"), using the term Iu Mien only in smaller script and parenthetically below the main caption. There has been a trend in Thailand toward local ethnic labels and away from the official terms that tend to carry various prejudiced connotations, but the Mien Association's banner shows no sign of that emphasis. The choice of the word for culture, *watthanatham*, is equally striking. The equivalent Mien term, *le* ("customs"), would translate as *prapheni* in Thai, which has connotations of local, non-elite cultural practices. There is no Mien equivalent to the term *watthanatham* (Thai, from Sanskrit), which literally means "progress of the Dharma [the Buddha's teachings]." Thus, notions of culture and the choice of an ethnic label both draw on an official and national reality. The Mien Association's president spoke in Mien at their meeting, but his opening discussion of the central issue of preserving Mien culture used the Thai term for culture and a series of Thai terms for its intended preservation (*anurak, raksa, pongkarn, sübsan* "preserve, protect, extend [into the future]").

In the language used as well as in the form that culture took at the fair, the issue of preserving and celebrating Mien culture and identity is very much in national terms. This is not accidental, in that the recent changes that undermined the household focus to Mien social and cultural life resulted from political economic changes that were an aspect of national integration. The process of national integration defined various manifestations of highland ethnic minority difference as backward practices that presented ecological, political, and social "problems" to the Thai nation. The national imagery that schools bring to Mien and other rural and ethnic minority villages provides models of presentability that replace previous social and cultural agendas and dynamics. These new models simultaneously reorient their engagements with their culture from households, kin-groups, and villages within ethnically specific and diverse schemes toward generalized forms that involve presenters and their audience—where the references for having, displaying, and preserving culture are all national.

Sports have provided a vehicle for realigning the Mien people as particular kinds of social entities. Sports and culture performances can be characterized as a particular kind of contact zone, not only between Thai and Mien models of sociality and identity but also between alternative Mien models of organizing themselves and in the relations of Mien to ethnically other co-villagers. The models of the world that these events assume and promote are tentative. Viewing the novel pan-ethnic fair in the context of similar but smaller events that took place about a decade earlier, the emerging combination of sports and ethnic culture suggests how the Mien, when in public, are a kind of Thai. Sports competitions obfuscate the political dynamics of defining a particular public reality and create national spaces for the Mien to act out their identity through the engagements of audiences and expert performers on stages and sports fields.

This practice also configures village populations in a particular way, one that counters the contemporary fact of their multi-ethnic composition. Pangkhwai (Jao Mae) village also has Thai Yai (Shan), Khon Muang (Northern Thai), Lisu, Jin-Haw (Yunnanese Chinese), and Palong (Karen) inhabitants, but in its representation through sports it was a uniformly Mien village. Mien sports contribute to a particular social imagery and preclude others. The Mien Association's project is delimited by the boundaries of the Thai nation-state, excluding non-Mien co-villagers from its village-centered gathering. While the association does not have a political ambition toward a Mien-land, its board deliberated on organizational practicalities (office, finances) as an ethnic entity, its president proposed a unique body language (the Mien greeting), and the event included a display of supposed key elements of Mien cultural heritage.

Culture and identity have been placed within a national sphere. At the fair, elements of the national gaze were evident in the orientation of the opening ceremony and in the sponsorship of a member of the national parliament. The legibility of the sports and culture performances for a general audience, the mobilization of the Housewives' Group for "domestic" duties, and the clause about monitoring the identities of the sports contestants all point to the nation-state as the model for the Mien festival. The national sphere has facilitated the embodiment of the Mien as an entity, and sports activities have played a central role in mapping the ethnic community through the nation's administrative units into a league that identifies the Mien to themselves.

The voices of many Mien people contributed to the formation of the Mien Association. Among the older and village-based constituents, there was a general sense of a cultural crisis. Young men were not training to become spirit mediums, younger people in general did not know the archaic song language that was used at weddings, and households had entered a precarious situation as more of the young people went away for work or education. Mien village life as the older people knew it was in danger of disappearing. These voices appear largely marginalized in the Mien Association's manifestation of the ethnic group, and the Mien-ness that was on display at the fair belongs squarely "in a global context where collective identity is increasingly represented by having a culture (a distinctive way of life, tradition, form of art, craft)" (Clifford 1997, 218). The dynamics of the Mien case have many parallels in Jackson's description of Tukanoans in the Colombian Amazon region, where "ethnicity" and "culture" are fundamentally informed by engagements with the nation-state and where "organizational efforts to promote cultural autonomy [serve] integration into the national society" (1995, 17). In staging their culture as presentable to a general audience, the Mien Association partakes in the widespread activation of "local culture" in the Thai countryside, which in many ways is a response to globalization (C. Reynolds 1998, 134–38). The emphasis on a presentable heritage that can be shared within the nation, such as the portrayal of Mien culture as dress, dance, and music, belongs to a more general move in Thailand to seek delight in an ethnically diverse heritage within national boundaries. This quest for heritage is in important ways conditioned by a view of the forces of modernity as constituting a threat to Thai identity.

Representatives from IMPECT, the non-governmental organization concerned with ethnic minority highlanders' culture, identity, and development, were involved in these activities and the organization of the pan-ethnic fair. They neither have nor seek control over the Mien Association, but they are one dimension of what constitutes the Mien as an ethnic group in contemporary Thailand and in an international context of indigenous peoples. During the festivities in Pangkhwai, IMPECT representatives called an evening meeting and asked that each village present send two participants. The process mimics that of the democratic nation-state, but the politics did not. Central to the agenda of IMPECT representatives was to extract local ecological wisdom that might contribute to Mien claims regarding land rights. Because of knowledge about medicinal plants, indigenous forms of forest preservation, and the like, the Mien could then make a case to control land as community forest. This is an increasingly important issue in Thailand, one that strives to counter the systemic erosion of local control over resources in the context of commercial exploitation, plantations, and land grabs associated with capitalist expansion (Anan 2000; Sato 2003). The issues raised at the meeting were the focus of some discussion the following morning. One Mien man in his fifties, whose bearing was that of an urban merchant, said that the organizers of the meeting had no understanding or knowledge of Mien culture; "it is about soul callings, wedding ceremonies, and ritual ordinations."

In the attempts to align ethnic identity with a claim to rights and livelihood, the agendas of IMPECT representatives provide a closer match than do sports competitions and culture shows to the concerns of the older, non–middle-class villagers who view highland farming as fundamental to their identity. The local practices of farming and identity are played out increasingly on a national terrain. The national context of farming includes not only markets for local produce and official decisions on the market price for crops but also legal definitions that sometimes inform settlement erasure and other violence by agents of the state, all of which relate in many ways to matters of Mien culture and identity in contemporary Thailand.[11]

The recent prominence of villages as the focus of identity and social life is indicative of the dynamics of national integration, in that registered villages are the smallest administrative units of the state. They can be seen as analogous to the titled chiefs in the tributary era as the link between locales and the state's structures. Claims regarding identity have long been couched in terms of official recognition. Mien attempts to play up their ethnic identity as they manifest their modernity and thus compatibility with the modern nation-state are variations on this trend in that they seek to gain legitimacy for the previously denigrated ethnic category. Of the highland peoples, the Karen have emerged as the most legitimate, based on Thai understandings of their compatibility with Buddhist conservation values (Hayami 1997; Andrew Walker 2001). Hmong ethnicity is still considered very problematic in the public sphere, whereas Mien identity is less stigmatized. Attempts by IMPECT staff to consolidate Mien eco-wisdom draw on a combination of global and national notions of sustainability and legitimacy in order to carve out a space where Mien identity can be acknowledged in ways that might bring them some rights to livelihood. All the highland ethnic minority groups have very tenuous claims to land, and so far there have been very clear limits to how much they can play up their difference from mainstream Thai society in the attempt to bargain for rights and recognition. This marginalization has accentuated ethnic consciousness at the same time that the structures that reproduce the marginalization have placed various limits on the expression of ethnic minority identities.

CHAPTER   FIVE

On National Terrain

We are allowed to vote but nothing for our benefit ever
comes out of elections. In this situation it would be better for
us to send the domestic animals to vote for representatives in
the parliament.
> —Women's Representative for a Mien village in
> Phachangnoi Sub-district at a meeting with
> Provincial authorities, October 1999

Recent Mien attempts to forge an identity in relation to the state
have emphasized village identities, primarily through sports competitions,
and more recently the ethnic group as a unit of culture. Both models concern
ways of forging a recognizable identity and bargaining position toward the
Thai nation and state that still entertain considerable ambivalence about *chao
khao* as disorderly, uncivilized, and a threat to the natural environment
through their farming practices—the "un-modern" that must be brought in
sync with "the present socio-economic and political situation of the country"
(Tribal Research Institute 1995, 2). Along with these village politics of alignment with the nation-state, some Mien efforts suggest important revisions of
history that draw on national temporality and ideas of national heroes, centering on Phaya Khiri Srisombat (Tang Tsan Khwoen). Other and more confrontational recent politics has also centered on defining Mien populations
in relation to the landscape of national history. Only by explicitly situating
themselves within the landscape of hegemonic understandings can the Mien
avoid being discredited in their quest for recognition and rights, because as
chao khao they have no legitimate claim on the national authorities.

A few days after his opening speech at the Phulangka Fun Fair in early 1993, the politician was again in the village of Pangkha. This time he arrived with his family and some policemen as his bodyguards. The visiting politician had been invited to go on a pleasure trip, and he was joined by local people in a pickup truck; the group consisted of the headmaster, headman, a few other villagers, and me. The purpose was to visit Phulangka, the place where the Pangkha population used to live. On the way there, we stopped in a Hmong village, where their headman joined us. The politician's wife and daughter picked poppies and hemp plants from nearby fields for decorating their home.[1] Then we spent hours at a waterfall, chatting and drinking some of the liquor that had been brought along. The subsequent hike to the old Phulangka site was the brainchild of the headmaster. His plan was to revive the area as a resort for Thai tourists. As he envisioned this, the increasingly marginalized farming economy could benefit from the jobs that the resort would create. This planned economic development is an indication of a class bias from a salaried, middle-class schoolteacher. It resonates with many projects aimed at keeping people rooted in their home villages through income generation, which in most cases pays significantly less than low-paid jobs in towns and cities.[2]

The headmaster's plans also included erecting a statue of the initial local leader of the Mien population, Phaya Khiri Srisombat, to assert the status of ethnic minorities in the area. Nothing came of the plan for a resort and a statue. The idea for a statue concerns the forging of Phaya Khiri as a founder of the Mien population in Thailand. It connects to the rhetoric of national significance that has been mapped on administrative units, particularly provinces. Statues have become common at the provincial level (Tannenbaum 2002). There is no precedent for a statue at the *tambol* level, but this is the highest administrative unit to which Mien can make a claim. Another dimension of the charting of the Mien past through their "founder" on national terrain came up at a party in Pangkha village held by Ung Lo, the headmaster's brother, to which he invited about sixty villagers. The third brother, Lao San, who sells insurance in the city of Phayao, conducted a pop quiz in the style of national television, asking, "Who has contributed most to the *tambol*?" The answer given was Phaya Khiri Srisombat, which was somewhat puzzling, since he died before the *tambol* was formed. The logic of the contribution to the *tambol* before there ever was one is common in the retrospective commemoration of heroes and history as people recast their identity on national terrain (Hoskins 1993, 306–32).

The historical Phaya Khiri was a strongman leader with connection to a lowland king and then the provincial administration and a trade monopoly. His position as a connection between communities and the authorities can be compared to that of lowland strongmen (*nakleng*) who mediate between communities and the state in terms of personal connections to police, politicians, and the like. These were patron-client ties with agents of the state, and the state itself was in many ways an assembly of such alliances as well as a site of contestation among rival strongmen (cf. Hanks 1962; Thak 1979). Phaya Khiri's recent transformation is indicative of changes in the political landscape, not only regarding nationalism but also in the connections that communities have with the national administration and in the language of bargaining for benefits and attention. By placing themselves on the national landscape of administrative units, the Mien make themselves accessible to various forms of state control. Through various enactments of allegiance to the nation and modernization, Mien communities are positioning themselves within the orbits of official recognition. This may give them access to benefits as well as protection against settlement evictions and the like. The changes in how communities connect to the administration involve a shift from strongmen leaders to more formal associations that employ the language of democracy and appeal to the media in consolidating their bargaining position.

Aspects of these changes can be seen equally in urban and rural areas of Thailand. In 1973, student-led demonstrations and calls for democracy influenced social organization in Bangkok communities, while this was less pronounced in the countryside. Most of the reforms were crushed with a brutal military takeover in 1976 (Anderson 1977), but political structures and processes in Bangkok gradually took a more democratic form. As Ockey describes the case of Ban Khrua in Bangkok, external threats to the community led to the establishment of a Community Organization and Special Working Committees, and these organizations forged various links to academics interested in the community's cultural heritage (Cham, Muslim), non-governmental organizations concerned with development and democracy, Muslim organizations and politicians, and the media (1997, 9–17).

For visibility in the public sphere, it was very important to maintain connections with sympathetic journalists and with the academics who write for newspapers. But the state agencies that wanted to take over some of the community's land for a highway project also had good connections in the media, and they used these to suggest that the residents of Ban Khrua were to blame for the city's traffic problems (10–13). Through resistance, public protests, and petitions to authorities, residents were able to stall the road project. Ockey relates how distressed farmers, workers, and slum dwellers from across Thailand assembled at the prime minister's official residence and formed an umbrella organization, Assembly of the Poor, to press for their rights. With a protest of about 13,000 people, they gained great media coverage. The threat of evictions, to slum dwellers as much as to farmers, did not go away, but through their organization, tactics, and links to the media and Thai and foreign NGOs, the Assembly of the Poor appeared not easily suppressed (21–23; see also Baker 2000, Missingham 2003).

The shift from strongmen to formal organizations and public petitions relates to changes in the opportunities for the expression of political demands. The growing importance of links to the media is indicative of the prominent place of the national mediascape in everyday affairs. The quest for agency, identity, and rights is increasingly played out on a national stage. Because of the place of *chao khao* in Thai public imagery, it is rare that their agendas regarding land issues and citizenship get aired in the media. One of the important exceptions to this silence about upland ethnic minorities occurred in the context of a Karen protest against the logging of a forest (Hayami 1997). The Forest Industry Organization (FIO), which is within the Royal Forestry Department, intended to log a pine forest in the vicinity of a Karen village in Chiangmai Province. Villagers initially protested, in 1989, with a letter to the deputy provincial governor. When the FIO built a sawmill in the village in 1992, opposition became more intense, and it received significant media coverage in terms of Karen villagers' ecological sensibilities and respect for nature (Hayami 1997, 570–72). In 1993, after the FIO had formally opened the sawmill, villagers protested in a letter to the Prime Minister, and then

> monks and 50 residents of the district, along with 200 villagers . . . gathered behind FIO's sawmill to perform the ceremony of ordination for 1,000 pine trees. They wrapped the trees in saffron monks' robes, thereby rendering the trees sacred. . . . FIO tore the robes off in preparation for the visit of officials from the National Economic and Social Development Board, for fear of tainting the image of the project. . . . When this act was reported in the media, it was emphasized that the Karen villagers are not non-Buddhist destroyers of forest resources as [the term *chao khao* implies] but, rather, Buddhists who are concerned with conserving the forest. (572–73)

As Mountain People, ethnic minority highlanders have no claim to recognition because they are seen as un-Thai. Thailand's public sphere avails no agency or rights to ethnic minority peoples in terms of their own local concerns or priorities, and it was as the opposite of *chao khao* that this group of Karen was able to garner positive media attention.

Tree ordinations do not have a long history as Buddhist practice. Used primarily in the context of defending the rights of poor farmers to forest land, they draw on the hegemonic and sacred imagery of monks' ordina tions (Darlington 1998; Tannenbaum 2000). Tree ordinations were also part of the celebrations surrounding the fiftieth anniversary of the reign of the current king. The resonance of tree ordinations in contemporary Thai-land has to do with a recent redefinition of forests from uninviting wilder-ness (*pa thüan*) to pleasant nature (*thammachat*, "birthplace of the Dharma" [the Buddha's teachings], see below). The recent concern with nature is an element in a debate about the shape of national society, and it is aimed against the destructive greed associated with capitalism, military rulers, and so on. Journalists and various NGO movements and their sym-pathizers have taken a great liking to the image of Karen as people who have a tradition of living in harmony with the forest (Andrew Walker 2001; Pinkaew 2001). This image then provides some options for Karen peoples themselves, and Hayami shows some of the complexity of the issue by not-ing that while the protest employed Buddhist imagery, it drew on the idea of animist Karen ecological sensibilities (1997).

The notion of a shared ethnic agenda in the village masks the fact that many landless villagers were keen to gain wage work at the project. The local concern for preserving the watershed was particularly pronounced among villagers with wet-rice fields, while the public action assumed that Karen ecological sensibilities were rooted in their swidden farmer concern for the forest (Hayami 1997, 567–76). Hayami suggests that "Karen resis-tance to the pine forest project arose from an acute awareness of their pow-erless position" (576), as they had no legal claims to land in the area.

Protest and Shows of Strength

The politics of livelihood and rights is about identity in relation to state control. Attempts by Thailand's Mien to be acknowledged as post–*chao-khao* and to map themselves on the administrative terrain provide a back-drop to the political mobilization of the villages in Phachangnoi sub-district that had been given an evacuation order in 1992. In the aftermath of the amnesty granted to members of the Communist Party of Thailand in 1982, many of the previous forest areas where they had their bases were turned into nature reserves or national parks. This includes the southern portion of Phachangnoi *tambol*, and among the reasons for the eviction order to the five villages in this area was the expansion of a wildlife sanctu-ary (*khet anurak phan sat pa*) in light of a redefinition of the forest as 1A, making it completely exempt from utilization (cf. Pinkaew 2001).

There was no immediate action on the eviction order. Among the reasons for the standstill were the lack of a site for resettlement of the villagers. Also, there was a standoff between two ministries of the national government. The Royal Forestry Department was invested in the expansion of the nature reserve, while the Royal Highway Department was concerned to expand the road network in the region. Meanwhile, the people in the targeted villages grew increasingly uneasy about their predicament. Given the current "Master Plan on the Environment," which reinforces the position of the Forestry Department, the road to the villages cannot be paved, electricity lines cannot be led to the villages, and no structures in the villages can be built with permanent materials like cement. Villagers were frustrated with this, not only because it made transportation challenging in the rainy season, when the road was sometimes not passable for days at a time, but also because they were unable to have a decent school building because everything had to be made from wood.

In September 1999, while things were still unclear about their future status, villagers from this area proceeded to burn buildings at the Wildlife Sanctuary as a form of protest against the Forestry Department. The event contrasts sharply with the kinds of agency and identity expressed at sports competitions and village fairs, where allegiance to the nation and national forms of sociability are very prominent. It also comes across as genuinely collective action, in contrast to the celebratory displays that appear to play primarily to the interests of headmen, schoolteachers, and other local leaders. On the day of the burning, September 30, villagers sent out a letter "to whom it may concern":

> Village No. 2, Phachangnoi Subdistrict
> Pong District, Phayao Province, 56140
> 30 September, 1999

Dear:

The enclosed, an account of the village, one letter. Concerning Village No. 2, Phachangnoi Subdistrict. It was established in this place in the year 1901 [2443 Buddhist Era], and [the inhabitants] have Thai citizenship since 1915 [BE 2457]. It has had a village boundary since 1950 [BE 2493], and in the year 1979 [BE 2522] Road No. 1188 was built through village No. 2. It is a proper road and according to law. Later, on 1 January 1981 [BE 2524], a nature reserve was announced behind [the village] but the extent of the reserve was not explained to the villagers. The work of the Phachangnoi Wildlife Sanctuary has obstructed the lives and the progress of the villagers here. Among the examples are:

Fig. 8: On the road to Huai Kok village during summer of 2000. In the rainy season the road is sometimes impassable; this time the car nearly went off the edge.

1. The Royal Project [for Hilltribe Development] has encouraged the planting of flowers and fruit suited to cold climate. When the Armed Forces Development Command was to lay the access road, the Wildlife Sanctuary prohibited it from being built in village No. 2, and the Project was moved to village No. 7 of Phachangnoi Subdistrict [Sipsongphatthana Village].[3]

2. Public health issues in Village No. 2. The village is over 13 kilometers away from the health center in the village of Pangkha, and it is appropriate to build a health center in Village No. 2. There is budget for it, and sufficient wood for its construction. But the Wildlife Sanctuary has persistently prohibited its construction in Village No. 2, and instead it was built in Village No. 7 of Phachangnoi Subdistrict.

3. The school in Village No. 2, Huai Kok, is a branch of the school in Pangkha village, that is 14 kilometers away from Village No. 2. There is sufficient number of students for grades 1 through 6 to build an independent school, and Bangkok university students are ready to come and build it for us. But the Wildlife Sanctuary does not allow the construction of any permanent buildings that would

improve the village. Each and every day the students have to travel to Pangkha village, a distance of 14 kilometers which they must cover on foot in the rainy season when Road No. 1188 is not passable [by vehicles]. This is because since 1979 [BE 2522] it has been within the jurisdiction of the Wildlife Sanctuary that does not allow for any improvements.

Villagers have held meetings and written documents to ask for assistance and justice in the improvement of the village. Villagers have rented tractors to repair the road to the villages of Sanam Tai, Huai Ien, Sanam Nüa, and Nam Puk Nüa. All five are [classified as] Village No. 2. Each time [they have the road repaired], the villagers have been arrested by Wildlife Sanctuary staff. They will not allow any repairs. The Director of the Wildlife Sanctuary used a tractor to build a road into the Sanctuary. Why was it built? Everyone at the station ought to know. Everyone involved states that it was done for the officials who allowed him to take this action. Because of these matters, villagers' trust in these officials deteriorated significantly, and the forest within the jurisdiction of the Sanctuary is absolutely destroyed. Anyone with questions about this can pay a visit and we invite people to come and see it with their own eyes. When villagers want to transport their crops [to market] through the Sanctuary checkpoint, they have to pay. Sanctuary staff persistently fleeces the villagers.

Because of the matters related above, the people (*ratsadorn*) in Village No. 2 have been under severe pressure for full eighteen years. Consequently they burned the Wildlife Sanctuary station. The citizens of Village No. 2 acted reasonably given the circumstances, and there was no instigator behind this act. This took place because the needs of the citizens in Village No. 2 were clear. We had to find an outlet in the vicinity of Village No. 2. We chose place 1A within the reserve. We ask for assistance from various agencies. The people in Village No. 2 need progress, education, and healthcare. Thus we call on you to ask for justice from various authorities, and for land from the Wildlife Sanctuary.

> Respectfully,
> The People of Village No. 2
> Phachangnoi Subdistrict
> Pong District, Phayao Province

This letter revolves around the legitimacy of a violent act based on the claim to legitimate subjectivity. The people are Thai citizens, the village territory has been official for a long time, and a "proper road and according to law" was laid to the village in 1979. The establishment of the Wildlife Sanctuary has "obstructed the lives and progress" of the villagers, precluding the establishment of an agricultural development project and a health center, both of which were later built in another village too far away to be of any benefit to the agitated villagers. Furthermore, there is a need for a proper school building in the village, and the villagers have the materials and ready outside help, but this too is held back by the obstinacy of the Wildlife Sanctuary. On top of everything, villagers may not even keep up the (proper and legitimate) dirt and gravel road that connects their villages and links them to the outside. Assumed in the letter is the people's right to improvements in their lives and their right to education and health care. The Wildlife Sanctuary has not only denied people this right, but its director has acted in a confrontational and destructive way by arresting people for maintaining the road and destroying the crops they plant to improve their lot. The destruction of the Wildlife Sanctuary buildings was not an act of sabotage by evildoers, but the only course of action left to people, after eighteen years of pressure, as a way to reach outsiders who might help their cause.

For much of the month of October, following these events, there were meetings aimed at finding a solution to the problems, where villagers met with police and other authorities as well as with fellow-inhabitants in the *tambol* and with representatives from IMPECT. The course of events was documented by IMPECT staff for distribution in order to publicize the plight of the villagers and in the hopes of winning them outside support. But the Mien protest did not get any media coverage, and the villagers' attempt to publicize the illegal logging within the sanctuary came to nothing because of the journalists' fear of retribution.[4]

On September 26, 1999, people from the five villages that form Village No. 2 met in Huai Kok, and they all shared the opinion that they would burn offices of the Wildlife Sanctuary on the thirtieth of that month. From 6 o'clock that morning, people started to come together in Huai Kok. By 9 a.m., between four and five hundred villagers had assembled. They held a meeting to decide on the course of action, and by 9:30 they took off in single file, heading for the sanctuary's offices. At 10 o'clock they made phone calls to IMPECT and some other offices to inform them of the upcoming action. By 10:30 they had arrived at the Wildlife Sanctuary, and they told the officials to take away any valuables and leave the area. The officials at first rushed at the group, attacking six or seven people. There was some fighting, but the officials then fled. Some officials brought a gun and fired three shots, but in the end they fled too. Villagers then began to spread gasoline that they had brought and set some of it on fire, burning down one office building, two officials' residences, a guard booth, and an inspection booth. At 11:30 a.m. the people returned home in single file. They then called to inform the district office, the police, the provincial authorities, and the people in charge of services at the *tambol* level. The villagers waited in the Huai Kok school building for a response until 4 p.m., at which point the deputy director for district security arrived with his staff to inspect the fire and to find out more details from the villagers. They left again in two hours, and by 6:30 p.m. the villagers had all returned to their homes.

On October 2, the headman of Huai Kok village met with district officials for consultation regarding the aftermath of the burning and to set a meeting time to seek a solution in the matter. That same morning, the headmaster of the Pangkha school arrived for discussions with villagers regarding a possible solution, and late in the afternoon the *kamnan* and his committee arrived for a briefing and discussions; a meeting was set for the sixth. Before noon on the October 4, police and district authorities met with the Pangkha headmaster and the *kamnan,* and called a meeting for 4 o'clock that day, which was attended by representatives from the five villages. The police stated that they "had to proceed in the matter" (*tawng damnoern khadi*). Villagers stated their case about their problems and showed their letter asking for justice. The police said there were two possible solutions: either the guilty villagers surrender or the police arrest the six people they alleged had been in charge. The police stated that they had a list of their names already. Also, the perpetrators were to pay a fine of one million Baht ($25,000). The meeting ended without any resolution, and two days later the villagers met to complete a document asking various outsiders for help in achieving justice. They decided that all 995 of them would collectively surrender to the police at the Huai Kok schoolhouse on the ninth.

On October 9, villagers from all across the *tambol* came together at the field by the Huai Kok school, where locals showed their letter calling for justice, which they had sent to various state agents and non-governmental organizations. That afternoon, provincial authorities including the district official arrived, and they were given the villagers' letter. The officials talked with the villagers, discussing possible solutions. Another meeting for the village representatives was set for the fourteenth, and a date was set for a meeting with the provincial governor. During October 15 and 16, village representatives aired their problems at a meeting of the ethnic group. On the seventeenth, the director of the Forestry Department, provincial officials, police, and rangers—about one hundred people in seventeen vehicles—arrived in Huai Kok. Most of them were armed. They conferred with the headman and the Village Committee, asking that someone take responsibility and surrender.

The headman asked for a few days to respond to that request. Later that day, staff from IMPECT arrived in the village and held a meeting, and then another meeting was set for the twenty-first. They met on that day, and set another meeting for the following day when the headman would respond to the Forestry Department request. On the morning of the twenty-second, some officials met with the villagers, and in the early afternoon the villagers held a ritual to ensure harmony among those who had joined hands and minds in the confrontation that expressed the need for justice. Villagers then conferred with IMPECT and wrote a letter to the police stating that no one would surrender. They then set another meeting for the twenty-fourth. On that day they met with a committee from IMPECT and with Mr. Nopphawan (former advisor to the government of PM Chaowalit Yongchaiyut), who came with a police committee to look for a potential solution. He was presented with the letter, which he was going to share with the human rights committee of the national parliament, and he promised to find a solution before the end of the month. Villagers called a meeting for the following day.

The Meeting with the Authorities

Village Headman[5]: He welcomed people, briefed them on the issues, and emphasized how the Wildlife Sanctuary had impeded progress in the area. A letter had been sent to state offices at the district and provincial level, to members of parliament, and to the Prime Minister, but there had been no response at any level. He also talked about a road into the Wildlife Sanctuary, used for illegal logging by capitalists. Then he listed villagers' demands, and the first was that the Wildlife Sanctuary be moved away. Another was that the Wildlife Sanctuary not preclude development in the area. If the villagers cannot improve their lot where they are, then find another area for them outside the influence of the Wildlife Sanctuary. The last was that villagers meet with relevant state officials about illegal logging. Then the floor was opened for discussion.

Villager 1: He gave dates, the villages go back to 1901, they were officially recognized in 1951, but the declaration of a nature reserve only dates to 1981, and there were no buildings at the reserve until 1985.

Villager 2: he spoke of oppression by the Wildlife Sanctuary, that they often demand road tax of the villagers. This taxation is even more expressed when villagers take their crops to sell in town. Villagers suffered this oppression until 1995, and then matters became worse as the Wildlife Sanctuary would close the road. The road deteriorated, children had to walk to school in Pangkha, and there were several cases when people had to be taken to hospital and the road was not passable. People have lost their lives because they could not be taken to hospital. This the police also know.

Representative from Sanam Tai Village: he began with the difficulties of school-age children. Local children experience only suffering, and if they had a choice they would not want to be born in the area. Villagers who own cars have to pay taxes and registration, but they can barely use the bad road. Their crops get damaged on the way to market, so they get a very low price. The Wildlife Sanctuary Director oppresses them. He demands drugs [*ya ba,* methamphetamines] of them, which they don't have. He demands money, which villagers have to hand over. Villagers have had to serve the Wildlife Sanctuary officials liquor and food many times. The Director arrived to run a wildlife sanctuary, but he has mostly brought frustrations to the villagers. Since the Director arrived, all the very large trees in the area have been felled. If the Director stays on, it will be the death of the villagers, the forest, and the wild animals in the area. Ultimately, villagers could not take any more of this oppression. Thus they came together and burned the Wildlife Sanctuary's buildings, for the improvement of their lives in the future.

Village Headman: Previously the forest was very rich in trees and wildlife, and there had been no need to get someone specifically appointed to protect it. Then when the Sanctuary was established, officials arrived and they allowed capitalists in the region to come and cut forest to the point that very little is left. How can they declare this a wildlife sanctuary? They should have given more power to the villagers, who have lived here for much longer and have protected the forest, instead of overly limiting villagers' power, as has been the case.

A Women's Representative: Wildlife Sanctuary staff had stolen pigs from villagers. We are allowed to vote, but nothing for our benefit ever comes out of elections. In this situation it would be better for us to send the animals to vote for representatives in the parliament.

A Village Headman: The theft of domestic animals, pigs, and horses has not only occurred but is an ongoing problem.

Representative from Sanam Nüa Village: The village has 20,000 *rai* (3,200 hectares, or 8,000 acres) of land suited for making irrigated fields, but the Wildlife Sanctuary Director has not allowed plowing of the area. It is impossible to imagine how the next generation is to make a living without some expansion of current land holdings. The children must walk in all weather and must supply rice when they go to school in Pangphrik or Pangkha.

The Headman of Huai Kok: He seconded this view of children's difficulties. He added that he has repeatedly asked for a vehicle to repair the road.

A vehicle was sent to plough land where the Sanctuary offices were built, but it was impossible to get a permit to have this vehicle plough villagers' land, and thus people have only meager harvests. The suffering of sick and injured people has been accentuated by the road situation, and some have died on the road. Villagers' various sufferings brought them to a point of explosion. Therefore they joined together and burned the Sanctuary offices. If they hadn't burned the buildings they would have simply had to continue suffering. Then to be alive or dead would have been about the same. Villagers could not withstand any more oppression. They did what had to be done. There was no instigator. There was no outside influence. What took place arose from the collective feeling of the villagers, who took action for their collective benefit. He reiterated his points; there was no instigator behind the burning, no one was acting in the villagers' shadow. The villagers acted completely in unison. Acting together, they take collective responsibility for this action that was for the benefit of future generations in the village.

Representative for the Housewives Association of Nam Puk Nüa: She complained about their suffering from the hands of Sanctuary officials, whom they must serve liquor and food and pay them road tax. They also will not allow villagers to take some of their crops to market, but which the officials can freely take to sell. It is very hard to raise children with this limited harvest. Reporters came on October 6, but they dared not go to where illegal logging had taken place because they feared the power of those behind the logging. But there are many who can testify and show where this took place. The road situation for Nam Puk Nüa is a major source of villagers' anger. Villagers laid the path entirely on their own, and they themselves have kept it up. Many development projects have been concerned to assist the village, but they have all been driven away [by the sanctuary]. Answering questions from the floor, she said that taking children to and from school every Monday and Friday on the bad road has resulted in several injuries. She added that they have photos showing cut trees and sawed wood within the Wildlife Sanctuary. If people do not believe her, she can show them. People were unable to put up with any more suffering, and thus had to go and burn the Sanctuary buildings. They had with them about a gallon of gasoline. Sanctuary staff has killed animals to eat within the Sanctuary. If a villager were to do that, the animal and the gun would be confiscated. We are worried and do not want to go to jail, but we had to do this, we could not withstand any more of the pressure. If the Sanctuary staff shows us understanding, we will reciprocate that and will cooperate with them concerning development (*kan phatthana*). What has gone on before has all been contrary to the emphasis on development.

The Director of the Welfare Department for Phayao Province: He introduced himself, Mr. Surakit. This is his first time in the village and he is
from far away. He understands that there has been real anger. He has read
reports stating that the problem in the area is of long standing. He has sym-
pathy and understanding and promises his full assistance. Before he came
he met with the Provincial Governor and received directives for solving the
problem. Development of various kinds in the locality is an absolute necessity. Villagers predate the Sanctuary, and have their customary ways with
many things. Of the three demands, I can only address villagers' livelihood,
that it must not take place within the Sanctuary. Our cooperation is very
important. The Governor is himself going to come here in about two weeks
to solve the problem and asks that people keep calm in the meantime. The
Hilltribe Welfare Center is pleased to be involved in solving this matter. I
ask for representatives to meet with the Governor at the future date. I believe that the Governor will solve your problem with sincerity. If you have
future problems, the whole Welfare Center will help you solve them.

Mr. Somnuk: Introduced himself. He learned of the problem a week ago
but now has the full information from the villagers. He is disappointed that
other state officials could not come, particularly District authorities and a
representative for the Forestry Department. It is good to hear from the
Welfare Department Director that the Provincial Governor will come, that
will surely contribute to a solution and to development in the area in the
future. Mr. Somnuk was going to share the villagers' document with many
concerned and asked they also send it to the District Office and the Provincial Governor. The document is important for gaining some power and for
finding a solution to the problem.

The village headman then thanked everyone who had come and adjourned the meeting. Lunch was served at 1:30 p.m., but at 2 p.m. the Assistant Provincial Governor and the District Governor arrived with some
District staff. This was unexpected, and the villagers were called back to a
new meeting at 2:30. The headman opened the meeting and laid out the villagers' objectives and what had led them to burn the Sanctuary's buildings.
He then opened the floor to others. When the first person spoke, the District Governor stopped the proceedings to ask who the speaker was and
what official position he held in the village. When it was clear that this was
an ordinary villager who held no official position, the Governor did not
allow him to speak further and asked the Village Committee and the Village
Development and Defense Organization to make a list of all those attending the meeting.

Khe Wanasangopsuk [member of the village committee]: He gave some
dates concerning the history of the village since it split from Suan Ya Luang

village [the settlement where Phaya Khiri and his followers were first allowed to grow opium] in 1901 and then about the Wildlife Sanctuary that has both oppressed people and obstructed development since it was established but particularly as of 1995 when a national birdlovers' association sent the Forestry Department a letter about the destructive impact of roads on wildlife sanctuaries, petitioning that the road from Pangphrik to Huai Kok must not be given a hard surface. At that time, the Highway Department had already covered the road to Pangphrik. The Forestry Department halted further roadwork, and further obstruction has followed these events.

Kasem Kraiklakhiri [Sanam Tai village representative]: Villagers have suffered in many ways, and the Sanctuary Director halted the road construction. The Sanctuary Director has prevented the construction, expansion, and improvement on the school, a health station, electricity, and a multi-purpose building. The forest has been nearly depleted since the director arrived. Villagers had long taken care of the forest. We have places for making a living and places we collectively protect. The Sanctuary Director had a road built to make it more convenient for capitalists to cut the forest that "belongs to the people" (*khong prachachon*). When villagers have cut a tree to use in house construction they have been arrested. The Sanctuary has confiscated wood meant for partition walls. If we make a petition, the Sanctuary will keep a constant watch over construction, repeatedly demanding liquor, money, and food from villagers. All of this has plagued us for over eighteen years already.

Another village representative then spoke, listing many of their grievances. Then villagers' demands were declared; that the Sanctuary be moved away from Village No. 2; if it is not moved then at least it shall not obstruct development; that Sanctuary areas be clearly set apart from where villagers make a living; and that something be done about Sanctuary staff destroying the forest. Then a Huai Kok Housewives' Group representative, Moei Wanajaroenphrai, listed many of the villagers' grievances and frustrations and stated that villagers must have a response to their requests.

Assistant Governor Mr. Phot Uthana: Today the Governor has a meeting with a Member of Parliament, so he sent me for him, but he is well informed about the issues. The burning would not have taken place if both sides had shown understanding. According to law, no construction can take place in forests classified as 1A, but the village of Huai Kok was built prior to the Sanctuary. Highway 1188 was built in 1979. It was not against the law, but more cannot be allowed. The road builders had misunderstood matters [when they laid the hard surface road to Pangphrik]. Villagers should contact District and Province authorities [to learn that more roadwork cannot take place] and cooperate toward a solution. About the Royal

Project being unable to bring development to here, they dare not go against the Forestry Department. Villagers must call a meeting and find a solution. Other development projects are similar. About bad Forestry officials, inform the District and the Province. If the officials are really bad then they will be removed. About villagers' demands: The first one is difficult because it concerns the law. On each of the remaining three he gave an identical response, the District will discuss possibilities for a solution. In the future, the Province shall keep a close watch on the Sanctuary Director. He is a special case, and villagers please do not do anything further that goes against the law.

Pong District Official: This is only his second time in the area. About identity cards, more cannot be issued this year. Exception is made regarding school-age children, and many have been issued for children going to the school in Pangkha. We will work on the issues that have angered villagers. Villagers, in the future, please think before you act.

Assistant Governor [continuing]: Electricity will surely come, because it can certainly be brought to the area. There have been misunderstandings. People must file for a permit and then wait their turn. I ask the village officials to please help in guarding the forest. Any outsider cutting trees will be dealt with. This also holds for any villager cutting trees. People must live together peacefully in the future. A village representative asked him about the situation of the police proceedings. The Assistant Governor said that the Province could not interfere with police proceedings. But a solution will be found. Please do not work up any more anger. In the future, everything will improve. The headman then thanked everyone attending and adjourned the meeting.

Contestations

As of December 2002, when I made inquiries via e-mail, nothing further had happened in the matter. No arrests had been made, and no fines had been imposed on the villagers. The sanctuary and its director were still in place, and the situation of the villagers and the road had not changed. But neither had there been any statement made regarding the police proceedings, and without a declaration on that matter villagers were wary of putting much trust in what officials said at the meetings. The officials never made any statement regarding the police case beyond saying that they could not interfere in police matters. On a brief visit to Huai Kok in March 2005 I learned that the sanctuary had had a new director for some months. The director was viewed as quite reasonable. But the only change in the matter is that villagers in this *tambol* have been deprived of their land-use papers. For a few years their livelihood has been illegal, and the whole population could be evicted in the name of watershed protection.

The Mien protest can be seen as informed by the villagers' sense of their marginalization, much like the Karen tree ordination described by Hayami (1997). The Mien protest did not employ any Buddhist imagery, unlike the Karen case, but it was still an explicit declaration of allegiance to the nation, modernization, and the preservation of nature. From that perspective, it is as much a dissociation from *chao khao* imagery as was the Karen presentation of themselves in their protest. The Mien petitions depict villagers as agitated farmers, people who desire development, education, and health care and who are held back by an overbearing government official. The needs that the Mien expressed were identical to the agendas of the modernizing state, which through national integration and military force had undermined uplanders' autonomy during the 1960s and 1970s. Furthermore, the villagers expressed concern for the forest and its animals by alleging various abuses by reserve staff who killed animals and facilitated illegal logging. The villagers' call for justice against abuses by reserve staff belongs squarely within the national democracy rhetoric of the 1990s, while the villagers also stated that, as democracy had not served any of their interests, they might as well send their domestic animals to the polls. The humor of that statement, which appears to have gone unnoticed by the authorities, is that the supposed democracy of the country was no democracy at all.

The course of events displays a keen sense of the modern political landscape, with people repeatedly convening for meetings before and after the burning, making cell phone calls to inform sympathetic agencies right before the events, and sending their statement to NGOs and to various levels of the state. It is very likely that in the absence of such connections, people would simply have been arrested and fined, possibly even evacuated. Had this happened prior to 1982, a large-scale military action would undoubtedly have ensued, such as in the case of retaliation for police abuse in 1968 that became known as the Red Meo Revolt. But evictions of upland minority peoples still take place, and the peculiarity of the situation in Phachangnoi must also have played a part in preventing state violence against the villagers. This is one of the very few ethnic minority areas in Thailand where the *tambol* headman is an upland ethnic minority person, and as a result most people in the area have been able to get citizenship papers. The Huai Kok villagers have kinship and other relations with the *kamnan* and headmaster of Pangkha, and these connections undoubtedly served them well. And as was repeatedly brought up at the meetings, the villagers have a long history in the area, and their dismal road was initially built quite properly and according to law. Their protest, too, was proper—it was the collective action of all the villagers, and there was no instigator or outside agitator. Going to and from the burning of the sanctuary buildings, the villagers walked in single file; this was no mob but an orderly event. The IMPECT documentation emphasized that the villagers walked in single file. The point has at least two references. One is the emphasis on orderliness that characterizes public ceremonies, and the other is the "mob" discourse that was prominent in the discrediting of the street protests in Bangkok during May 1992 (see Callahan 1998, 35–84) and resurfaced in the official dismissal of the Assembly of the Poor in 1997 and more recently (Baker 2000, 25; Missingham 2003, 201–3).

The display of democratic orderliness at meetings; the connections to local authorities and to IMPECT; the desire for development, education, health care, and a decent road; and the complaints about corrupt officials—and possibly also the collective protest—showed the Mien villagers to be model citizens. All their demands were fully legitimate in the contemporary political climate. As the director of the provincial Welfare Department stated, development in rural areas was an absolute necessity. But like other officials, he insisted that agency lie with the state. Villagers were to trust the authorities to solve their problems, and they should rely on government officials. The agency of the state was most pronounced in the visit of October 17, when authorities, police, and rangers, in an impressive and intimidating convoy of one hundred people in seventeen vehicles, demanded that someone take responsibility and surrender. This visit repeated the police demand of October 4 for the surrender of the instigators. Only the state should act. A further expression of the emphasis on the state's exclusive agency came from the district governor, who declared that only the state could speak when he silenced an "ordinary villager" and limited the proceedings to those with official position.

The emphasis on the state's agency and power is evident in how the sanctuary officials conducted themselves, in everything from collecting road tax and (sometimes) closing the road to the demands for liquor, food, money, and drugs and their disregard for the stated purpose of the Wildlife Sanctuary. What sanctuary officials did as part of their duties seems limited to placing themselves above the villagers. This concern to teach villagers their lowly place, so to speak, is evident from many of the official comments at the meetings with villagers regarding the primacy of the law, the province's inability to influence how the police conducted their work, and the police statement that they "must proceed in the matter."

In important ways, the protest is all about agency. The protest consolidated agency and simultaneously created its subject, the people of Village No. 2. The focus on striking at the sanctuary unified the villagers in ways that are not evident in other collective expressions, where many people have been mobilized for projects that serve an emerging elite in local affairs. Underlying the protest and its unifying force is not an ethnic subject (the Mien) but rather a frustrated national subject (the Thai). It is as rural nationals desiring the basics of modern life in a democratic society that the villagers expressed their frustrations, as much in the violence of the burning as in the orderliness of their meetings and petitions and in the collectivity of their responsibility for the act. The unified subject of action comes with its own historicity, the founding of the village, the date of the official road 1188, and the arrival of the Wildlife Sanctuary and how it has precluded development and basic services.

While the state is far from a unified subject, as can be seen in the tensions between the Highway Department and the Forestry Department, the independence of the police from provincial authorities, and other factors, it emerges through the confrontation as unified in the quest to situate farmers exclusively as docile recipients of its guidance and initiative, particularly its law. The unrest would have not taken place if villagers and Wildlife Sanctuary officials had shown each other understanding, and this message was given only to the villagers with the implication that they were the problem. No action was taken against the sanctuary's staff. As villagers were told: "A solution will be found [by the Governor]. Please do not work up any more anger. In the future, everything will improve."

The state creates itself as the guardian of order, and this order resides in a particular hierarchical chain of command, from which agency and identity are suspended. The protest by villagers against the Wildlife Sanctuary in Phachangnoi *tambol* posed a fundamental challenge to the state because it claimed not only rightful grievances (eighteen years of oppression by sanctuary officials who furthermore were not guarding the forest or the animals it contained) by proper subjects (Thai citizens in a registered village by a lawful road) but because it appropriated agency; villagers used violence in order to press for changes that would improve their position toward that of the ideal modern village (access to markets, health care, and a local school). The response to this action crystallized the state as the only legitimate source of temporality and agency—villagers were to wait for the governor to fix the matter—at the same time as "the state" shut up anyone who was not its manifestation, such as ordinary villagers who held no official position. The state also showed itself as the legitimate agent of violence in the intimidating visit in which the authorities threatened to arrest the supposed perpetrators of the crime.

The case is also instructive about the relationship between scale and complexity. On the most general level, the issue concerns a confrontation between villagers and the state. But the lack of a solution in the case is instructive. The protesting villagers had the support of the *kamnan* and the headmaster of the Pangkha school—agents of the state and its civilizing mission—and they are Thai citizens. Had this taken place during the 1970s or 1980s, the confrontation would most likely have been labeled a communist revolt and been "solved" by shooting or bombing the villagers and burning down the villages. Neither the state nor highland ethnic minorities during the 1990s are identical to their respective subject positions a few decades earlier; it is only in the most abstract terms that the terms "hegemony" and "resistance" capture the interactions of villagers and the state's agents (cf. Ortner 1995). And in the 1990s, the Highway Department and the Forestry Department were at odds about how to proceed within this *tambol.* What constitutes the state is equally these rival departments, provincial authorities, military and police units, as well as its local embodiments in the *kamnan* and headmaster. To define communities as opposed to or as fundamentally distinct from the state would require a dismissal of the connections that constitute contemporary villages and the imagery that animates their self-presentation at festivals and their attempts to bargain for recognition and benefits.

Ever since upland peoples came about as a category, their identity and political status has had regional dimensions and involved lowland states. The worlds of the Mien and the other upland peoples have never been merely local in the sense of being cut off from the regional dynamics of political economy and history. Recent events such as the protest and the prominence of sports competitions are creative engagements with the political landscape of classification that can potentially alter the character of state control and the categorizations of people and politics that animate social life and thus lend shape to the region. These efforts have been motivated attempts to dissociate contemporary uplanders from the Thai image of *chao khao.* This notion has not only been about the official marginalization of certain ethnic minority populations, it has equally been about the definition of the nation and that of the state's mission, a larger landscape of inequality and the threat of military violence that has repeatedly been anchored to particular renderings of history. The term *chao khao* engenders a conflation of national time and space that leaves ethnic minority highland peoples with no claim to legitimate identity in Thailand. This is what the protesting farmers' rhetoric was aimed against when they repeatedly insisted on the dates of their settlement and official recognition. The protest concerned the right to livelihood and the problem of an overbearing government official. At a deeper level, it also concerned the alignment of a group of people with the coordinates of time and space that rendered them legitimate actors on the national terrain. That is, the event and its rhetoric were simultaneously about identity and rights and the landscape of classification on which they came into agency and being—it created a subject (the citizens in Village No. 2 of Phachangnoi *tambol*) as it declared the people's action both legitimate and necessary in relation to the state.

Conclusions: The Work of Classification

About 1,000 residents yesterday threatened to turn a road in Phon Sai district into a rice farm after it was left in disrepair for 28 years. The 4.5 kilometer stretch of the Hong Sang-Chado road, beginning at kilometer marker 28 in Nong Thum village, serves tambons Sam Kha, Yang Kham, and Tha Hat Yao. The residents yesterday brought ploughing machines, hoes, and rice shoots which they planted in craters in the road. The road has not been repaired despite complaints to the provincial authority and even cabinet members, said resident Narong Thonsi. The protest was an attempt to bring their grievance to the attention of the authorities, he said.

—*The Nation*, August 30, 2003

Having waited almost thirty years for the government's highway department to improve their road, farmers in Roi-Et Province in northeast Thailand (Isan) pulled the rug out from under the definition of a road by turning it into a rice field, wielding humor via the national media in an attempt to embarrass the authorities and thus regain their road in good shape. By planting rice, the farmers suggested that the road was not a road, which is comparable with surrealist painter René Magritte's famous painting of a pipe that was not a pipe. As a public performance through the national media, the event made a mockery of the Royal Highway Department for letting the road disintegrate for decades. In that respect, the protest-performance has some resemblance to the "emperor's new clothes" story in revealing the nakedness of the authorities. This was not protest for art's sake or for the sake of a good story, though the performative aspect is important; it was a call for improvement.

Like the manifestations of the Mien in the 1990s, those of the state are partial expressions of larger potential collectivities and structures that are crystallized in and through particular projects. What lends shape to state control, and to the state as such, is the attempt to monopolize agency and to control the parameters of how people engage with history and identity. Politics concerns classification, of people as much as of forests and roads, for instance. Identity and rights rest on such classifications. As people engage with classifications of who they are through compliance, confrontation, or subversion, they contribute to redefining the social landscape and the shape of history. In Thailand, there has been a major change in the classification of forests from an uncivilized territory of savages, wild animals, and dangerous spirits, to that of nature, a sacred realm and a national treasure, guarded by the state's agents, as in the wildlife sanctuary in Phachangnoi *tambol.* This recent process of re-signification in Thailand is comparable to the United States, where nature became the opposite of "society" and was placed under state control as national parks (Olwig 1995; Stevens 1997).

Between the two Thai formulations of forests, *pa thüan* and *thammachat,* there was a period of logging that lasted until 1988, when logging was declared illegal. While the change is significant, it also obscures a fundamental continuity. The origins of the Yao and Lawa suggest that the making of the forest and forest people as socially relevant categories was entangled with state control from the very beginning. Similar dynamics are evident in the recent conversion of forests into nature reserves. The state's classification of social and natural environments rests on the consolidation of society in relation to its opposite—barbarians in the former case, communists in the latter. By the 1960s, mountain people's difference from Thai ideals of society and livelihood was then re-signified as insubordination, one made equivalent to the communist insurgency. These entanglements of identity with realms of state control show continuity in the conflation of domains that are often viewed as distinct; culture, politics, agriculture, nature, and religion. These supposedly separate domains draw their distinctions from categorical divisions that are reinforced through separate branches of state control and that inform the constitution of identity, rights, and power relations.

The notion of *pa thüan,* "forested wilderness," once indexed the uncivilized Lawa in contrast to the subjects of Buddhist kingdoms. In the early twentieth century, the term was recast in light of the evolutionary ranking of peoples to index primitiveness, as national identity was forged in relation to modernity and civilization. Phi Tong Lüang were "the wildest (*pa thüan thi sut*) of all races (*manut-chat*)" (see chapter 2). According to Davis, among the lowland peoples of Nan Province, "contraband articles such as bootleg whiskey and unregistered firearms are called 'things of the forested wilderness' (*khaung paa khaung theuan*). Undisciplined and immoral people are designated in the same fashion. To 'go to the forest' (*pai paa*) means, in addition to its literal sense, to defecate or enter a cemetery. The forest is the domain of aboriginals, wild animals, and malevolent spirits" (1984, 81). Davis further describes how notions of the beauty of settlements are determined by their place in a hierarchy (81–85), but the emphasis on worldview tends to obfuscate how state control prefigures this ranking and bifurcation.

Moonshine and unlicensed guns are of the 'forested wilderness' because they are beyond state control. State control creates the idea of this "wildness," because in the absence of a national control, on alcohol and firearms, including registration and taxation, there is nothing illicit about home-distilled alcohol or a household weapon. This is somewhat analogous to the ideas of isolation and backwardness that are apparent in the disparaging remarks about the filth and self-sufficiency that characterized the Mien and other highland settlements in early twentieth-century Siam. To stand outside the realms of regulation and taxation is to be defective or illicit. The notion of piracy rests on the same premise.

The idea of the forested wilderness is no longer diacritical for the classification of mountain peoples relative to Thai society. To some extent, it has been replaced with the image of nature as a sacred realm (*thammachat*). Recent notions of mountain peoples imply that image as they cast them as a threat to national resources such as forests and watersheds. Much of the identity work of highland ethnic minority people in recent decades has concerned their dissociation from these Thai images of destructive outsiders. In the Thai public sphere, allegiance to the nation most often takes the form of explicit reverence for the markers of nationhood: the monarchy, the Buddhist religion, and the Thai flag. Love for the nation is an important criterion for marking insider status. Love for the monarchy is simultaneously an expression of the love for nation. A slogan that was common on billboards during the 1990s declared, "Love the king, be concerned for future generations, together [we will] fend off drugs" (*rak nai luang, huang luk lan, ruam kan tan ya sep tit*). One such billboard stood at the intersection next to the schoolgrounds where the Mien came together for their ethnic festival in 2001. While this is a rather banal statement, it is of the kind that has informed various negative constructions of highland people and others as un-Thai, which to some extent is an invitation to violence against groups categorized in this fashion. The slogan leaves both the in-group and the out-group unspecified, but both are created in relation to the diacritical love of the monarchy.

Fig. 9: Billboard in the village of Pang Khwai: "Love the King, be concerned for future generations, together we will fend off drugs."

The pillar of Thailand's national identity, nation-religion-king, produces history in that it offers a genealogy of Thai Buddhist rulers whose virtue and power have protected the Thai people and constituted society. This foundation myth assumes that society is under threat from un-Thai forces. The idea of hill tribes was consolidated as one such external threat.[1] The nation-religion-king model of history and identity is very much of the twentieth century, and it tends to erase the possibility of divergent histories as it produces historical continuity. Outside the framework of nationalist history, the position of the Thai monarchy as a constituting element of national identity is problematic. A coup in 1932 ended the absolute monarchy in favor of a parliamentary system, and the king was only reinstalled as an important component of public life in the late 1950s—at a time when *chao khao* were taking shape as another aspect of what defined Thai-ness.[2]

This related consolidation of the top and bottom of society is important not only for an understanding of the construction of particular social visions and categories in contemporary Thailand. It also suggests regulatory continuities with premodern states, in which leaders established their prominence by drawing the parameters of social life, defining identity and difference as they consolidated particular boundaries. Such projects set society and history in motion through embodied practices that repeatedly dissolved the boundaries of the mythical and the mundane. "Mountain people" are both a new construction and an old one, as are "Thailand" and "the monarchy." In 2003, the Thai government dissolved the Tribal Research Institute. The Tribal Museum stays, and it now has a website that is run with the support of the Tourism Authority of Thailand. The relevance of mountain peoples to Thailand's national image within the country may fade. As it is, matters concerning ethnic minority highlanders have been moved squarely within the Provincial Hill Tribe Welfare and Development offices. That is, they have been demoted from a national to a provincial concern. At the same time, the hill tribe image has become more important to the fashioning of Thailand as a destination for international tourism.

By situating the Mien in region and history, this book has attempted to identify the shifting social landscapes in which the Mien people have come into particular kinds of agency and being, paying some attention to the repeated inequalities in the representations of Mien-ness. This has also been an attempt to recast history away from taking ethnic groups and bounded national territories for granted and toward some understanding of the social contexts in which states and highlander identities were forged and reproduced, dynamics that set particular histories in motion. The effort is not intended to settle the historical landscape but rather to open it up for new ways of doing ethnography with old material. Mien forms of subjectivity have always assumed larger settings, from the origins of chiefs and their subordinate settlements on the southern fringes of the Chinese empire through the strongman-dominated settings of tributary states to household prominence once such tributary links were erased. That last setting is the context of a recent nostalgia for the days when children stayed at home and then married to set up their own farming household. It expresses a configuration of being and agency that, in some areas at least, was the prerogative of better-off households. There was a time when such household autonomy was novel. Tsan Khwoen's leadership had many novel attributes, ones that his sons were not able to replicate because the context for Mien social life had changed in important ways by the time they engaged with the terms and boundaries of social action.

In their recent attempts to consolidate eco-wisdom, which may gain them rights to land, some Mien people are attempting creative ways to retain some control over their own lives in a national setting in which some of the most positive statements about them suggest that they are not disorderly or dangerous. The Mien woman's suggestion of sending the pigs to vote for them in the national elections is a playful denial of the state's premises of control and well-being. It flirts with the possibility of redrawing the boundaries of rights, power, and acceptable social action. This corresponds to the related action against the wildlife sanctuary that combined an orderly, single-file march with the destruction of official buildings and formal petitions, the establishment in letters and at meetings of village history on national terrain, and the reiteration of farmers' primary identity as citizens and thus as legitimate players on the landscape of development.

This last image of farmers, whose agriculture and aspirations are in line with the modernizing nation-state, shows how relations of unequal power prefigure Mien self-fashionings. Farmers tend to have no means of setting the terms of their relations with state power. Such inequality has been one of the recurring features of this region in history; as tributary state power ranked and classified people and settlements, it set the terms in which mountain peoples came into being as a recognizable category in relation to forests as society's outside. The upland-lowland divide was a product of history at the same time that it was productive of history and identity. A focus on this structure allows for and requires a regional perspective, within which the Yao and Mien can be viewed as simultaneously an outcome and among the constitutive elements of the upland-lowland divide. Mien people engaged with spirits and lowland rulers in terms of contracts that could be revoked, and such relations informed the identities and structural poses that people assumed—as householders, chiefs, and the like.

If such contracts were sustained over long periods of time, they could inform assertions about history and identity. Reading history in terms of an ethnic label erases the complexity and contingency of structural poses within the Mien category. Ethnic histories are products of the modern era of nation-states, in which claims to rights and recognition rest in part on state-classified identities and the control of history. As mountain people, the Mien have no political rights in contemporary Thailand, which is why they emphasized their national credentials as they tried to improve their lot in the recent confrontation with the wildlife sanctuary. Aspects of this situation suggest some historical continuity, in that the origins and reproduction of the Yao category concerned claims to rights and recognition in the era of tributary states. This continuity is a product of the state's command over identity and political position, and it compromises the often-asserted fundamental difference of the nation-state from previous state formations (cf. Anderson 1991). The historical expectation that a fundamental break separates tradition from modernity is itself a product of modernity's worldview (cf. Knauft 2002, 9–10; Hayami 2003, 237–39). Characterizing the relations of past to present as either a linear progression (the nationalist perspective) or as a fundamental break (the modernist perspective) is contingent on cosmographic narratives that often relate to frameworks for defining identity, rights, and the subjects of history (Duara 1995; Greenhouse 1996).

By taking a regional and historical approach, this book has attempted to make explicit certain cosmographic narratives that have structured social life and identities in the region, particularly those that have contributed to defining the position of mountain peoples. The examination of Mien social formations is an attempt to highlight this historicity and contingency of patterns that previous ethnography defined as the structure of an ethnic group. In this perspective, the notion of a traditional culture or social structure emerges as a product of specific encounters among Mien people, ethnographers, and particular forms of state control. The resonance of this notion of tradition was dependent on a given set of expectations that assumed the binary relationship of tradition and modernity. This relationship was reinforced by the ideology of the modernizing state, and it has become one of the parameters of the social landscape within which Thailand's Mien situate themselves, variously highlighting their modernity or tradition or creatively combining the two, as in the recent ethnic festival. The character of the recent protest against the wildlife sanctuary was also informed by this binary relationship—the farmers made no reference to their ethnic identity, as it would have discredited them as *chao khao*.

The entanglements of identity with rights and political position emerge as one of the persistent features of the social landscape, strongly linked to the state's ability to inscribe its classifications into social life. This feature of state control is a main factor in the apparent continuity of ethnic groups, as ethnic identities have served as the terms of engagement with the state. While states have set the terms for claims about rights and recognition, the resulting social life cannot be reduced to the state's designs. The varied effects of state control are deeply entwined with the classifications that inform notions of society and nature, ones that have long served as reference points for articulations of identity and practices of livelihood. Mien politics has not simply been about rights and resources such as citizenship and access to land. It has equally been about the work of classification, on which rest the articulations of politics that concern modernity, democracy, livelihood, citizenship, and the like.

The Mien case is rather telling about the ongoing work of defining history and region, and it is productive for an understanding of the state. Making a case about the Mien does not ultimately rest on there being a particular set of features that one may define as Mien-ness. The term *Mien* is an anchor for writing ethnography as much as it has been a framework for livelihood and cultural practice. It offers a perspective on the relationships among mountain peoples, ethnography, and state control that have lent shape to a region. That is, the Mien offer a perspective on the varied, non-linear dynamics of history and identity in a context that is simultaneously global, national, and local.

There is nothing merely local about the Mien people, and their words can be wielded to put tribal ethnography in perspective. The point of suggesting that the pigs should be sent to vote in the next elections is a critique of the authorities and a subversion of their rhetoric of democratic rule. It also suggests a twist on the ethnographic prominence of pigs in ritual and social life among so-called tribal peoples. Focusing on "pigs for the ancestors" (Rappaport 1968; cf. Miles 1974) is likely to convey a closed world of society, ecology, and ritual; it is also to suggest that the real Mien, in this case, stand outside history and regional dynamics. The ecology of "pigs for the polling booths" better captures their situation of democratic participation in the modern nation-state as well as their despair in the context of the state's theatrics of public representation.[3]

Public statements that suggest this is not a road, a wildlife sanctuary, or a democracy are attempts to align the political landscape in favor of particular actors. They match Sumit Mandal's description of activist art in Indonesia and Malaysia as "aesthetically multidimensional and complex, thereby giving creative protests the capacity to be illuminating, instructive, memorable as well as sharply critical. Arts activism is thus positioned to engage society and politics as a whole, besides the state" (2003, 204). The Mien protest and the suggestion of deploying the pigs to mock the electoral process are both funny and memorable, and the Mien woman's send-up of the seriousness of the state's democratic ritual deserves the same social and ethnographic recognition as the more successful projects of defining Mien through meetings, sports, and cultural performances.

The Diacritics of Mountain People's Identity

In the old days, a massive flood swept across the earth, and the only people who were not drowned were a brother and sister who hung on to a gourd. When the flood ceded, they went around looking for spouses but found no one. They met a turtle that advised them to marry, since they were the only two people left in the world. The siblings were very upset with this advice, smashed the shell of the turtle, and then proceeded to build their separate huts, plant separate trees, and to each make their own fire. But the smoke from the two fires joined in the air above them, and then the branches of the two trees intertwined. The brother and sister came to see that the turtle had spoken the truth. Going back to look for the turtle to apologize for their action, they found out that this had been a divinity taking the guise of a turtle. This divinity told them to get married, which they did. Later, the woman became pregnant. She gave birth, but to a melon rather than a human offspring. The spirit advised the woman to take the melon and cut it up, to scatter the seeds in the hills and the meat in the lowlands. The woman passed the advice to her husband, but he confused the instructions, scattering the seeds in the lowlands and the meat in the hills. Therefore, we high-forest-people are few and the lowlanders are many. But we are good and honest people while lowlanders are a bunch of thieves and murderers.

This is a rather common origin story among the Mien, and I heard it from several people between 1992 and 1994.[4] This particular version was from a woman in her fifties. Variants of this story are known among other upland groups, such as Lisu and Kmhmu (Wohnus and Hanks 1965; Proschan 2001). The melon/gourd story addresses the division between upland and lowland peoples in a cosmographic manner and as a mix-up of the advice from a divinity to the original couple. The story is based on the notions that there are spirits and people and that spirits can advise people about how to go about their lives. But what does the story say about Mien origins? It does not make social distinctions beyond that of high-forest people versus lowlanders, but this is also the key point of the story; "we (*i-bua mien* is simultaneously 'us [people]' and the Mien ethnic group) are good and honest people, while lowlanders are a bunch of thieves and murderers." The fundamental difference between uplanders and the more numerous lowlanders is that you can trust the former and not the latter.

As a manifestation of local ethnology, one that treats human origins and subsequent history as being about the difference between two kinds of people, the story suggests a basic difference in conduct. Many Mien people of the same generation as the woman who told the gourd story, people who were adults by the time that Thailand's national integration entangled their lives with national realities and marginalized them in many ways, aired similar views, such as that "there is no Thai word for honesty, the Thai don't have it [the practice or the notion]." As a self-identification, *Mien* stands in contrast to *Jan*, which implies any kind of outsider. Lowland Thai are generally referred to as *jan-thai*. There are three ways in which Mien can become *jan*; they may become *jan-tza* (thief), *jan-put-ndin* (crazy person), or *jan-tai* (corpse). That is, in this implicit and normative definition of Mien-ness, their ethnic identity requires life, sanity, and honesty.

The story suggests that the upland-lowland divide was the outcome of a divinity's instructions for repopulating the earth after a catastrophic flood. The story does not state that either the uplands or the lowlands are a better place to live, it focuses on internal cultural dimensions as manifest in conduct. In these terms, there is no doubt that the highlands are a good place to live, while the lowlands are not. The story is of the kind that commonly evokes the label "myth" among western scholars and that western scholarship commonly contrasts with "history." Lemoine, for instance, brings up this distinction in relation to two Mien origin stories. He contrasts the story of Pien Hung as "of course pure mythology" and the story "Crossing the Ocean," which he finds of historical value since it can be plotted on a map and dated with apparent precision (1983, 196–99).

This distinction between myth and history, between accounts concerning actual events, places, and peoples and those that are made up, is politically charged. To classify the melon/gourd story as a myth—and thus with no basis in reality—is to undermine a particular construction of identity and history. At the same time, this classification attributes reality to a different construction, one that is most often associated with state power and with western colonial expansion. Given that the identity of the Mien and other upland peoples in the hinterlands of China and Southeast Asia has been forged in an often-ambivalent relationship with state power, the depiction of Mien stories as myths can only serve to undermine their claims to legitimacy, agency, and historicity. The distinction between myth and history serves to locate historicity with the state, whose chronicles have a format that matches western notions of "real" history—dates, places, named peoples and events.

These dynamics simultaneously serve to locate the parameters of identity within the science and history that have been closely tied to colonial expansion and other forms of administrative hegemony that include the nation-state (Duara 1995, 17–50; Skaria 1999, 6). Greenhouse argues that history cannot be neatly separated from time or structure, and further that "the mythic core of history is in the system of social distinctions which divides the past from the present in the present. In the modern United States, for example, racial and class differences are the canvas of myth in this precise sense" (1996, 216).

In some versions of the above story, the woman gives birth to a pumpkin. Two botanists who present a Yao version that they recorded in Yunnan, China, exhibit a rather typical scientific attitude that might be called "botanical correctness" when they argue that since pumpkins are a New

World crop, they cannot have been the story's original component: "It is uncertain why ethnographers choose to use the word 'pumpkin.' . . . Accounts written in English of the creation stories of Asia and India [*sic*] do not mention that the sister gave birth to a fruit of [*Benincasa*] *hispida*" (Marr and Xia 2001, 575–76). Versions of reality that stand outside the realms of scientific verification are thus defined as defective or illicit, similar to dominant understandings of the position of some people as outside the realms of regulation, taxation, and other forms of state control. Like Thai notions of forests as wilderness and common notions of piracy, scientific notions of the veracity of history and culture (and thus identity) can reinforce a state-centered understanding of the world that undermines the legitimacy and rights of various groups of people.

Mien stories are indications of who the Mien people are; it is out of their historical experiences that they construct their narratives, and they bring their own biases to what elements they select and combine. Stories are not clearly separate from experience, and they often suggest the terms through which people filter the experience of events (Kapferer 1988). The story of the brother and sister who repopulated the earth after a flood makes a general cosmographic point, and it connects to other stories that concern kingroups and ritual practice, but it was also about current events in the village at the time of the telling, which was 1993. The woman who told me the story went on to complain about one of her neighbors, an ethnically Thai woman who had invited a number of her Mien fellow villagers to a restaurant in Chiangkham town and who did not contribute anything to the roughly $100 cost of the food and drink: "See, lowlanders are dishonest people." The teller of the story is of the generation that is increasingly frustrated by the entanglements of younger people with lowland worlds and their disconnection from the farming life.

Stories are somewhat like currency, their efficacy is contingent on a set of guarantees for reliable returns. In the absence of such guarantee, currency is at best of interest to collectors, who assume a separate framework for agency, value, and play from those who rely on it for the necessities of life.[5] Stories become true through their resonance with the routines of social life, or because they speak to the truths that underlie social reality. Sports competitions, competitive feasting and ritual ordinations, and practices of farming have repeatedly cast the Mien subject as particular and ethnic. But in each case these have been projects in and of their time, which have evoked history as they shaped society and local inequalities. Their versions of history are all true, and in most cases they contradict one another and do not accumulate. They are cosmographic, like the story of Pien Hung in *Kia Shen Pong*; it is from their creation of a world that they derive their truth claims. The identity of mountain peoples as savages, slaves, forest people, hill tribes, illegal immigrants, indigenous peoples, and "Mountain Thai" indicate the range of diacritical stories that have defined the social land-scape of Southeast Asia and adjacent regions over the last millennium or longer. While any one of these appellations implies an essence, they are each a term of engagement that defines hinterland farmers' position vis-à-vis the lowland states and a regional landscape of unequal rights. Taken in historical context, these terms dissolve the assumed shift from tradition to modernity at the same time that they suggest that the identity of mountain peoples has always been entangled with the shaping of a larger region.

Stories set history and society in motion as they create peoples and places. Their efficacy rests on establishing the diacritics of identity and dif-ference. Honesty was diacritical to the articulation of the Mien story that I was told, and the assumed lack of it among Thai peoples was what made the lowlands so undesirable. The story rang true for the teller at the time; it both explained the improper conduct of the lowland woman in the village and served as the context for defining lowland people more generally and thus for establishing who the Mien were as an upland people. Within Mien settlements in Thailand, the idea of honesty was also central to ritual life; people who did not maintain a ritual contract with ancestor spirits were perceived as dishonest and below the standard of normative Mien practices of culture and exchange.

These diacritical notions of Mien-ness and of the upland-lowland divide do not ring true among the younger people whose lives are quite signifi-cantly informed by Thai realities of education, labor, entertainment, and the like. It is quite conceivable that ritual contracts with ancestors and other spirits will lose their status as a diacritical marker of Mien identity, since the household-based agriculture and rituals that framed it are no longer central to Mien social life. In recent years, sports competitions and culture shows have been most prominent in defining Mien to themselves and to the nation. In that setting, the diacritical features of being a village and an ethnic group have been defined within the larger landscape of the nation-state. Mien identity has repeatedly been framed by their relations with the worlds of states and spirits, so the quest for an essence of Mien identity internal to their social and cultural dynamics may be misguided in principle—unless it is also focused on these two "outsides" that have served to delimit the Mien social universe in particular times and places.

Ritual contracts have been central to particular internal constructions of Mien identity and history. The particular identities of migration groups, in-dividual villages, and of households have tended to disappear along with the specific contracts. The ethnic label *Mien* (and more so, *Yao*) offers a historical continuity that is not dependent on such individual contracts. One possible implication of this understanding is that there is no such thing as the Mien. But if so, then neither is there any such thing as the Thai or the state, since both are brackets for constructions of identity, rights, and history that invoke a past in terms of present concerns. Ethnic categories and state structures imply projects that are present- and future-oriented and concern the diacritics of identity and difference that inform social relations and various definitions of rights. Sports festivals make certain diacritics of identity routine and have imported a particular social division of labor and recognition. The protest against the Phachangnoi wildlife sanctuary was not simply a call for the improved situation of a given set of villages, it was equally an attempt to establish particular parameters of relations among villagers, authorities, and the forest that might have altered the diacritics of identity and rights.

Establishing rights and identity through history on the landscape of national administration was central to the farmers' petition, and they referred to themselves as "the people" (*ratsadorn*), using the rhetoric of Thai democracy. When the women's representative complained that democracy had not served their interests so far, she was equally establishing history and defining the social landscape. Her suggestion of sending the pigs to vote is not trivial; it implies the same kind of embodied practice as that which has animated constructions of the Mien as village people on the landscape of development and administration. But it was also a send-up of the assumed grassroots benefits of the political system that might have redrawn the connections of communities to the state. While the mockery of the administration and the violence of the burning of the sanctuary's buildings may be taken as anomalous in the contemporary setting of culture shows and sports festivals, they may also be seen along a continuum of attempted contracts through which communities maneuver to improve their position through relations with more powerful others. That is, depending on one's understanding of history and of the Mien in relation to the state and to ethnography, the same event can be interpreted as traditional or anomalous, trivial or compelling.

The pigs have not yet been sent to select the candidates for parliament, but the idea of doing so is no more implausible than the range of events and practices that have lent shape to social, cultural, and political realities among Thailand's Mien over the last century and over the long run of the region's history. Any one of these projects has not only lent shape to the Mien in particular times and places, it has also been an attempt to inscribe history, society, and identity from specific points of view in settings that have been as local and unique as they have been regional and general. The

Mien and their ethnography both rest on such relations between parts and wholes, between the singular and the universal, where any particular event or practice can set history and identity in motion and thus redefine ethnography and the significance of the past. Deliberately, the last words are reserved for the suggestive encounters that Mien people have had with the spirits of their ancestors.

Send-Off

Mien people have long constituted themselves explicitly through relations with spirits. The following fragments of a chant suggest some of the connections among economy, ritual, health, propriety, and exchange relations that have informed the reproduction of Mien people, households, and settlements. Mien people have long relied on ancestor spirits for their well-being, but they only bring them in temporarily. Spirits, as essential as they may be, are of another world, and they must be sent off so that life can continue: "When I have matters to discuss, I will invite you to come. When I do not have any matters to discuss, I will not talk in jest. When I invite you then I make preparations for each of you invited. Now return."[6] Spirits, if provoked without good reason, can bring violence and destruction on people. They are rather like the state authorities that Mien people have dealt with throughout history in that they can procure many good things that are otherwise out of reach to poor people in the countryside and they can also leave people and places in ruins. People without the requisite resources cannot afford to engage in some of the practices that have been diacritical to Mien-ness or those that have constituted the Mien through their relations with more powerful others. Spirits have to be paid to give any attention to their dependents and paid more to bring them good things (analogous to the state's "fee for enforcing this order 50, fee for receiving this document 100"):

> During the year with four seasons, if there is illness, have it not reach us, throw it away. If there is misfortune, throw it away. In this year of four seasons, make us stay well, bring good health and fortune to us. Use your power (*liing*) and your formulas (*faat*) to keep all these people healthy and strong. Please sit down. We have prepared the incense stand, the water cup, the five liquor cups, the liquor pot, the chicken, the pig. I pour liquor for you now. The day of our ceremony has come. Please come, eat and drink, sing and dance.

Fig. 10: A medium burns household-stamped spirit money, paying the spirits in advance for householders' requests. If the request proves successful, the householders are obliged to pay up or otherwise risk losing their relationship with the ancestors.

> The money bills: ten coins, descend from your chariots and horses.
> Ten coins, bring luck.
> Ten coins, enter the new year.
> Ten coins, keep us well.
> Ten coins, enter the new year.
> We bring you gold and bring you silver. Eat and drink.
> Ten coins, keep away bad luck stars.
> Ten coins, let our souls return.
> Ten coins, let souls return to strengthen our bodies.
> Ten coins, extend our lives.
> Ten coins, throw away illness and pain.

Let our animals prosper. In this year of four seasons, if illness arrives then have it not reach us. If misfortune comes, don't have it reach us. Let us all be well. Let health and well-being reach us. Keep away illness, *su-a*. We burn the spirit money and it becomes gold and silver, becomes coins. Collect it all for the first time, for the second time, for the third time, *su-a*.

Ancestors, each and every one, in the relic jars (*po mo le tao*). Males who have ordained to *lu-kwoen-jua-long*, females who have ordained to *nam-pa-nye-king* (in the heavens); help us get shoes and get shade. Wherever we go, to the District center or elsewhere, look after us. We have a house that you can come to (for offerings). You can go back to your homes now. We thank you all, you can now return, *su-a*.[7]

References

Abadie, Maurice. 1924. *Les Races du Haut-Tonkin, de Phong-Tho à Lang-Son.* Paris: Société d'Editions Géographiques, Maritimes et Coloniales.

Adams, Kathleen M. 1997. "Nationalizing the Local and Localizing the Nation: Ceremonials, Monumental Displays and National Memory-Making in Upland Sulawesi, Indonesia." *Museum Anthropology* 21, no. 1: 113–30.

Anan Ganjanapan. 1997. "The Politics of Environment in Northern Thailand: Ethnicity and Highland Development Programs." In *Seeing Forests for Trees: Environment and Environmentalism in Thailand,* edited by Philip Hirsch, 202–22. Chiangmai: Silkworm.

——. 2000. *Local Control of Land and Forest: Cultural Dimensions of Resource Management in Northern Thailand.* Chiangmai: Regional Center for Social Science and Sustainable Development, Faculty of Social Science, Chiangmai University.

Anderson, Benedict. 1977. "Withdrawal Symptoms." In *The Specter of Comparisons: Nationalism, Southeast Asia, and the World,* 139–73. New York: Verso, 1998.

——. 1978. "Studies of the Thai State: The State of Thai Studies." In *The Study of Thailand,* edited by Eliezer B. Ayal, 193–247. Athens: Ohio University Center for International Studies.

——. 1991. *Imagined Communities: Reflections on the Origins and Spread of Nationalism.* Revised edition. New York: Verso.

Appadurai, Arjun. 1996. *Modernity at Large: Cultural Dimensions of Globalization.* Minneapolis: University of Minnesota Press.

Aragon, Lorraine. 2000. *Fields of the Lord: Animism, State Development, and Christian Minorities in Indonesia.* Honolulu: University of Hawaii Press.

Archaimbault, Charles. 1964. "Religious Structures in Laos." Translated by Jane R. Hanks. *Journal of the Siam Society* 52, no. 1: 57–74.

Aroonrut Wichienkeeo. 2000. "Lawa (Lua): A Study from Palm-Leaf Manuscripts and Stone Inscriptions." In *Dynamics of Ethnic Cultures Across National Boundaries in Southwestern China and Mainland Southeast Asia: Relations, Societies, Languages,* edited by Hayashi Yukio and Yang Guangyuan, 138–53. Bangkok: Amarin.

——. 2002. "Lua Leading Dogs, Toting *Chaek,* Carrying Chickens: Some Comments."

In *Inter-Ethnic Relations in the Making of Mainland Southeast Asia and Southwestern China*, edited by Hayashi Yukio and Aroonrut Wichienkeeo, 1–22. Bangkok: Amarin.

———. 2003. "Commoners and Slaves in Ancient Lanna Society." In *Cultural Diversity and Conservation in the Making of Mainland Southeast Asia and Southwestern China: Regional Dynamics in the Past and Present*, edited by Hayashi Yukio and Thongsa Sayavongkhamdy, 78–94. Bangkok: Amarin.

Aroonrut Wichienkeeo and Gehan Wijeyewardene, trans. and ed. 1986. *The Laws of King Mangrai*. Canberra: Department of Anthropology, Australian National University.

Aung-Thwin, Michael. 1985. *Pagan: The Origins of Modern Burma*. Honolulu: University of Hawaii Press.

Baker, Chris. 2000. "Thailand's Assembly of the Poor: Background, Drama, Reaction." *South East Asia Research* 8, no. 1: 5–29.

Barmé, Scott. 1993. *Luang Wichit Wathakan and the Creation of a Thai Identity*. Singapore: Institute of Southeast Asian Studies.

Barth, Frederik. 1969. "Introduction." In *Ethnic Groups and Boundaries*, edited by Frederik Barth, 9–38. Olso: Universitetsforlaget.

Be, Viet Dang. 1975. "The Zao in Vietnam." *Vietnamese Studies* 11: 40–83.

Beard, Tim, Betsey Warrick, and Kao Cho Saefong, eds. 1993. *Loz-Hnoi, Loi-Hnoi Uov: In the Old, Old Days: Traditional Stories of the Iu Mien*. Vol. 1. Berkeley: Laotian Handicraft Center.

Bellwood, Peter. 1992. "Southeast Asia Before History." In *The Cambridge History of Southeast Asia*, edited by Nicholas Tarling, vol. 1, 55–136. Cambridge: Cambridge University Press.

Blofeld, John. 1960. *People of the Sun*. London: Hutchinson.

Boswell, David, and Jessica Evans, eds. 1999. *Representing the Nation: A Reader*. New York: Routledge.

Bowen, John. 1995. "The Forms Culture Takes: A State-of-the-Field Essay on the Anthropology of Southeast Asia." *Journal of Asian Studies* 54, no. 4: 1047–78.

Bowie, Katherine. 1988. "Peasant Perspectives on the Political Economy of the Northern Thai Kingdom of Chiang Mai in the Nineteenth Century: Implications for the Understanding of Peasant Political Expression." Ph.D. dissertation, University of Chicago.

———. 1996. "Slavery in Nineteenth Century Northern Thailand: Archival Anecdotes and Village Voices." In *State Power and Culture in Thailand*, edited by E. Paul Durrenberger, 100–138. New Haven: Yale Southeast Asia Studies.

———. 1997. *Rituals of National Loyalty: An Anthropology of the State and the Village Scout Movement in Thailand*. New York: Columbia University Press.

———. 2000. "Ethnic Heterogeneity and Elephants in Nineteenth-Century Lanna Statecraft." In *Civility and Savagery: Social Identity in Tai States*, edited by Andrew Turton, 330–48. Richmond, Surrey: Curzon.

Braudel, Fernand. 1972. *The Mediterranean and the Mediterranean World in the Age of King Philip II*. Translated by Sian Reynolds. New York: Harper and Row.

Breazeale, Kennon, and Snit Smuckarn (Sanit Samakkarn). 1988. *A Culture in Search of Survival: The Phuan of Thailand and Laos*. New Haven: Yale Southeast Asia Studies.

Bunchuai Srisawat [Boonchuay Srisawasdi]. 2493/1950. *30 Chat Nai Chiangrai* [30 Peoples of Chiangrai]. Bangkok: Uthai.

———. 2506/1963. *Chao Khao Nai Thai* [Mountain Peoples in Thailand]. Bangkok: Odeon Store.

Calavan, Kay Mitchell. 1974. "Aristocrats and Commoners in Rural Northern Thailand." Ph.D. dissertation, University of Illinois at Urbana-Champaign.

Callahan, William. 1998. *Imagining Democracy: Reading "the Events of May" in Thailand.* Singapore: Institute of Southeast Asian Studies.

Callender, Rev. C. R. 1915. "Among the Yao." *Laos News* 12, no. 3: 80–85.

Carsten, Janet. 1997. *The Heat of the Hearth: The Process of Kinship in a Malay Fishing Community.* Oxford: Clarendon Press.

Cary, Caverlee. 1994. "Triple Gems and Double Meanings: Contested Space in the National Museum of Bangkok." Ph.D. dissertation, Cornell University.

Chairat Charoensin O-Lan. 1988. *Understanding Postwar Reformism in Thailand.* Bangkok: Duang Kamol.

Chandler, David P. 1982. "Songs at the Edge of the Forest: Perceptions of Order in Three Cambodian Texts." In *Moral Order and the Question of Change: Essays on Southeast Asian Thought,* edited by David K. Wyatt and Alexander Woodside, 53–77. New Haven: Yale Southeast Asia Studies.

——. 1992. *A History of Cambodia.* 2nd ed. Boulder: Westview.

Chang, K. C. 1983. *Art, Myth, and Ritual: The Path to Political Authority in Ancient China.* Cambridge: Harvard University Press

Chaudhuri, K. N. 1990. *Asia Before Europe.* Cambridge: Cambridge University Press.

Chayan Vaddhanaputhi. 1991. "Social and Ideological Reproduction in a Rural Northern Thai School." In *Reshaping Local Worlds: Formal Education and Cultural Change in Rural Southeast Asia,* edited by Charles F. Keyes, 153–73. New Haven: Yale Southeast Asia Studies.

Chob Kacha-Ananda. 1997. *Thailand Yao: Past, Present, and Future.* Tokyo: Institute for the Study of Languages and Cultures of Asia and Africa.

Chou, Ta-Kuan. 1967. *The Customs of Cambodia.* Translated by J. Gilman d'Arcy Paul from the French translation by Paul Pelliot. Bangkok: The Siam Society.

Chuphinit Kesmanee. 1992. "The Masque of Progress: Notes from a Hmong Village." *Pacific Viewpoint* 33, no. 2: 170–79.

Clifford, James. 1997. *Routes: Travel and Translation in the Late Twentieth Century.* Cambridge: Harvard University Press.

Cohen, Erik. 2000. *The Commercialized Crafts of Thailand.* Honolulu: University of Hawaii Press.

Collier, Jane F. 1997. *From Duty to Desire: Remaking Families in a Spanish Village.* Princeton: Princeton University Press.

Condominas, Georges. 1990. *From Lawa to Mon, From Saa to Thai: Historical and Anthropological Aspects of Southeast Asian Social Spaces.* Canberra: Department of Anthropology, Research School of Pacific Studies, Australian National University.

Cooper, Robert. 1984. *Resource Scarcity and the Hmong Response: A Study of Settlement and Economy in Northern Thailand.* Singapore: Singapore University Press.

Court, Christopher. 1985. "Fundamentals of Iu Mien (Yao) Grammar." Ph.D. dissertation, University of California, Berkeley.

Cushman, Richard. 1970. "Rebel Haunts and Lotus Huts: Problems in the Ethnohistory of the Yao." Ph.D. dissertation, Cornell University.

Dang, Nghiem Van, Chu Thai Son, and Luu Hung. 2000. *Ethnic Minorities in Vietnam.* Hanoi: The Gioi Publishers.

Darlington, Susan. 1998. "The Ordination of a Tree: The Buddhist Ecology Movement in Thailand." *Ethnology* 37, no. 1: 1–15.

Davis, Richard. 1984. *Muang Metaphysics.* Bangkok: Pandora.

de la Cadena, Marisol. 2000. *Indigenous Mestizos: The Politics of Race and Culture in Cuzco, Peru, 1919–1991.* Durham: Duke University Press.

Demaine, Harvey. 1986. "Kanpatthana: Thai Views of Development." In *Context, Mean-*

ing, and Power in Southeast Asia, edited by Mark Hobart and Robert Taylor, 93–114. Ithaca: Cornell Southeast Asia Program.

Department of Public Welfare, Thailand. 1962. *Report on the Socio-economic Survey of the Hill Tribes of Northern Thailand*. Bangkok: Ministry of Interior, Department of Public Welfare.

Dessaint, Alain Y. 1971. "Lisu Migration in the Thai Highlands." *Ethnology* 10, no. 3: 329–48.

Dessaint, Alain Y., and William Y. Dessaint. 1982. "Economic Systems and Ethnic Relations in Northern Thailand." *Contributions to Southeast Asian Ethnography* 1: 72–85.

Dikötter, Frank. 1992. *The Discourse of Race in Modern China*. Stanford: Stanford University Press.

Diller, Anthony. 1993. "What Makes Central Thai a National Language?" In *National Identity and Its Defenders: Thailand 1939–1989*, edited by Craig Reynolds, 87–131. Chiangmai: Silkworm.

Dodd, William C. 1923. *The Tai Race: Elder Brother of the Chinese*. Cedar Rapids: Torch Press.

Douglas, Mary. 1966. *Purity and Danger*. London: Routledge and Kegan Paul.

Duara, Prasenjit. 1995. *Rescuing History from the Nation: Questioning Narratives of Modern China*. Chicago: University of Chicago Press.

Duncan, Carol. 1995. *Civilizing Rituals: Inside Public Art Museums*. New York: Routledge.

Duncan, Christopher, ed. 2004. *Civilizing the Margins: Southeast Asian Government Policies for the Development of Minorities*. Ithaca: Cornell University Press.

Durrenberger, E. Paul. 1975a. "Law and Authority in a Lisu Village: Two Cases." *Journal of Anthropological Research* 32, no. 4: 301–25.

——. 1975b. "Understanding a Misunderstanding: Thai-Lisu Relations in Northern Thailand." *Anthropological Quarterly* 48: 106–20.

——. 1983. "Lisu: Political Form, Ideology, and Economic Action." In *Highlanders of Thailand*, edited by John McKinnon and Wanat Bhruksasri, 215–26. Kuala Lumpur: Oxford University Press.

Eder, James. 1987. *On the Road to Tribal Extinction: Depopulation, Deculturation, and Adaptive Well-Being among the Batak of the Philippines*. Berkeley: University of California Press.

Englund, Harri, and James Leach. 2000. "Ethnography and the Meta-Narratives of Modernity." *Current Anthropology* 41, no. 2: 225–48.

Epple, Carolyn. 1998. "Coming to Terms with Navajo *nádleehí*: A Critique of *Berdache*, 'Gay,' 'Alternate Gender,' and 'Two-Spirit.'" *American Ethnologist* 25, no. 2: 267–90.

Fine Arts Department, Thailand. 1987. *Chao Nan: Khon Mu Mak Lae Khon Klum Noi Nai Muang Nan* [Nan People: Majority and Minorities]. Bangkok: The Fine Arts Department.

Fiskesjö, Magnus. 1999. "On the 'Raw' and the 'Cooked' Barbarians of Imperial China." *Inner Asia* 1: 139–68.

——. 2003. *The Thanksgiving Turkey Pardon, the Death of Teddy's Bear, and the Sovereign Exception of Guantanamo*. Chicago: Prickly Paradigm Press.

Fordham, Graham. 1995. "Whisky, Women, and Song: Alcohol and AIDS in Thailand." *Australian Journal of Anthropology* 6, no. 3: 154–77.

——. 2004. *A New Look at Thai AIDS: Perspective from the Margins*. New York: Berghahn.

Forsyth, Tim. 2002. "What Happened on 'The Beach'? Social Movements and the Governance of Tourism in Thailand." *International Journal of Sustainable Development* 5, no. 3: 326–37.

Freidman, Jonathan. 2002. "Modernity and Other Traditions." In *Critically Modern: Alternatives, Alterities, Anthropologies,* edited by Bruce Knauft, 287–313. Bloomington: Indiana University Press.

Gearing, Fred. 1958. "The Structural Poses of 18th-Century Cherokee Villages." *American Anthropologist* 60, no. 4: 1148–56.

——. 1962. *Priests and Warriors: Social Structures for Cherokee Politics in the 18th Century.* Washington, D.C.: American Anthropological Association, Memoir 93.

Geddes, William R. 1967. "The Tribal Research Centre, Thailand: An Account of Plans and Activities." In *Southeast Asian Tribes, Minorities, and Nations,* edited by Peter Kunstadter, vol. 2, 553–81. Princeton: Princeton University Press.

——. 1976. *Migrants of the Mountains: The Cultural Ecology of the Blue Miao (Hmong Njua) of Thailand.* Oxford: Clarendon Press.

——. 1983. "Research and the Tribal Research Centre." In *Highlanders of Thailand,* edited by John McKinnon and Wanat Bhruksasri, 3–12. Kuala Lumpur: Oxford University Press.

Geertz, Clifford. 1973. "Deep Play: Notes on the Balinese Cockfight." In *The Interpretation of Cultures,* 412–53. New York: Basic Books.

George, Kenneth M. 1996. *Showing Signs of Violence: The Cultural Politics of a Twentieth-Century Headhunting Ritual.* Berkeley: University of California Press.

Gillogly, Kathleen. 2004. "Developing the 'Hill Tribes' of Northern Thailand." In *Civilizing the Margins: Southeast Asian Government Policies for the Development of Minorities,* edited by Christopher Duncan, 116–49. Ithaca: Cornell University Press.

Gladney, Dru. 1994. "Representing Nationality in China: Refiguring Majority/Minority Identities." *Journal of Asian Studies* 53: 92–123.

Grabowsky, Volker. 1999. "Forced Resettlement Campaigns in Northern Thailand During the Early Bangkok Period." *Journal of the Siam Society* 87: 45–86.

——. 2003. "Cao Fa Dek Noi and the Founding Myth of Chiang Khaeng." In *Cultural Diversity and Conservation in the Making of Mainland Southeast Asia and Southwestern China: Regional Dynamics in the Past and Present,* edited by Hayashi Yukio and Thongsa Sayavongkhamdy, 95–143. Bangkok: Amarin.

——, ed. 1995. *Regions and National Integration in Thailand, 1892–1992.* Wiesbaden: Harrassowitz.

Greenhouse, Carol. 1996. *A Moment's Notice: Time Politics Across Cultures.* Ithaca: Cornell University Press.

Greenwood, Davydd J. 1985. "Castilians, Basques, and Andalusians: An Historical Comparison of Nationalism, 'True' Ethnicity, and 'False' Ethnicity," in *Ethnic Groups and the State,* edited by Paul Brass, 204–27. London: Croom Helm.

Hamilton, James W. 1976. *Pwo Karen: At the Edge of Mountain and Plain.* St. Paul: West Publishing.

Handler, Richard. 1985. "On Having a Culture: Nationalism and the Preservation of Quebec's *Patrimoine.*" In *Objects and Others,* edited by George Stocking, 192–217. Madison: University of Wisconsin Press.

Hanks, Jane R., and Lucien M. Hanks. 2001. *Tribes of the North Thailand Frontier.* New Haven: Yale Southeast Asia Studies.

Hanks, Lucien M. 1962. "Merit and Power in the Thai Social Order." *American Anthropologist* 64, no. 4: 1247–61.

——. 1972. *Rice and Man: Agricultural Ecology in Southeast Asia.* Chicago: Aldine.

Harrell, Stevan. 2001. *Ways of Being Ethnic in Southwest China.* Seattle: University of Washington Press.

——, ed. 1995. *Cultural Encounters on China's Ethnic Frontier.* Seattle: University of Washington Press.

Hayami, Yoko. 1997. "Internal and External Discourse of Communality, Tradition and Environment: Minority Claims on Forest in the Northern Hills in Thailand." *Southeast Asian Studies* (Kyoto) 35: 558–79.

——. 1998. "Challenges to Community Rights in the Hill Forests: State Policy and Local Contradictions." *Tai Culture* 5, no. 2: 104–31.

——. 2003. "Epilogue: From Modernity and Beyond." In *Gender and Modernity: Perspectives from Asia and the Pacific*, edited by Yoko Hayami, Akio Tanabe, and Yumiko Tokita-Tanabe, 237–50. Kyoto: Kyoto University Press.

——. 2004. *Between Hills and Plains: Power and Practice in Socio-Religious Dynamics among Karen.* Kyoto: Kyoto University Press.

Herzfeld, Michael. 2002. "The Absent Presence: Discourses of Crypto-Colonialism." *South Atlantic Quarterly* 101, no. 4: 899–926.

Hickey, Gerald C. 1982. *Sons of the Mountains: Ethnohistory of the Vietnamese Central Highlands to 1954.* New Haven: Yale University Press.

Hill, Ann Maxwell. 1998. *Merchants and Migrants: Ethnicity and Trade among Yunnanese Chinese in Southeast Asia.* New Haven: Yale Southeast Asia Studies.

Hinsley, Curtis. 1981. *Savages and Scientists: The Smithsonian Institution and the Development of American Anthropology, 1846–1910.* Washington, D.C.: Smithsonian Institution Press.

Hinton, Peter. 1979. "The Karen, Millenialism, and the Politics of Accommodation to Lowland States." In *Ethnic Adaptation and Identity: The Karen on the Thai Frontier with Burma*, edited by Charles F. Keyes, 81–94. Philadelphia: Institute for the Study of Human Issues.

——. 1983. "Do the Karen Really Exist?" In *Highlanders of Thailand*, edited by John McKinnon and Wanat Bhruksasri, 155–68. Kuala Lumpur: Oxford University Press.

Hirschman, Charles. 1987. "The Meaning and Measurement of Ethnicity in Malaysia: An Analysis of Census Classifications." *Journal of Asian Studies* 46, no. 3: 555–82.

Höllmann, Thomas O., and Michael Friedrich. 1999. *Botschaften an die Götter: Religiose Handschrifte der Yao* [Instructions to the Gods: Yao Religious Manuscripts]. Wiesbaden, Germany: Harrassowitz.

Hong, Lysa. 1984. *Thailand in the Nineteenth Century.* Singapore: Institute of Southeast Asian Studies.

Hoskins, Janet. 1993. *The Play of Time: Kodi Perspectives on Calendars, History, and Exchange.* Berkeley: University of California Press.

——, ed. 1996. *Headhunting and the Social Imagination in Southeast Asia.* Stanford: Stanford University Press.

Huang, Yu. 1991. "Preliminary Study of the Yao 'King Ping's Charter.'" In *The Yao of South China*, edited by Jacques Lemoine and Chiao Chien, 89–123. Paris: Pangu.

Hubert, Annie. 1985. *L'Alimentation dans un Village Yao de Thailande du Nord.* Paris: Editions du Centre National de la Recherche Scientifique.

Hucker, Charles O. 1975. *China's Imperial Past.* Stanford: Stanford University Press.

Iijima, Akiko and Koizumi Junko. 2003. "Engendering Thai History: 'I do not wish my people to be *that*.'" *Asian Research Trends: A Humanities and Social Science Review* 13: 21–46.

IMPECT [Inter Mountain Peoples Education, Culture, and Development in Thailand]. 1999a. "Karani Duan: Nad Mawb Tua Chao Ban 995 Khon" [Urgent Case: Scheduled Surrender of 995 Villagers]. Chiangmai: IMPECT.

——. 1999b. "Lamdab Hetkan Karani Ban Huai Kok" [An Account of the Case in Huai Kok Village]. Chiangmai: IMPECT.

———. 1999c. "Prawatisat Ban Huai Kok" [The History of Huai Kok Village]. Chiangmai: IMPECT.

———. 1999d. "Saphab Thuapai Khong Tambol Phachangnoi" [General Conditions in Phachangnoi *tambol*]. Chiangmai: IMPECT.

Irvine, Walter. 1982. "The Thai-Yuan Madman and the Modernizing, Developing Thai Nation as Bounded Entities Under Threat: A Study in the Replication of a Single Image." Ph.D. dissertation, University of London.

Izikowitz, Karl Gustav. 1944. *Över Dimmornas Berg* [Over the Misty Mountain]. Stockholm: Bonniers.

———. 1951. *The Lamet: Hill Peasants of French Indochina.* Gothenburg: Etnografiska Museet.

Jackson, Jean. 1995. "Culture, Genuine and Spurious: The Politics of Indianness in the Vaupes, Colombia." *American Ethnologist* 22: 3–27.

Jao, Tsung-I. 1991. "Some Remarks on the 'Yao Documents' Found in Thailand and edited by Yoshiro Shiratori." In *The Yao of South China: Recent International Studies*, edited by Jacques Lemoine and Chiao Chien, 125–44. Paris: Pangu.

Jenks, Robert D. 1994. *Insurgency and Social Disorder in Guizhou: The 'Miao' Rebellion, 1854–1873.* Honolulu: University of Hawaii Press.

Jonsson, Hjorleifur. 1999. "Moving House: Migration and the Place of the Household on the Thai Periphery." *Journal of the Siam Society* 87, 1/2: 99–118.

———. 2001a. "Does the House Hold? History and the Shape of Mien (Yao) Society." *Ethnohistory* 48, no. 4: 613–54.

———. 2001b. "French Natural in the Vietnamese Highlands: Nostalgia and Erasure in Montagnard Identity." In *Of Vietnam: Identities in Dialogue*, edited by Jane Winston and Leakthina Ollier, 52–65. New York: Palgrave.

———. 2001c. "Serious Fun: Minority Cultural Dynamics and National Integration in Thailand." *American Ethnologist* 28, no. 1: 151–78.

———. 2002. "Identity and Historicity in the Northern Regions of Thailand and Vietnam: Museums and the National Appropriation of Diversity." Workshop on Interethnic Relations and Globalization in the Making of Mainland Southeast Asia and Southwest China, Center for Southeast Asian Studies, Kyoto University.

———. 2003a. "Encyclopedic Yao in Thailand." *Asian Ethnicity* 4, no. 2: 295–301.

———. 2003b. "Mien Sports and Heritage, Thailand 2001." Video. Camera and editing by Karl Coogan. Distributed by the Program for Southeast Asian Studies, Arizona State University.

———. 2003c. "Mien through Sports and Culture: Mobilizing Minority Identity in Thailand." Ethnos 68, no. 3: 317–40.

———. 2004. "Mien Alter-Natives in Thai Modernity." *Anthropological Quarterly* 77, no. 4: 673–704.

Kahn, Joel. 1993. *Constituting the Minangkabau: Peasants, Culture, and Modernity in Colonial Indonesia.* Providence: Berg.

Kalb, Laurie Beth. 1997. Nation Building and Culture Display in Malaysian Museums." *Museum Anthropology* 21, no. 1: 69–81.

Kamala Tiyavanich. 1997. *Forest Recollections: Wandering Monks in Twentieth-Century Thailand.* Honolulu: University of Hawaii Press.

Kandre, Peter. 1967. "Autonomy and Integration of Social Systems: The Iu Mien Mountain Population and their Neighbors." In *Southeast Asian Tribes, Minorities, and Nations*, edited by Peter Kunstadter, vol. 2, 583–638. Princeton: Princeton University Press.

——. 1971. "Alternative Modes of Recruitment of Viable Households among the Yao of Mae Chan." *Southeast Asian Journal of Sociology* 4: 43–52.

——. 1976. "Yao (Iu Mien) Supernaturalism, Language, and Ethnicity." In *Changing Identities in Modern Southeast Asia*, edited by David J. Banks, 171–97. The Hague: Mouton.

Kandre, Peter, and Lej Tsan Kuej. 1965. "Aspects of Wealth Accumulation, Ancestor Worship, and Household Stability among the Iu Mien Yao." In *Felicitation Volumes of Southeast Asian Studies, Presented to H. H. Prince Dhani Nivat*, vol. 1, 129–48. Bangkok, Thailand: The Siam Society.

Kapferer, Bruce. 1988. *Legends of People, Myths of State: Violence, Intolerance, and Political Culture in Sri Lanka and Australia*. Washington: Smithsonian Institution Press.

Kauffmann, Hans E. 1972. "Some Social and Religious Institutions of the Lawa." *Journal of the Siam Society* 60: 237–306.

Keen, F. G. B. 1973. *Upland Tenure and Land-Use in North Thailand*. Bangkok: SEATO.

Keesing, Felix M., and Marie Keesing. 1934. *Taming Philippine Headhunters: A Study of Government and Cultural Change in Northern Luzon*. Stanford: Stanford University Press.

Keesing, Roger M. 1987. "Anthropology as Interpretive Quest." *Current Anthropology* 28, no. 2: 161–76.

Kelly, John, and Martha Kaplan. 2001. *Represented Communities: Fiji and World Decolonization*. Chicago: University of Chicago Press.

Kelly, Kristin. 2001. *The Extraordinary Museums of Southeast Asia*. New York: Harry N. Abrams.

Keyes, Charles F. 1971. "Buddhism and National Integration in Thailand." *Journal of Asian Studies* 30: 551–68.

——. 1979. "The Karen in Thai History and the History of the Karen in Thailand." In *Ethnic Adaptation and Identity: the Karen on the Thai Frontier with Burma*, edited by Charles F. Keyes, 25–61. Philadelphia: Institute for the Study of Human Issues.

Khajadphai Burusaphatana. 1985. *Chao Khao* [Mountain Peoples]. Bangkok: Phraephitthya.

Kia Shen Pong. 1991. *Kia Shen Pong: Passport for Travelling in the Hills. Perpetual Redaction of the Imperial Decree of Emperor Ping Huang for Protection when Travelling in the Hills* [Guo Shan Bang]. English translation by Richard Goldrick, Thai translation by Kosak Thammajaroenkit, edited by Theraphan L. Tongkum. Bangkok: Linguistics Research Unit, Faculty of Arts, Chulalongkorn University.

King, Victor T., and William D. Wilder. 2003. *The Modern Anthropology of South-East Asia*. New York: Routledge Curzon.

Kipp, Rita Smith. 1993. *Dissociated Identities: Ethnicity, Religion, and Class in an Indonesian Society*. Ann Arbor: University of Michigan Press.

Kirisci, Kemal. 1998. "Minority/Majority Discourse: The Case of the Kurds of Turkey." In *Making Majorities*, edited by Dru Gladney, 227–45. Stanford: Stanford University Press.

Kirsch, A. Thomas. 1973. *Feasting and Social Oscillation: Religion and Society in Upland Southeast Asia*. Ithaca: Cornell Southeast Asia Program.

——. 1984. "Cosmology and Ecology as Factors in Interpreting Early Thai Social Organization." *Journal of Southeast Asian Studies* 15: 253–65.

Klein Hutheesing, Otome. 1990. *Emerging Sexual Inequality Among the Lisu of Northern Thailand*. Leiden: Brill.

Knauft, Bruce. 2002. "Critically Modern: Introduction." In *Critically Modern: Alternatives, Alterities, Anthropologies*, edited by Bruce Knauft, 1–54. Bloomington: Indiana University Press.

Koizumi, Junko. 2002. "King's *Man*power Constructed: Writing the History of the Conscription of Labor in Siam." *South East Asia Research* 10, no. 1: 31–61.

Kraisri Nimmanhaeminda. 1965. "An Inscribed Silver-Plate Grant to the Lawa of Boh Luang." In *Felicitation Volumes Presented to His Highness Prince Dhaninivat*, vol. 2, 233–36. Bangkok: The Siam Society.

Kroeber, Alfred L. 1928. *Peoples of the Philippines*. New York: American Museum of Natural History.

Kuklick, Henrika. 1991. *The Savage Within: The Social History of British Anthropology, 1885–1945*. Cambridge: Cambridge University Press.

Kunstadter, Peter. 1967. "The Lua' and Skaw Karen of Maehongson Province, Northwestern Thailand." In *Southeast Asian Tribes, Minorities, and Nations*, edited by Peter Kunstadter, vol. 2, 639–74. Princeton: Princeton University Press.

———. 1983. "Highland Populations in Northern Thailand." In *Highlanders of Thailand*, edited by John McKinnon and Wanat Bhruksasri, 15–45. Kuala Lumpur: Oxford University Press.

Kuper, Adam. 1988. *The Invention of Primitive Society*. New York: Routledge.

Leach, Edmund R. 1954. *Political Systems of Highland Burma*. Boston: Beacon Press.

Ledgerwood, Judy. 1997. "The Cambodian Toul Sleng Museum of Genocidal Crimes: National Narrative." *Museum Anthropology* 21, no. 1: 82–98.

Lehman, F. K. 1967a. "Ethnic Categories in Burma and the Theory of Social Systems." In *Southeast Asian Tribes, Minorities, and Nations*, edited by Peter Kunstadter, vol. 1, 93–124. Princeton: Princeton University Press.

———. 1967b. "Kayah Society as a Function of the Shan-Burman-Karen Context." In *Contemporary Change in Traditional Society*, edited by Julian Steward, vol. 2, 1–104. Urbana: University of Illinois Press.

le May, Reginald. 1926. *An Asian Arcady: The Land and People of Northern Siam*. Cambridge: W. Heffer and Sons.

Lemoine, Jacques. 1982. *Yao Ceremonial Paintings*. Bangkok: White Lotus.

———. 1983. "Yao Religion and Society." In *Highlanders of Thailand*, edited by John McKinnon and Wanat Bhruksasri, 195–211. Kuala Lumpur: Oxford University Press.

———. 1991. "Yao Culture and Some Other Related Problems." In *The Yao of South China: Recent International Studies*, edited by Jacques Lemoine and Chiao Chien, 591–612. Paris: Pangu.

Lewis, David R. 1994. *Neither Wolf Nor Dog: American Indians, Environment, and Agrarian Change*. New York: Oxford University Press.

Lewis, Paul, and Elaine Lewis. 1984. *Peoples of the Golden Triangle: Six Tribes of Thailand*. London: Thames and Hudson.

Li, Mo. 1991. "The Ancient Distribution of Yao in Guangdong." In *The Yao of South China: Recent International Studies*, edited by Jacques Lemoine and Chiao Chien, 143–73. Paris: Pangu.

Li, Tania M., ed. 1999. *Transforming the Indonesian Uplands*. Newark: Harwood Academic Publishers.

Lieberman, Victor. 1984. *Burmese Administrative Cycles: Anarchy and Conquest, c. 1580–1760*. Princeton: Princeton University Press.

———. 1987. "Reinterpreting Burmese History." *Comparative Studies in Society and History* 29, no. 1: 162–94.

Litzinger, Ralph. 1995. "Making Histories: Contending Conceptions of the Yao Past." In *Cultural Encounters on China's Ethnic Frontiers*, edited by Stevan Harrell, 117–39. Seattle: University of Washington Press.

———. 2000. *Other Chinas: The Yao and the Politics of National Belonging.* Durham: Duke University Press.

———. 2002. "Tradition and the Gender of Civility." In *Chinese Femininities/Chinese Masculinities*, edited by Susan Brownell and Jeffrey N. Wasserstrom, 412–34. Berkeley: University of California Press.

Loos, Tamara. 1998. "Issaraphap: Limits of Liberty in Thai Jurisprudence." *Crossroads* 12, no. 1: 35–75.

Luang Wichit Wathakan. 1950. "Foreword." In *30 Chat Nai Chiangrai*, by Bunchuai Srisawat. Bangkok: Uthai.

Luke, Timothy W. 2002. *Museum Politics: Power Plays at the Exhibition.* Minneapolis: University of Minnesota Press.

Malkki, Liisa. 1995. *Purity and Exile: Violence, Memory, and National Cosmology among Hutu Refugees in Tanzania.* Chicago: University of Chicago Press.

Mandal, Sumit. 2003. "Creativity in Protest: Arts Workers and the Recasting of Politics and Society in Indonesia and Malaysia." In *Challenging Authoritarianism in Southeast Asia: Comparing Indonesia and Malaysia*, edited by Ariel Heryanto and Sumit Mandal, 178–210. New York: Routledge Curzon.

Manndorff, Hans. 1967. "The Hill Tribe Program of the Public Welfare Department, Ministry of Interior, Thailand: Research and Socio-Economic Development." In *Southeast Asian Tribes, Minorities, and Nations*, edited by Peter Kunstadter, vol. 2, 525–52. Princeton: Princeton University Press.

Marr, Kendrick L., and Xia Yong Mei. 2001. "Botanical Note: *Benincasa hispida* (Cucurbitaceae), the 'Pumpkin' of Asian Creation Stories?" *Economic Botany* 55, no. 4: 575–77.

Maurer, Bill. 2000. "A Fish Story: Rethinking Globalization on Virgin Gorda, British Virgin Islands." *American Ethnologist* 27, no. 3: 670–701.

McCarthy, James. 1900. *Surveying and Exploring in Siam.* London: John Murray.

McCaskill, Don, and Ken Kampe, eds. 1997. *Development or Domestication? Indigenous Peoples of Southeast Asia.* Chiangmai: Silkworm.

McCoy, Alfred W. 1991. *The Politics of Heroin: CIA Complicity in the Global Drug Trade.* New York: Lawrence Hill Books.

McKinnon, John. 1989. "Structural Assimilation and the Consensus: Clearing Grounds on Which to Rearrange Our Thoughts." In *Hill Tribes Today: Problems in Change*, edited by John McKinnon and Bernard Vienne, 303–59. Bangkok: White Lotus and ORSTOM.

McKinnon, John, and Wanat Bhruksasri, eds. 1983. *Highlanders of Thailand.* Kuala Lumpur: Oxford University Press.

McKinnon, John, and Bernard Vienne, eds. 1989. *Hill Tribes Today: Problems in Change.* Bangkok: White Lotus and ORSTOM.

Miles, Douglas. 1967–1968. "Research in the Yao Village of Phulangka, Ampur Pong, Changwad Chiengrai, vol. 1–8." Chiangmai: Tribal Research Center.

———. 1972a. "Land, Labor, and Kin Groups among Southeast Asian Shifting Cultivators." *Mankind* 8: 185–97.

———. 1972b. "Yao Bride-exchange, Matrifiliation, and Adoption." *Bijdragen tot de Taal-Land- en Volkenkunde* 128: 99–117.

———. 1973. "Some Demographic Implications of Regional Commerce: The Case of North Thailand's Yao Minority." In *Studies of Contemporary Thailand*, edited by R. Ho and E. C. Chapman, 253–72. Canberra: Australian National University.

———. 1974. "Marriage, Agriculture, and Ancestor Worship among the Phulangka Yao." Ph.D. dissertation, Sydney University.

———. 1990. "Capitalism and the Structure of Yao Descent Units: A Comparison of Youling (1938) and Phulangka (1968)." In *Ethnic Groups Across National Boundaries in*

Mainland Southeast Asia, edited by Gehan Wijeyewardene, 134–48. Singapore: Institute of Southeast Asian Studies.

Mills, Mary Beth. 1999. *Thai Women in the Global Labor Force: Consuming Desires, Contested Selves.* New Brunswick: Rutgers University Press.

Ministry of Finance [Krasuang Kankhlang], Thai Government. 1938. *Report of the Financial Adviser on the Budget of the Kingdom of Siam for the Year B.E. 2481* [1938–1939]. Bangkok: Ministry of Finance.

Missingham, Bruce. 1997. "Local Bureaucrats, Power, and Participation: A Study of Two Village Schools in the Northeast." In *Political Change in Thailand: Democracy and Participation,* edited by Kevin Hewison, 149–62. New York: Routledge.

———. 2003. *The Assembly of the Poor in Thailand: From Local Struggles to National Protest Movement.* Chiangmai: Silkworm.

Moerman, Michael. 1965. "Ethnic Identification in a Complex Civilization: Who are the Lue?" *American Anthropologist* 67: 1215–30.

———. 1967. "A Minority and Its Government: The Thai Lue of Northern Thailand." In *Southeast Asian Tribes, Minorities, and Nations,* edited by Peter Kunstadter, vol. 1, 401–24. Princeton: Princeton University Press.

———. 1968. "Being Lue: Uses and Abuses of Ethnic Identification." In *Essays on the Problem of Tribe,* edited by June Helm, 153–69. Seattle: American Ethnological Society.

———. 1975. "Chiangkham's Trade in the 'Old Days.'" In *Change and Persistence in Thai Society,* edited by G. William Skinner and A. Thomas Kirsch, 151–71. Ithaca: Cornell University Press.

Nai Chan Rangsiyanan and Luang Bamrung Naowakarn. 1925. "The Yao," translated by E. G. Sebastian. *Journal of the Siam Society* 19, no. 2: 83–128.

Nash, Roderick. 1982. *Wilderness and the American Mind.* 3d ed. New Haven: Yale University Press.

Naquin, Susan, and Evelyn S. Rawski. 1987. *Chinese Society in the Eighteenth Century.* New Haven: Yale University Press.

Ockey, James. 1997. "Weapons of the Urban Weak: Democracy and Resistance to Eviction in Bangkok Slum Communities." *Sojourn* 12, no. 1: 1–25.

O'Connor, Richard A. 1983. *A Theory of Indigenous Southeast Asian Urbanism.* Singapore: Institute of Southeast Asian Studies.

———. 1989. "From Fertility to Order, Paternalism to Profits." In *Culture and Environment: Symposium of the Siam Society,* 393–414. Bangkok: The Siam Society.

———. 1995. "Agricultural Change and Ethnic Succession in Southeast Asian States: A Case for Regional Anthropology." *Journal of Asian Studies* 54, no. 4: 968–96.

Ohnuki-Tierney, Emiko. 1998. "A Conceptual Model for the Historical Relationship Between the Self and the Internal and External Others." In *Making Majorities,* edited by Dru Gladney, 31–51. Stanford: Stanford University Press.

Olwig, Kenneth R. 1995. "Reinventing Common Nature: Yosemite and Mount Rushmore—A Meandering Tale of a Double Nature." In *Uncommon Ground: Rethinking the Human Place in Nature,* edited by William Cronon, 379–408. New York: Norton.

Ortner, Sherry. 1995. "Resistance and the Problem of Ethnographic Refusal." *Comparative Studies in Society and History* 37, no. 1: 173–93.

Pan, Caiwan. 1991. "Distribution and Origin of Yao in Ru Yuan." In *The Yao of South China: Recent International Studies,* edited by Jacques Lemoine and Chiao Chien, 175–88. Paris: Pangu.

Park, David. 1907. "Report from Nan." *Laos News* 4, no. 4: 107–8.

Pels, Peter and Oscar Salemink, eds. 1999. *Colonial Situations: Essays on the Practical History of Anthropology.* Ann Arbor: University of Michigan Press.

Pemberton, John. 1994. *On the Subject of "Java."* Ithaca: Cornell University Press.

Penth, Hans. 2000. *A Brief History of Lanna: Civilizations of North Thailand.* Chiangmai: Silkworm.

Picard, Michel. 1999. "The Discourse of *Kebalian*: Transcultural Constructions of Balinese Identity." In *Staying Local in the Global Village: Bali in the Twentieth Century,* edited by Raechelle Rubinstein and Linda H. Connor, 15–49. Honolulu: University of Hawaii Press.

Pinkaew Laungaramsri. 2001. *Redefining Nature: Karen Ecological Knowledge and the Challenge to the Modern Conservation Paradigm.* Chiangmai: Regional Center for Social Science and Sustainable Development, Chiangmai University.

———. 2002. "Ethnicity and the Politics of Ethnic Classification in Thailand." In *Ethnicity in Asia,* edited by Colin Mackerras, 157–73. New York: Routledge Curzon.

Piot, Charles. 1999. *Remotely Global: Village Modernity in West Africa.* Chicago: University of Chicago Press.

Pourret, Jess G. 2002. *The Yao: The Mien and Mun Yao in China, Vietnam, Laos, and Thailand.* London: Thames and Hudson.

Proschan, Frank. 1996. "Who are the 'Khaa'?" *Proceedings of the 6th International Conference on Thai Studies. Theme 4: Traditions and Changes at Local/Regional Levels,* 391–414. Chiangmai: Chiangmai University.

———. 2001. "Peoples of the Gourd: Imagined Ethnicities in Highland Southeast Asia." *Journal of Asian Studies* 60, no. 4: 999–1032.

Purnell, Herbert. 1991. "The Metrical Structure of Yiu Mien Secular Songs." In *The Yao of South China, Recent International Studies,* edited by Jacques Lemoine and Chiao Chien, 369–96. Paris: Pangu.

Race, Jeffrey. 1974. "The War in Northern Thailand." *Modern Asian Studies* 8, no. 1: 85–112.

Radley, Howard. 1986. "Economic Marginalization and the Ethnic Consciousness of the Green Mong in Northwestern Thailand." Ph.D. dissertation, Corpus Christi College, Oxford University.

Rappaport, Roy A. 1968. *Pigs for the Ancestors: Ritual in the Ecology of a New Guinea People.* New Haven: Yale University Press.

Ratanaporn Sethakul. 1989. "Political, Social, and Economic Changes in the Northern States Resulting from the Chiangmai Treaties of 1874 and 1883." Ph.D. dissertation, Northern Illinois University.

Reid, Anthony. 1983. " 'Closed' and 'Open' Slave Systems in Pre-Colonial Southeast Asia." In *Slavery, Bondage, and Dependency in Southeast Asia,* edited by Anthony Reid, 156–81. New York: St. Martin's Press.

———. 1988. *Southeast Asia in the Age of Commerce, Vol. One: The Lands Below the Winds.* New Haven: Yale University Press.

———. 1993. *Southeast Asia in the Age of Commerce, Vol. Two: Expansion and Crisis.* New Haven: Yale University Press.

Renard, Ronald D. 1980. "Kariang: History of Karen-T'ai Relations from the Beginnings to 1923." Ph.D. dissertation, University of Hawaii.

———. 1986. "The Integration of Karens in Northern Thai Political Life During the Nineteenth Century." In *Anuson Walter Vella,* edited by Ronald D. Renard, 229–48. Honolulu: Center for Asian and Pacific Studies, University of Hawaii at Manoa.

———. 1988. *Changes in the Northern Thai Hills: An Examination of the Impact of Hill Tribe Development Work, 1957–1987.* Chiangmai: Research and Development Center, Phayap University.

———. 1996. "Blessing and Northern Thai Historiography." In *Merit and Blessing in Main-*

land Southeast Asia in Comparative Perspective, edited by Cornelia Ann Kammerer and Nicola Tannenbaum, 159–80. New Haven: Yale Southeast Asia Studies.

———. 2000. "The Differential Integration of Hill People into the Thai State." In *Civility and Savagery: Social Identity in Tai States*, edited by Andrew Turton, 63–83. Richmond, Surrey: Curzon.

———. 2002. "On the Possibility of Early Karen Settlement in the Chiangmai Valley." In *Inter-Ethnic Relations in the Making of Southeast Asia and Southwest China*, edited by Hayashi Yukio and Aroonrut Wichienkeeo, 59–84. Bangkok: Amarin.

Reynolds, Craig J. 1998. "Globalization and Cultural Nationalism in Modern Thailand." In *Southeast Asian Identities: Culture and the Politics of Representation in Indonesia, Malaysia, Singapore, and Thailand*, edited by Joel Kahn, 115–45. Singapore: Institute of Southeast Asian Studies.

———, ed. 1993. *National Identity and Its Defenders: Thailand, 1939–1989.* Chiangmai: Silkworm.

Rosaldo, Renato, ed. 2003. *Cultural Citizenship in Island Southeast Asia: Nation and Belonging in the Hinterlands.* Berkeley: University of California Press.

Rousseau, Jerome. 1995. "The Subject of Knowledge." In *Beyond Textuality: Asceticism and Violence in Anthropological Interpretation*, edited by Gilles Bibeau and Ellen Corin, 289–302. Berlin: Mouton de Gruyter.

Sahlins, Marshall. 1985. *Islands of History.* Chicago: University of Chicago Press.

Saimuang Wirayasiri. 1986. *Chao Khao Nai Thai* [Mountain Peoples in Thailand]. Bangkok: Khurusapha.

Salemink, Oscar. 2003. *The Ethnography of Vietnam's Central Highlanders: A Historical Contextualization, 1850–1990.* Honolulu: University of Hawaii Press.

Sangkhit Janthanaphoti. 2540/1997. *Saneh Sao Phukhao* [The Charm of Mountain Girls]. Bangkok: Samakkhisan.

Sanit Wongprasert. 1988. "Impact of the Dhammacarik Bikkhus' Programme on the Hill Tribes of Thailand." In *Ethnic Conflict in Buddhist Societies: Sri Lanka, Thailand, and Burma*, edited by K. M. de Silva, Pensri Duke, Ellen S. Goldberg, and Nathan Katz, 126–37. Boulder, Co.: Westview Press.

Sao Saimong Mangrai. 1981. *The Padaeng Chronicle and the Jengtung State Chronicle Translated.* Ann Arbor: University of Michigan Papers on South and Southeast Asia.

Sato, Jin. 2003. "Public Land for the People: The Institutional Basis of Community Forestry in Thailand." *Journal of Southeast Asian Studies* 34, no. 2: 329–46.

Schein, Louisa. 2000. *Minority Rules: The Miao and the Feminine in China's Cultural Politics.* Durham, N.C.: Duke University Press.

Schiller, Anne. 1997. *Small Sacrifices: Religious Change and Cultural Identity among the Ngaju of Indonesia.* New York: Oxford University Press.

Schrauwers, Albert. 1999. "Negotiating Parentage: The Political Economy of 'Kinship' in Central Sulawesi, Indonesia." *American Ethnologist* 26, no. 2: 310–23.

Scott, James C. 1998. *Seeing Like a State: How Certain Schemes to Improve the Human Condition Have Failed.* New Haven: Yale University Press.

Seidenfaden, Erik. 1954. "Siam's Tribal Dresses." In *Selected Articles from the Siam Society Journal*, vol. 2, 84–94. Bangkok: The Siam Society.

———. 1958. *The Thai Peoples.* Bangkok: The Siam Society.

Seri Phetyaprasert. 2476/1933. "Saphap Chonchat" [The Condition of Ethnic Groups]. In *Nakhorn Nan, Chabab Phathomruk* [An Introduction to Nan], 272–85. Bangkok: Bamrungkulkit and Thaphrajan Presses.

Shiratori, Yoshiro. 1978. *Visual Ethnography of the Hill Tribes of Southeast Asia.* Tokyo: Sophia University.

Skaria, Ajay. 1997. "Shades of Wildness: Tribe, Caste, and Gender in Western India." *Journal of Asian Studies* 56, no. 3: 726–45.

———. 1999. *Hybrid Histories: Forests, Frontiers, and Wildness in Western India.* Delhi: Oxford University Press.

Smalley, William A., Chia Koua Vang, and Gnia Yee Yang. 1990. *Mother of Writing: The Origin and Development of a Hmong Messianic Script.* Chicago: University of Chicago Press.

Sophon Ratanakhon. 1978. "Legal Aspects of Land Occupation and Development." In *Farmers in the Forest,* edited by Peter Kunstadter, E. C. Chapman, and Sanga Sabhasri, 45–53. Honolulu: University of Hawaii Press.

Steedly, Mary M. 1999. "The State of Culture Theory in the Anthropology of Southeast Asia." *Annual Reviews in Anthropology* 28: 431–54.

Steinberg, David Joel, ed. 1987. *In Search of Southeast Asia: A Modern History.* Rev. ed. Honolulu: University of Hawaii Press.

Stevens, Stan. 1997. "The Legacy of Yellowstone." In *Conservation Through Cultural Survival,* edited by Stan Stevens, 13–32. Washington, D.C.: Island Press.

Stewart, Susan. 1984. *On Longing: Narratives of the Miniature, the Gigantic, the Souvenir, the Collection.* Baltimore: Johns Hopkins University Press.

Stocking, George W., Jr. 1968. *Race, Culture, and Evolution: Essays in the History of Anthropology.* Chicago: University of Chicago Press.

Streckfuss, David. 1993. "The Mixed Colonial Legacy of Siam: Origins of Thai Racialist Thought, 1890–1910." In *Autonomous Histories, Particular Truths: Essays in Honor of John R. W. Smail,* edited by Laurie J. Sears, 123–53. Madison: Center for Southeast Asian Studies, University of Wisconsin.

Strickmann, Michel. 1982. "The Tao among the Yao: Taoism and the Sinification of South China." In *Collected Essays in Honor of Professor Tadao Sakai on his Seventieth Birthday,* 23–30. Tokyo: Kokusho Kankukai.

Strong, John. 1990. *The Legend and Cult of Upagupta: Sanskrit Buddhism in North India and Southeast Asia.* Princeton: Princeton University Press.

Sujibatr. 2544/2001. "Sujibat Kan Khaengkila Iu Mien Samphan Khrang thi 13" [Program for the Thirteenth Iu Mien Games], 24–27 March. Village No. 6, Mae Ngon *tambol,* Fang District, Chiangmai Province.

Swearer, Donald, and Sommai Premchit. 1998. *The Legend of Queen Cama.* Albany: SUNY Press.

Tambiah, Stanley J. 1976. *World Conqueror and World Renouncer: A Study of Buddhism and Polity in Thailand against a Historical Background.* Cambridge: Cambridge University Press.

Tan, Chee Beng. 1975. "A Legendary History of the Origins of the Yao People." In *Farmers in the Hills,* edited by Anthony Walker, 55–59. Singapore: Suvarnabhumi.

Tanabe, Shigeharu. 2000. "Autochtony and the Inthakhin Cult of Chiang Mai." In *Civility and Savagery: Social Identity in Tai States,* edited by Andrew Turton, 294–318. Richmond, Surrey: Curzon.

Tang, Hui. 1991. "The Yao in China Today." In *The Yao of South China: Recent International Studies,* edited by Jacques Lemoine and Chiao Chien, 459–66. Paris: Pangu.

Tannenbaum, Nicola. 1995. *Who Can Compete Against the World? Power-Protection and Buddhism in Shan Worldview.* Ann Arbor: Association for Asian Studies.

———. 2000. "Protest, Tree Ordination, and the Changing Context of Political Ritual." *Ethnology* 39, no. 2: 109–27.

———. 2001. "Foreword." In *Tribes of the North Thailand Frontier,* by Jane R. Hanks and Lucien Hanks, xi–xxxix. New Haven: Yale Southeast Asia Studies.

——. 2002. "Monuments and Memory: Phaya Sihanatraja and the Founding of Mae-hongson." In *Cultural Crisis and Social Memory: Modernity and Identity in Thailand and Laos*, edited by Shigeharu Tanabe and Charles F. Keyes, 137–53. Honolulu: University of Hawaii Press.

Tapp, Nicholas. 1989. *Sovereignty and Rebellion: The White Hmong of Northern Thailand.* Singapore: Oxford University Press.

——. 2002. "In Defense of the Archaic: A Reconsideration of the 1950s Ethnic Classification Project in China." *Asian Ethnicity* 3, no. 1: 63–84.

Tarling, Nicholas, ed. 1992. *The Cambridge History of Southeast Asia.* Cambridge: Cambridge University Press.

Taylor, Keith W. 1986. "Authority and Legitimacy in 11th Century Vietnam." In *Southeast Asia in the 9th to 14th Centuries*, edited by David G. Marr and A. C. Milner, 139–76. Singapore: Institute of Southeast Asian Studies.

——. 2001. "On Being Muonged." *Asian Ethnicity* 2, no. 1: 25–34.

Taylor, Nora A., and Hjorleifur Jonsson. 2002. "Other Attractions in Vietnam." *Asian Ethnicity* 3, no. 2: 233–48.

ter Haar, Barend J. 1998. "A New Interpretation of the Yao Charters." In *New Developments in Asian Studies*, edited by Paul van de Velde and Alex McKay, 3–19. London: Kegan International.

Terwiel, B. J. 1983. "Bondage and Slavery in Early Nineteenth-Century Siam." In *Slavery, Bondage, and Dependency in Southeast Asia*, edited by Anthony Reid, 118–37. New York: St. Martin's Press.

——. 1993. "Thai Nationalism and Identity: Popular Themes of the 1930s." In *National Identity and Its Defenders, Thailand 1939–1989*, edited by Craig J. Reynolds, 133–55. Chiangmai: Silkworm.

Thak Chaloemtiarana. 1979. *Thailand: The Politics of Despotic Paternalism.* Bangkok: Social Science Association of Thailand.

Thapar, Romila. 1971. "The Image of the Barbarian in Early India." *Comparative Studies in Society and History* 13, no. 4: 408–36.

——. 1992. *Interpreting Early India.* New Delhi: Oxford University Press.

Thawin Chotichaipiboon. 1997. "Socio-Cultural and Environmental Impact of Economic Development on Hill Tribes." In *Development or Domestication? Indigenous Peoples of Southeast Asia*, edited by Don McCaskill and Ken Kampe, 97–116. Chiangmai: Silkworm.

Thawit Jatuworapruk. 2541/1998. *Siang Priak Jak Khon Chai Khob* [Marginalized Voices]. Chiangmai: Social Science Department, Chiangmai University.

Thaworn Fufüang, ed. 2543/2000. *Chaokhao: Tamnan Chonphao Tang Watthanatham* [Mountain Peoples: Chronicle of Tribes of Varied Cultures]. Chiangmai: Tribal Research Institute.

Theraphan L. Thongkum. 2534/1991. "Botnam" [Introduction], in *Kia Shen Pong: Perpetual Redaction of the Imperial Decree of Emperor Ping Huang for Protection when Travelling in the Hills*, edited by Theraphan L. Tongkum, 1–10. Bangkok: Chulalongkorn University, Faculty of Arts, Linguistics Research Unit.

Thomas, Nicholas. 1989. *Out of Time: History and Evolution in Anthropological Discourse.* Cambridge: Cambridge University Press.

——. 1994. *Colonialism's Culture: Anthropology, Travel, and Government.* Princeton: Princeton University Press.

Thompson, Virginia. 1941. *Thailand: The New Siam.* New York: Macmillan.

Thongchai Winichakul. 1994. *Siam Mapped: The History of the Geo-Body of a Nation.* Honolulu: University of Hawaii Press.

———. 1995. "The Changing Landscape of the Past: New Histories in Thailand Since 1973." *Journal of Southeast Asian Studies* 26, no. 1: 99–120.

———. 2000a. "The Others Within: Travel and Ethno-Spatial Differentiation of Siamese Subjects, 1885–1910." In *Civility and Savagery: Social Identity in Tai States*, edited by Andrew Turton, 38–62. Richmond, Surrey: Curzon.

———. 2000b. "The Quest for 'Siwilai': A Geographical Discourse of Civilizational Thinking in the Late Nineteenth and Early Twentieth-Century Siam." *Journal of Asian Studies* 59: 528–49.

———. 2002. "Remembering/Silencing the Traumatic Past: The Ambivalent Memories of the October 1976 Massacre in Bangkok." In *Cultural Crisis and Social Memory: Modernity and Identity in Thailand and Laos*, edited by Shigeharu Tanabe and Charles F. Keyes, 243–83. Honolulu: University of Hawaii Press.

Thornton, Robert. 1988. "The Rhetoric of Ethnographic Holism." *Cultural Anthropology* 3, no. 3: 285–303.

Tooker, Deborah. 2004. "Modular Modern: Shifting Forms of Collective Identity among the Akha of Northern Thailand." *Anthropological Quarterly* 77, no. 2: 243–88.

Tractenberg, Alan. 1982. *The Incorporation of America: Society and Culture in the Gilded Age.* New York: Hill and Wang.

Tribal Research Institute, Thailand. 1995. *The Hill Tribes of Thailand.* 4th ed. Chiangmai: Tribal Research Institute.

Trouillot, Michel-Rolph. 1991. "Anthropology and the Savage Slot: The Poetics and Politics of Otherness." In *Recapturing Anthropology: Working in the Present*, edited by Richard G. Fox, 17–44. Santa Fe, N.M.: School of American Research Press.

———. 1995. *Silencing the Past: Power and the Production of History.* Boston: Beacon Press.

Tsing, Anna Lowenhaupt. 1993. *In the Realm of the Diamond Queen: Marginality in an Out-of-the-Way Place.* Princeton: Princeton University Press.

———. 1996. "Telling Violence in the Meratus Mountains." In *Headhunting and the Social Imagination in Southeast Asia*, edited by Janet Hoskins, 184–215. Stanford: Stanford University Press.

———. 1999. "Becoming a Tribal Elder and Other Green Development Fantasies." In *Transforming the Indonesian Uplands*, edited by Tania M. Li, 159–202. Newark, N.J.: Harwood Academic Publishers.

———. 2000. "The Global Situation." *Cultural Anthropology* 15, no. 3: 327–60.

———. 2003. "Cultivating the Wild: Honey-Hunting and Forest Management in Southeast Kalimantan." In *Culture and the Question of Rights*, edited by Charles Zerner, 24–55. Durham, N.C.: Duke University Press.

Turton, Andrew, ed. 2000. *Civility and Savagery: Social Identity in Tai States.* Richmond, Surrey: Curzon.

Vatthana Pholsena. 2002. "Nation/Representation: Ethnic Classification and Mapping Nationhood in Contemporary Laos." *Asian Ethnicity* 3, no. 2: 175–97.

Vella, Walter F. 1978. *Chaiyo! King Vajiravudh and the Development of Thai Nationalism.* Honolulu: University of Hawaii Press.

Volkman, Toby. 1985. *Feasts of Honor: Ritual and Change in the Toraja Highlands.* Urbana: University of Illinois Press.

Walker, Andrew. 1999. *The Legend of the Golden Boat. Regulation, Trade, and Traders in the Borderlands of Laos, Thailand, China and Burma.* Honolulu: University of Hawaii Press.

———. 2001. "The 'Karen Consensus,' Ethnic Politics and Resource-Use Legitimacy in Northern Thailand." *Asian Ethnicity* 2, no. 2: 145–62.

Walker, Anthony R. 1983. "The Lahu People: An Introduction." In *Highlanders of Thai-*

land, edited by John McKinnon and Wanat Bhruksasri, 227–37. Kuala Lumpur: Oxford University Press.

——, ed. 1992. *The Highland Heritage: Collected Essays on Upland North Thailand.* Singapore: Suvarnabhumi.

Westermeyer, Joseph. 1982. *Poppies, Pipes, and People: Opium and Its Use in Laos.* Berkeley: University of California Press.

Wohnus, William, and Lucien Hanks. 1965. "The Brother and Sister Who Saved the World: A Lisu Folktale." In *Ethnographic Notes on Northern Thailand*, edited by Lucien Hanks, Jane R. Hanks, and Lauriston Sharp, 68–71. Ithaca: Cornell Southeast Asia Program.

Wolf, Eric R. 1982. *Europe and the People Without History.* Berkeley: University of California Press.

Wolters, O. W. 1999. *History, Culture, and Region in Southeast Asian Perspectives.* Rev. ed. Ithaca: Cornell Southeast Asia Program.

Wong, Deborah. 2001. *Sounding the Center: History and Aesthetics in Thai Buddhist Performance.* Chicago: University of Chicago Press.

Wood, W. A. R. 1925. *History of Siam.* Bangkok: Chalermnit Press.

——. 1935. *Land of Smiles.* Bangkok: Krungdebarnagar Press.

——. 1965. *Consul in Paradise.* Chiangmai: Trasvin Publications.

Wyatt, David K., trans. and ed. 1994. *The Nan Chronicle.* Ithaca: Cornell Southeast Asia Program.

Wyatt, David K., and Aroonrut Wichienkeeo, trans. and eds. 1998. *The Chiangmai Chronicle.* Chiangmai: Silkworm.

Yoshino, Akira. 1995. "Father and Son, Master and Disciple: The Patrilineal Ideology of the Mien Yao of Thailand." In *Perspectives on Chinese Society: Anthropological Views from Japan*, edited by Suenari Michio, J. S. Eades, and C. Daniels, 265–73. Kent: Centre for Social Anthropology and Computing, University of Kent at Canterbury.

Young, Gordon. 1962. *The Hill Tribes of Thailand.* Bangkok: The Siam Society.

Zerner, Charles, ed. 2003. *Culture and the Question of Rights: Forests, Coasts, and Seas in Southeast Asia.* Durham, N.C.: Duke University Press.

NOTES

Introduction

1. *Mien* is one of many ethnic labels within the more inclusive term *Yao*. According to a 1990 census, Yao people in China number 2,134,013 (Schein 2000, 70). All of Thailand's Yao, according to recent statistics about forty thousand people, are Mien speakers (Thaworn 2000, 134). In Laos, there are both Mien and Lantien Yao, about fifteen thousand people (Pourret 2002, 39), and in Vietnam there are roughly 474,000 Yao of various subgroups (Dang, Chu, and Luu 2000, 183). The linguistic, cultural, and other diversity of Yao peoples is greatest in China (Cushman 1970; Tang 1991). But the issue of ethnic identity is not a simple correlation from language or dress to an ethnic label. To a large degree, the contemporary Yao peoples in China, Vietnam, Laos, and Thailand are acknowledged and thus counted in terms of official projects of identifying the nation's peoples, where ethnology is made to serve state- and nation-building (see Litzinger 2000; Pinkaew 2001; Vatthana 2002; and Salemink 2003). The two published ethnographies of Thailand's Mien, Hubert (1985) and Chob (1997), neither widely distributed, both portray a traditional people with a shared culture.

2. The Mien language has three forms that are quite distinct, the everyday language (*mien wa*), the archaic song language (*nzung wa*), and ritual language (*zie wa*). See Court (1985) and Purnell (1991).

3. When Kachin "became Shan," the shift involved a move from upland shifting cultivation and an "animist" religion to lowland wet-rice farming, adherence to Buddhist practice, and positions as (usually) a peasant within a state. Location, ecology, livelihood, religious practice, and political organization were all part of the boundary markers between the ethnic categories of Kachin and Shan (cf. Barth 1969).

4. See, for instance, Volkman (1985), Radley (1986), Tapp (1989), Kahn (1993), Hoskins (1993) and (1996), George (1996), Thawit (1998), T. Li (1999), Aragon (2000), Turton (2000), Hanks and Hanks (2001), Pinkaew (2001), Salemink (2003), and Hayami (2004). The distinction between island and mainland Southeast Asia is common in studies of the region, and to some extent it also informs an academic divide that not many scholars appear to cross. The mainland consists of Burma (Myanmar), Thailand, Cambo-

dia, Laos, and Vietnam, and the islands Malaysia, Indonesia, Singapore, Brunei, the Philippines, and East Timor. For Southeast Asia and trends in the anthropology of the region, see Bowen (1995), Steedly (1999), and King and Wilder (2003). The collections edited by Zerner (2003) and Rosaldo (2003) situate new ethnographic efforts on marginal populations in relation to culture, identity, and basic rights in island Southeast Asia. For state policies in relation to ethnic minorities and marginal areas across the region, both island and mainland, see Christopher Duncan (2004).

5. See, for instance, Pemberton (1994), Schein (2000), Litzinger (2000), Cohen (2000), Taylor and Jonsson (2002).

6. The notion of acting subjects combines Rousseau's discussion of the "trans-individual subject" (1995; he draws on Michel Foucault and other theorists) and Gearing's (1958, 1962) account of eighteenth-century Cherokee politics in terms of "structural poses." In Rousseau's terms, "subject" refers to "the entity which engages in an activity." Individuals are not "organized totalities, but the locus of various structures, which are trans-individual" (1995, 290, 298). Gearing proposes that "the social structure of a human community is not a single set of roles and organized groups, but is rather a series of several sets of roles and groups which appear and disappear according to the tasks at hand" (1958, 1148). He outlines four structural poses that characterized Cherokee social life, the different structurings implied in householding, lineage matters, warfare, and ceremonials and agriculture (1962, 13–29). One can read Leach's ethnography as describing similar issues, but his explicit analytical statements concern individuals' quest for power in relation to three different models of society. That is, he does not elaborate on the vast middle ground between individuals and social organization, which is precisely the strength of the notion of acting subjects.

7. In the countryside, the smallest administrative units of the modern Thai nation state are villages (*mu-ban*), several of which form a sub-district (*tambol*); several *tambol* constitute a district (*amphoe*), which in turn are governed by a province (*jangwat, changwad*), which is under the nation's government (*ratthaban*) and its ministries (*krasuang*). A village is governed by a headman (*phu yai ban*), who is elected locally, and the headman of the administratively central village of a *tambol* is the *kamnan*. The authorities of the higher levels of the bureaucracy (such as the district official, *nai amphoe,* and the provincial governor, *phu-wa rachakan jangwat*) are externally appointed. In the countryside where I did most of my research, not all households are registered, nor do all the settlements in the area have recognition as *mu-ban*. In at least one case, five separate settlements were grouped together as a single *mu-ban*.

Chapter One. Yao Origins and the State of Nature

1. This remark from a Chinese observer draws on a one-year stay at the court of Angkor (present-day Cambodia) at the end of the thirteenth century. Chou Ta-Kuan (Zhou Daguan) was there as part of a diplomatic mission. Trade had already connected China to various parts of Southeast Asia for a long time, and China's rulers sometimes required tribute or homage in order to facilitate trade. Chinese proto-ethnography was entangled with trade and politics, and it also reflected and informed the Chinese worldview. Chou referred to Angkor's population as "coarse people, ugly and deeply sunburned . . . [their customs are similar to those of] the southern barbarians" (1992, 13). His work cannot be reduced to trade, politics, and the Chinese worldview; it does reveal glimpses of late–thirteenth century life in Cambodia, which local scribes might not have found notable and which are valuable for understandings of upland peoples in relation to the region's history. But the account itself has long been entangled in politics, trade, and

transnational connections. Versions of this account were included in various subsequent Chinese volumes on people and places produced between the fourteenth to the seventeenth centuries. A French translation was published in 1902, when Cambodia was a French colony. The English translation (published in Bangkok, originally in 1967) is from the French, and international cultural tourism has been a major factor in sustaining a market for the book. It was republished in 1992, when Cambodia opened again for tourism after an international trade embargo had been lifted, and reissued in 2003 with new illustrations.

2. A systematic historical comparison of social categorizations across India, China, Japan, and Southeast Asia would serve as the ultimate test of this argument. There was considerable traffic in goods and religious ideas across this area, which also extended by sea and via the Silk Road to the Mediterranean region. The most ambitious attempt to employ Braudel's (1972) regional approach to the formation of "Asia before Europe" dismisses highland shifting cultivators: "A situation of chronic under-population and an abundance of forested land justified the survival of swidden culture through the centuries" (Chaudhuri 1990, 220). Reid's (1988, 1993) regional study of Southeast Asia on the eve of colonial encounters only mentions highland peoples in passing, whereas they were one of the key elements in the structuring of the region and its histories. The formation of the historical record makes hinterland populations disappear. Rather than work from the historical record, a theory is needed that can explain the recorded history and its omissions.

3. The *Muang Pai Chronicle,* from a kingdom that lies between Chiangmai and Jengtung, relates a sixteenth-century event that suggests how things could go wrong between a ruler and the nonsubject highland peoples over whom he claimed power. The king had ordered highland Yang (Karen) to bring him logs for his palace as a form of tribute. Presumably because they viewed themselves as not owing this ruler any obligation, the Karen people brought logs to the palace and then stabbed the ruler to death (Renard 1980, 53–54). The chronicle does not say if the Karen took the logs back with them when they left.

4. Grabowsky (2003) provides a fascinating discussion of Tai-Kha/Lawa dichotomies and relations regarding the now-defunct state of Chiang Khaeng.

5. Bowie (1996) and Aroonrut (2003) provide further discussion of slavery in relation to Lanna society. See Terwiel (1983) for Siam.

6. *Guo Shan Bang* in Chinese; "License for Crossing the Mountains," also called "King Ping's Charter." See Huang (1991), Jao (1991).

7. See Be (1975); Cushman (1970); Huang (1991); Shiratori (1978); Tan (1975); Kia Shen Pong (1991); Lemoine (1982) and (1991). The version I am using is from a *Kia Shen Pong* scroll that currently belongs to Tang Tsoi Fong (Phaisal Srisombat) in the village of Pangkha, northern Thailand (see chapter 4).

8. On the Chinese chronicles' preoccupation with the suppression of Yao rebellions, see Litzinger (1995) and (2000). These are "Yao rebellions" only in the context of Chinese conceptualizations of the mass of people they refer to as Yao (cf. Jenks 1994 for "Miao" rebellions). Rather, these were local uprisings in the context of relations with particular local rulers. The category "Yao rebellion" consolidates the state as the source of order through an identification of external threat. It is in this context that the stipulations regarding the exemptions of Yao from service to authorities contribute to an understanding of the reissue of *Kia Shen Pong* as repeated attempts to limit the reach of lowland rulers into the hinterlands that might provoke rebellion. It is possible that the source of these rebellions lay in the tensions between the imperial statement regarding the reach of local officials and the relations that the latter worked out, through force or benevolent means, with neighboring Yao populations.

9. As with the term *li* among Thailand's Lisu (Klein Hutheesing 1990, 16), *le* has had no stately connotations in recent times. As manifestations of regional and transregional contact zones, these terms can be compared with *adat* in Indonesia, which now refers to "customs" and non-state religions. *Adat* ultimately derives from Arabic and the consolidation of state societies in the precolonial Malay world through Islam but was reified in relation to Dutch colonial rule and later the modern Indonesian state (cf. George 1996, 260; Picard 1999, 36, 44).

10. The *Padaeng Chronicle*'s statement about what "is not done" hints at a significant historiographic problem. In stating that sub-class people and outsiders such as Lawa were not to be ordained in the main temple's ordination hall, the chronicle may be aimed against common practice that some authorities disapproved of. As with the upland-lowland divide, public statements may have insisted on a separation in part because such was not the case in everyday life.

11. In China, some *Man* ("barbarians") later became known as Yao. Around Lao domains, the term *Kha* was the most common reference to highland peoples. In Lao and Thai, the term means "slave," and their settlements were no doubt sometimes raided for subjects. But more importantly, the term implies the outsider position of highland people in the lowlanders' worldview and society (Proschan 1996). Ethnic labels such as *Dayak* on Borneo, *Batak* on Sumatra, and *Toraja* in Sulawesi indexed uncivilized highland or hinterland peoples (Schiller 1997, 3; Kipp 1993, 24–32; Volkman 1985, 2–5). These terms were place-specific references, while others drew on long-distance networks of ideas and trade. The Batak identity of a group of foragers on the island of Palawan in the Philippines (Eder 1987) may have drawn on translocal imagery within the precolonial Malay world that connected Sumatra and the Philippines through relations of trade and religion (Reid 1988; Wolters 1999). One example of such traffic in identities comes from a twelfth-century inscription from the Cham regions of present-day southern Vietnam commemorating the king's victory over "Khmer, Vietnamese, Randaiy, Mada, and other Mlecchas" (Hickey 1982, 2). Mleccha referred to "wild savages who lived in the forest" (Wolters 1999, 110). A Cham inscription from southern Vietnam used the Sanskrit term *kiratas,* "mountain peoples" (Hickey 1982, 83), but the Vietnamese term *Moi* ("savages") became most common and was later routinized by French colonial rule. For the American borrowing of the French term *Montagnard,* which by 1948 had replaced *Moi* as the official reference to Vietnam's highland peoples, see Jonsson (2001b). The colonial Spanish term *Moro,* indexing the identity of Muslim peoples in the southern Philippines, is another example of the translocal circulation of identities. It draws on the identity of Moors on the Iberian peninsula, and the transplanting had much to do with the continued consolidation of Spanish state society in terms of Christianity. American colonial forces in the Philippines inherited from the Spanish the terms "infidels" and "non-Christians" as ethnic references to highland populations (Keesing and Keesing 1934, 12).

12. The charting of society through a contrast with internal and external outsiders is not specifically Asian or pre-modern. The history of the United States shows similar dynamics, perhaps most clearly in the related processes of dispossession focusing on African Americans as slaves and Native Americans as savages that complemented the consolidation of "White" society (see Nash 1982, Tractenberg 1982, and Lewis 1994). At the same time as white America constructed a narrative about itself through notions about Indians, it defined "Blacks" and "Chinese" in particular ways: "Blacks could be understood as a special category of American: formerly enslaved but now enfranchised and (presumably) on the way to equality. Chinese, on the other hand, were clear 'aliens' whose right to occupy space in the country was completely at the mercy of American sovereignty. . . . Both groups were targets of intensifying racial hostility in these years. . . . But the Indian repre-

sented a special case in that the right to space lay bound up with the very right to exist" (Tractenberg 1982, 27).

13. For accounts of ranking, hierarchies, and peasant-state relations in Southeast Asia more generally, see Steinberg (1987, 9–95). See Tarling (1992) for the history of Southeast Asia since "before history." After completing revisions of this manuscript, I read Koizumi's critique of Thai historiography, which suggests that predominant understandings of the Ayutthyan society have little or no basis in historical records and were informed by the priorities of nation-building in the early 1900s (2002). Her case shows quite clearly that the "Thai state" was far from integrated and that its historical trajectory has repeatedly been a politically motivated projection (cf. Duara 1995). Thongchai's emphasis on the change from personal to political relations echoes familiar anthropological arguments about the shift from primitive or traditional life to modern society (cf. Kuper 1988). Perhaps the most significant change concerned the emergence of individual subjects as accountable to the state (for military service in particular) whereas in earlier times various local overlords had been prominent intermediaries, a situation that had reinforced the link between group identity and tributary status (see Koizumi 2002, 52–55).

14. See Stocking (1968), Hinsley (1981), Kuklick (1991), and de la Cadena (2000).

Chapter Two. Twentieth-Century Highlanders

1. This story does not appear in Wood's revised memoir, *Consul in Paradise,* where he instead stated, "The Yao are a clean people. They bathe daily, and are usually well dressed" (1965, 147). What remains constant is the emphasis on personal hygiene as a measure of civilization.

2. Seidenfaden's rationale for the miniaturization of Siam's ethnic diversity in 1937 was to fit the display "on top of the book cases of our Library" (1954, 84). This effort can equally be seen as an attempted dollhouse of Siam's disappearing cultural diversity (cf. Stewart 1984). The exhibit has a dollhouse-effect not only through the difference in scale between objects and the viewers. It also implies that ethnic diversity through dress was a feature of Siam's past (childhood), prior to the homogenizing impact of international dress and media in the countryside.

3. See Abadie (1924) for Vietnam and Kroeber (1928) for the Philippines; for an analysis of this process in Malaysia, see Hirschman (1987).

4. There were and are many Shan speakers in Chiangrai. Bunchuai spells *lui* ("shirt") as *dui, hop* ("to drink") as *huap,* and *luang* ("village") as *raang* (1950, 372). What is "ua" in Siamese is "o" in Shan (e.g., *muak* and *mok,* "hat"). The Shan *liaw,* "instance," matches the Siamese *diaw.*

5. Grabowsky (1995) is the best overview of national integration and includes several chapters on northern Thailand. See also Reynolds (1993).

6. In the context of looming and violent aspects of national integration, the Western anthropologists tended to draw clear lines between tribal and Thai realities. Kunstadter's (1967) distinction between "traditional" and "Thai-ized" Lawa is in this mold. Durrenberger (1975b) describes Lisu society as "egalitarian" in contrast to the "hierarchic" Thai society. The then-frequent settlement migration among highland peoples was characterized in ethnic terms and implicitly in contrast to the sedentary Thai lowlanders. For Geddes, Hmong migrations were the result of ecology, particularly the cultivation of poppy: "We believe that the Miao [Hmong] behavior [migration] is largely due to the types of crops they grow" (1976, 33). For Dessaint, migration is "an integral element in this dynamic [Lisu] social structure. Each move is an opportunity to cooperate with or separate

from other individuals and households within the potential social field" (1971, 340). One aspect of this relationship between migration and social structure is political, a response "to an assertive or despotic headman"; he adds that "the stories Lisu tell of murdered headmen are legion" (337). Each ethnic group was described as having a structure, usually defined in terms of the basic units of households and villages: "The basic social unit in Lahu society is the autonomous household. . . . Households are bound together into a relatively stable village community by economic convenience, long association, kinship, marriage, friendship, or a combination of such ties. But, at any time, the village may split up, with one or more households moving elsewhere. Among Lahu there are no enduring ties [that] bind a household to one village rather than another" (Anthony Walker 1983, 233–34). Some studies took the image of timeless structures a step further, toward their destruction as they would be incorporated into Thai society: "Each ethnic group tends to occupy an ecological niche propitious to certain types of economic activity, more or less to the exclusion of others. From this situation derive certain patterns of ethnic relations in view of the fact that economic transactions take place largely between people belonging to different ethnic groups, since they correlate to a large extent with different types of ecology and economy" (Dessaint and Dessaint 1982, 72). In this particular study, the analytical point is that modernity—that is, "recent economic and political changes"—is fundamentally challenging a prior condition of "social and cultural pluralism—in which ethnic groups maintain different ways of life, but interact economically and politically. . . . Such a drastic disruption of the previously existing *modus vivendi* is likely to lead to an unhappy situation rife with tension and conflict" (83).

7. The best points of entry into this ethnographic tradition are McKinnon and Wanat (1983) and Anthony Walker (1992). Many of the chapters in McKinnon and Vienne (1989) and MacCaskill and Kampe (1997) suggest the destruction of tribal worlds.

8. I learned of this from Peter Hinton (personal communication, 2002), who indicated that Geddes had found the statues problematic on aesthetic and ethnographic grounds. Geddes died in 1989 and Hinton in 2003.

9. Because of the apparent dissimilarity with the nation-building project of the Socialist Republic of Vietnam, it is worth noting some parallels in ethnographic museums in Vietnam's north—the Vietnam Museum of Ethnology in Hanoi that opened in 1997 and the Museum of the Cultures of Vietnam's Ethnic Groups in Bac Thai, about sixty miles north of Hanoi, which dates to 1960. In northern Vietnam, history and historicity reside in the struggle against foreign enemies (ancient China, colonial France, and postcolonial United States) that is situated with reference to the Red River Delta origins of the Vietnamese people and to the leadership of Ho Chi Minh. In these terms, the unity of the Vietnamese people as members of geographical regions and/or language families is then displayed in a hierarchic fashion that is premised on the centrality of Viet-Muong peoples. Vietnam's turbulent twentieth-century history of revolution and warfare is the symbolic gate through which people (and peoples) have entered national history. Thailand's different history in the twentieth century does not avail historicity to commoners, minority or not. Rather, history resides squarely with royalty and the state, most often in relation to Buddhism. Within this framework, people can enter the sacred realm of identity and historicity through submission to Buddhist authorities. For all their other differences, the dominant mode of categorizing and presenting history and identity in both countries' museums revolves around the nation's modern leadership and the structures of the state (Jonsson 2002). For parallels elsewhere in Southeast Asia, see Adams (1997), Kalb (1997), Ledgerwood (1997); for the United States, Luke (2002); and for Europe and more generally, Carol Duncan (1995) and Boswell and Evans (1999).

10. The imagery draws on the Buddha's footprints, which are important sacred ob-

jects. Chronicles sometimes refer to the footprints of the Buddha as preordaining certain sites for settlement by Buddhist peoples. The footprints align time, space, and sanctity with the destiny or mission of particular peoples.

11. This is an increasingly prominent topic in China studies. See Gladney (1994), Harrell (1995), Litzinger (2000), and Schein (2000), and, for a different angle, Harrell (2001) and Tapp (2002).

12. The dances included a "fingernail dance," a "northern Thai dance," a Chiangmai dance from 1909 that was composed for a royal visit from Bangkok, a sword dance, a combination Thai dance and a Burmese court dance, a courtly candle dance, and finally *ramwong*, "a typical Thai folk dance, very easy to do," in which the audience was invited to participate after a short introductory display. Wong (2001) describes the nationalization of heritage in Thailand, where "ethnic" and "traditional" music and dance are (like the national museums) under the Fine Arts Department and performed by graduates of the Fine Arts University in Bangkok.

13. The supposed Mien dances that are performed by women are based on ritual performances done by men for particular spirits. Only at the Old Chiangmai Cultural Center have these steps become ethnic dances. I do not know if the same is true for the dance routines of the other ethnic groups. The image of mountain people as safely un-modern is prevalent in recent cultural encyclopedias in Thailand; see Jonsson (2003a).

Chapter Three. From Strongmen to Farmers

1. Hong (1984) describes tax farming and monopoly trade in relation to state control and trends toward national integration.

2. By 1914 or so, the king of Nan also granted Phaya Khiri the family name Srisombat that many of his descendants carry (Jonsson 1999). The extent of Tsan Khwoen's wealth may have been an exaggeration on behalf of the missionary. The account appeared in *Laos News*, a journal aimed at mission supporters in America. To the missionaries and their home base, the Mien leader's wealth was a promise of the future prosperity of a station among the Mien. The missionaries were hopeful. In 1905, one of them reported from a visit to Mien villages that "the people [the villagers] declare that if the patriarch [the chief, Tsan Khwoen] did not object, they would like to 'enter the religion' in a body" (*Laos News* 2, no. 1, 12). That is, if the chief allows it, they would all convert. During a visit two years later, the Mien headman (most likely still Tsan Khwoen) said that "his tribe will come in as a tribe as soon as they fully understand" (*Laos News* 4, no. 4, 108). Again in 1910, "Their headman has said that when we accept Christ it will be as a tribe" (*Laos News* 7 no. 3, 79). Thus the ordinary villagers said this was a matter for their chief to decide, and the chief said it depended on the villagers. In an entry from 1915, the journal declared hopefully, "The signs are that the Yao may soon turn to Jesus Christ *en masse*" (*Laos News* 12, no. 3, 85). But this entry also suggests that Mien priorities lay in their relations with ancestor spirits. Initially, the Chief went along with discussions about conversion but declined when missionaries insisted on destroying shelves to ancestor spirits: "He said the spirits of their fathers and mothers live in these and that when they left their homes in China they promised solemnly to revere them in their new homes in this land; that if they should remove these shrines they would be breaking their promise and do violence to parental obligation. Moreover, their ancestors supposed to be living in these household shrines are used to indicate and locate the demons that afflict the people" (*Laos News* 12, no. 3, 84).

3. This list of domains is not common knowledge; it appears in a ritual chant in the annual renewal of a relationship with a particular spirit and acknowledges the domain-

spirits with which the population has had some relations. The Mien people who felt able to discuss this past with me indicated that the Müang of Siang, Khwa, and Tsa are within Müang Long, in Guangxi. Müang Lai and La are in northern Vietnam, Müang Hun in Laos, and Müang Nan (now Nan Province), though in recent versions of the chant Nan has been subsumed by *Siem Law,* Siam/Bangkok. National integration retrospectively informs ritual chants because they are in and of history. At the same time, the temporality of chants to spirits is more complicated. Spirit mediums give the date (month and year) each time they call on spirits, and during my research their calendar was that of the Chinese Republic (pre-revolution), where 1912 was year one. The mediums and spirits thus share a calendar with contemporary Taiwan.

4. "Chinese warlords" is a gloss that is neither precise nor necessarily accurate. The so-called Ho or Haw warlords that were causing trouble in northern Lao domains in the 1870s and 1880s were sometimes "Chinese" but Thongchai (1994, 103–4) shows that in some cases these were Lao rulers of Lao or Black Thai domains (see also Breazeale and Sanit 1988, 47–49) such as Müang Lai. The notion of Ho was in part to justify the Siamese military's violence against them.

5. There was a clear difference by place in these recollections, and their pattern appears related both to proximity to Thao La and to relative prosperity, which were related factors. The uniformly favorable memories of Thao La's rule came from his descendants in Phulangka village. The neutral recollections—that he mostly sat around in his house and dealt with matters brought to him there—came from people living in somewhat well-off villages not far from Phulangka. The one negative account that I heard was from a man too young to have known Thao La himself. He had learned this from his father, who at the time had lived in a poor village far away from Phulangka. The apparently positive assessment of wealthy and powerful people in Phulangka, as reported by Miles, in contrast to the ambiguity expressed to Kandre in Phale, may have only reflected the dominant view in the village at the time.

6. There was a thriving underground market for opium. After Phulangka people had sold the registered amount to the monopoly traders, itinerant merchants would visit the village to purchase the rest. This annual period of illicit trade is remembered as a very lively time.

7. Some studies make much of Daoism among the Yao and assume that Yao peoples are Daoist (Strickmann 1982; Lemoine 1982, 1983, 1991; Höllmann and Friedrich 1999). There is a similar descriptive problem regarding the Karens' engagements with Buddhism (Hinton 1979; Hayami 2004). Daoist practices, imagery, and texts are a part of the religious repertoire that Mien and other Yao have drawn on, but this does mean that Yao are Daoist. Only wealthier Mien people engage with the Daoist framework of rituals. Circumstantial evidence indicates that Thao La's redefinition of the household contributed to a reworking of Daoist rituals toward the goals of farming households. In Laos, Chao La sponsored a number of Daoist ordination rituals for the Mien subordinates who formed his army. Little is known of this, but Lemoine (1982) has several photographs of these ordinations that indicate their scope and Chao La's prominence. In all likelihood, Chao La's articulation of Daoist rituals has more in common with Phaya Khiri's emphasis on military prowess. The impulse to classify a people in relation to a religious doctrine is one dimension of the ethnic landscaping of modern state formations, though the practice has a much longer history. See Kipp (1993) for modern Indonesia, where religion and not ethnicity has been people's official identifier.

8. When a man acquires ritual rank, he gains access to a number of spirit soldiers (*paeng*) who assist him in the spirit world. Once a household head has ritual rank, the household has to engage in a series of more expensive rituals beyond those to ancestors. In

general, these rituals require an offering of one or more pigs, instead of the chicken that is sufficient for ancestor spirits. The greater the offering, the greater the expected rewards in terms of good harvest, wealth, and the health of household members. Thus there is a clear economic correlation to Mien ritual activity, and ritual practice serves as a means of differentiating wealthy and poor households. Ritual rank carries obligations for several generations, as ranked ancestors have to be cared for with more costly offerings. Such an elevation in status also exposes a farming household to risks that do not pertain to those of commoner status. One example is a ritual called "collecting soldiers" (*syo paeng*). It is performed when households of ritual rank experience crop failure. The assumption is that the spirit soldiers were not adequately taken care of through offerings and hence were obliged to attack the household's fields for sustenance. This ritual involves men going into a trance and briefly diving on a pile of burning coals in order to assemble the spirit soldiers to their proper place. The somewhat ferocious spirit soldiers are lured with freshly killed chicken, the chicken blood being mixed with the liquor. The Daoist ritual scheme that Mien have appropriated provides a vehicle for status distinctions within Mien society. In important ways, Thailand's Mien have applied Daoist ritual practice toward household goals. But while this ritual complex is focused on household benefits, it is simultaneously a mechanism for differentiating Mien households by wealth and ritual rank. In wealthy households, people may conduct ordinary soul-callings for the benefit of a member, but they may also opt for the more expensive method of a bridge ceremony, which calls on big spirits to help find the lost soul and bring it back. The regular soul-calling ceremony takes about an hour to perform and involves the offering of a chicken with a chant in ritual language. In contrast, the bridge ceremony takes from six to twelve hours and requires a pig; the medium chants from a text in Chinese and writes letters in Chinese to the higher spirits.

9. The logic of adoptions in the Mien context concerned intergenerational relations of exchange and obligations, both among parents and children and among householders and their ancestor spirits. The non-Mien background of children purchased for adoption was not of local concern, as the children became Mien through taking part in householding and social life more generally. Like brides brought into a household or children, adoptees were introduced to a set of ancestors during a ceremony and implicated in the exchange relations a household had with its ancestor spirits.

10. The Nan kingdom controlled and taxed access to salt (McCarthy 1900, 80–81), and Chiangmai had conquered Nan in the fifteenth century to take over this source of wealth (Wyatt 1994, 19).

11. Cooper (1984) is the best study of the highlands during this violent period of national integration.

Chapter Four. Village People

1. The exchange rate at the time was Baht 25 to $1 (U.S.). During the 1997 Asian financial crisis, the Baht was devalued to 50 to the dollar, and since then the exchange rate has settled at about Baht 40.

2. *Sanuk* means "fun/pleasure" in Thai. For a description of the concept and its relevance in the anthropology of Thailand, particularly regarding "peasant personality," see Jonsson (2001c), 154–55.

3. Both the dances and the races separated the contestants by age, thus using on the grades of the school system as a model for social categorization. In the dance contests, accompanied by music from a cassette player, this ranking had an interesting evolutionary

dimension. The youngest students performed a "classical" Thai dance and were dressed in the stereotypical outfit of pre–twentieth century Thai society that is somewhat common in TV programs. The dances and the accompanying tunes were progressively more "modern" as the performers got older, and the show/contest culminated in seventh-graders lip-synching to a Thai pop song, dressed in imitations of the sexy outfits of modern pop stars.

4. The implicit background for this discussion is Clifford Geertz's (1973) famous study of cockfights in Bali, in which his analytical point is that through their cultural practice, people tell themselves stories about themselves.

5. Schools have served as a tool of national integration in Thailand since the early twentieth century, while they did not become much of a presence in rural areas until about 1960, following concerted efforts toward "national development" (Thak 1979; Missingham 1997). Chayan (1991) has shown how much of what schools instill in students in the northern countryside is a firm sense of their lowly place in a national hierarchy. His findings apply equally to ethnic minority areas. The emphasis on "re-education" is fundamental to the official effort because of the firm sense that ethnic minority cultures are an impediment to national integration, progress, and sensible land use practices. But it would be an analytical shortcut to say that through schools, populations such as the Mien and Hmong in Phachangnoi sub-district "become Thai." This would imply that they "were" Mien and Hmong before, as if the ethnic reference provided a description of social dynamics in this "before" period. Through schools, populations such as Thailand's upland minorities become part of contemporary Thai society. But references to official integration policies, national imaginaries, and the placement of rural villagers in a national hierarchy provide only a partial understanding of the restructuring that schools contribute to in upland areas.

6. I occasionally came under questioning that revolved around my character since I was not living with or taking care of my parents and was not making offerings to the spirits of my ancestors. According to notions held by better-off Mien regarding honesty and integrity, these shortcomings were serious, though people were quite forgiving about them in my case.

7. Mills (1999) describes similar tensions regarding lowland peasants in northeastern Thailand, where young labor migrants to the city are under pressure to save money for their parental household and for Buddhist merit-making at the village level. In the northeast, there is little pressure on men and considerable pressure on women, a gender difference that I did not sense in Mien settlements.

8. The issue of compiling a handbook on Mien culture for Mien people speaks to changes in understandings of culture and identity. Collier (1997) describes a similar dynamic for Andalusia in Spain, where an interest in cultural preservation and revival was accompanied by an encyclopedia of Andalusian culture. There, many of the cultural practices were stigmatized as un-modern. The emphasis was more on knowledge of the cultural ideas and practices—as heritage belonging to the people collectively—than on the everyday practice of the culture. Similar dynamics surround Mien enactments of their traditions in Thai context (Jonsson 2004).

9. When the Mien Association met during the Pangkhwai festival in 2001, the only woman present was the representative from IMPECT, who was sitting in for a male representative who had to attend a meeting elsewhere. The other participants were mostly village headmen, men ranging in age from forty to seventy. The organization of events such as this tends to bring a clear gender distinction in that women take care of food, largely through the village Housewives' Group. Thus, a national framework for village organization, related to the nation-state's modernizing agenda in the countryside, contributes to

silencing the voices of women in the public affairs of Mien villages and in their recent organizing as an ethnic group.

10. Neither the outfits nor the women dancers were a feature at any weddings in the Pangkha area from 1992 to 1994. It is possible that this was a feature at some wedding in someone's living memory, but it was certainly not a regular occurrence. Instead, what is emerging is that some practices from one village emerge as typical and traditional not only for that village but also for the ethnic group as a whole. When Pangkha men performed their plate dance for a general audience during the Phulangka Fun Fair in 1993, a man from a neighboring village stated that the dancers were no good and that they did not even know how to really do this dance. According to this man, the way to do it was to have two teams, one each representing the groom's and the bride's sides, try to outdo one another with their skill in the dance. This was how people did it "correctly" in the village where he lived. Between 1992 and 1994, the only time I saw women do a Mien dance was when the group of male and female students performed at the opening of the Phulangkha Fun Fair. On at least one formal occasion, when a group of Chinese Yao and Yao scholars visited, young women in modified Mien clothing did a "classical" Thai dance. The shift from male to female dancers is most likely a product of increasing engagements with Thai notions of gender and culture.

11. Hayami (1998) and Sato (2003) discuss recent definitions and contestations regarding forests. Forsyth (2002) describes how some pro-environmentalist discourses in Thailand have aligned with critiques of the government.

Chapter Five. On National Terrain

1. This may be taken as an indication of how gender and space are reproduced in Thai social life through engagements with the *chao khao* Other in relation to the domestic sphere. Urban women pick beautiful, illicit plants to accentuate their domestic life, whereas men engage in drinking and sometimes sexual relations away from home. Masculine notions of the sexually loose highland women are not as routinized in Thailand as they are in China (see Schein 2000), but there are various similarities. See for instance Sangkhit's (1997) *Charm of Mountain Girls.* In the 1990s, ethnic minority highland men were increasingly placing themselves within national orbits of sociality and sexuality by visiting urban and suburban bars and brothels. In urban and national terms, the venues were all considered lower-class.

2. The politician's visit was largely occasioned by a political crisis involving the Hmong in this area, one that could not be made public, see Jonsson (2001c), 165–68.

3. The name of the village translates as "Twelve Development." The village is a resettlement, a part of the evacuation of the highlands, that was in the hands of a twelfth division of some branch of the military. The term "development" is a statement about the village's bright future in its new location, and it hints at the Thai sense of development's opposite in highland villages, accentuated by the Hmong identity of the bulk of the villagers. They had been, in rhetoric if not always in reality, associated with the CPT, and the new naming has to do with the transformation of a former threat into a manifestation of the authorities' gift of development, for which the villagers ought to be thankful and mindful—this is somewhat analogous to the Hmong statues in the TRC fountain and the T-shirt that declared the love of Thailand. The renaming of settlements is common. One Mien village is now *Muban Thai Phatthana,* "Thai Development Village," and some former "insurgent" villages in the north have become *Muban Rak Thai,* "The Village that Loves Thailand"; *Ban Thoed Thai,* "The Village that Respects Thailand"; and the like.

4. In describing the course of events, I draw on the documentation by IMPECT (1999a, b, c, d), as well as conversations with their staff and with Mien villagers in Huai Kok and elsewhere in the area during the summer of 2000. I copied the letter on a visit to Huai Kok village.

5. This section draws on minutes taken by an IMPECT representative at the meeting in Huai Kok. The minutes are too long for reproduction here, but at the same time they provide valuable insight into matters of rights, identity, and political negotiation between farmers and government officials. My translation variously summarizes or follows the text and shifts between first and third person perspective in an attempt to convey the issues and atmosphere while keeping the account brief.

Conclusions. The Work of Classification

1. Douglas (1966) describes how the classification of unclean matter contributes to social demarcation. For similar analytical attention in relation to large-scale political violence, see Malkki (1995) and Kapferer (1988) and, regarding Thailand, Irvine (1982) and Bowie (1997). Such violence is sometimes explicitly racist, but given the overlapping signifiers of race, culture, and identity, an emphasis on labels such as "racism" and "ethnic warfare" is likely to obscure the commonality of large-scale political violence in the contemporary world as much as in the past, some of which is now labeled peacekeeping, the war against terror, and the like.

2. Anderson (1978) describes the restoration of the monarchy in relation to changes in the composition of Thai society and to the ambitions of Prime Minister Sarit Thanarat.

3. The woman literally said *sat liang* ("domestic animals"), but I gloss this as "pigs" both to have some fun with my inheritance—the biases of previous anthropology—and because Mien have for the most part only kept pigs and chickens. I don't think the woman was plotting with the chickens, but I may be wrong.

4. There is a more elaborate and somewhat different version in Beard et al. (1993), 9–18, from Mien now in the United States who are refugees from the war in Laos and its aftermath.

5. The relationship goes the other way, too; currency works like stories. Maurer's fascinating study of capital and capitalism points out that "assumptions about historicity and historical development are built into dominant understandings of capital and its peregrinations." He suggests that we should question such understandings and offers a change in metaphors as a starting point regarding capitalism and globalization: "Less like a fiber optic network; more like a lava lamp" (2000, 672).

6. From a translation of his own chant into Central Thai and Mien by Tang Jiem Hin, 1993.

7. Translated by Tang Tsan Seng and Tang Khe Thseng into Mien and Northern Thai, 1993, from a previously recorded chant by Tsan Seng.

INDEX